Basic Issues of Philosophy

Experience, Reality, and Human Values

Basic Issues of Philosophy

Experience, Reality, and Human Values

MARVIN FARBER

HARPER TORCHBOOKS
Harper & Row, Publishers
New York, Evanston, and London

BASIC ISSUES OF PHILOSOPHY

Copyright © 1968 by Marvin Farber.

Printed in the United States of America.

All rights reserved. No part of this book may be used or reproduced in any manner whatsoever without written permission except in the case of brief quotations embodied in critical articles and reviews. For information address Harper & Row Publishers, Incorporated, 49 East 33rd Street, New York, N.Y. 10016.

First edition: HARPER TORCHBOOKS, 1968,
Harper & Row, Publishers, Incorporated,
New York, N.Y. 10016.

Library of Congress Catalog Card Number: 68-10864.

Contents

Preface   viii

I   THE NATURE AND FUNCTION OF PHILOSOPHY   1

- A. Philosophy and the Natural View of the World, 1
- B. The Origin of Western Philosophy and its Critical Function, 5
- C. The Divisions of Philosophy, 8
- D. The Ideal of a Rigorous Science of Philosophy, 10
- E. The Philosopher in the Human City, 15
- F. Historical Aspects of Philosophy, 21
- G. The "Great Tradition" of the History of Philosophy, 24
- H. The Philosopher and the Choice of a Philosophy, 32
- I. The Alleged Crisis in Philosophy, 36

II   PHILOSOPHY AND THE METHODS OF INQUIRY   39

- A. Knowledge and Methods, 39
- B. Direct Observation and Induction, 42
- C. Hypothesis and Speculation, 44
- D. Deduction, 45
- E. The Reflexive Method, 49
- F. The Descriptive Procedure of Phenomenology, 50
- G. Subjectivism and Objectivism as Methods of Approach, 52
- H. Metaphysical Interpretation, 57
- I. Other Varieties of Method, 60
- J. Has Philosophy a Distinctive Method?, 62

III   EXPERIENCE AND THE PROBLEMS OF PHILOSOPHY   66

- A. The Perceptually Founded Problems, 67
- B. The Conceptually Founded Problems, 79
- C. The Nature of Philosophical Problems, 82

IV Questions and Methods in Philosophy · 98

  A. The Method of Knowledge in Philosophy, 98
  B. The Question of the Autonomy of Philosophy, 101
  C. Aporetics as an Alleged Separate Discipline, 110
  D. Classification of Questions and Problems, 112
  E. The Treatment of Philosophical Questions, 114
  F. The Meaning of Radicalism in Philosophy, 116
  G. Philosophical Neutrality, 118

V Experience and Knowledge · 121

  A. The Locus of Experience and the Status of the Mind, 121
  B. The Problem of the Given, 124
  C. The Problem of Certainty, 127
  D. Sameness and the Ideality of Meaning, 135
  E. Judgment and Reality, 138
  F. Hypothetical Judgments and Conditions Contrary to Fact, 142
  G. The Social Conditions of Experience and Knowledge, 145

VI Monism and Pluralism · 149

  A. The Historical Problem of Monism, 149
  B. Royce's Argument for Monism, 151
  C. The Diversity of Systems and Domains, 153
  D. The Reality of Internal and External Relations, 158
  E. Basic and Formal Unity, 161
  F. Kinds of Pluralism, 165
  G. Application to the Problem of Monism, 168
  H. Real Unity and the Diversity of Systems, 171
  I. The Program of Unity, 176
  J. Summary: Frames of Unity, 179

VII Existence and its Interpretation · 184

  A. The Meaning of Existence, 184
  B. Existence and Possibility, 190
  C. Problems of Existence, 199

- D. The Dimensions of Existence, 202
- E. The World in Philosophy, 208
- F. The Destruction of the World in Phenomenology, 211

VIII HUMAN EXISTENCE AND ITS INTERPRETATION 213

- A. Man in the Tradition of Philosophy, 213
- B. The Place of Man in the Cosmos, 219
- C. Human Existence and Philosophical Anthropology, 222
- D. The Philosophy of Existence, 229
- E. Existence and Value, 233

IX APPROACHES TO A PHILOSOPHY OF VALUES 236

- A. Hedonism and the Principle of Quantity, 237
- B. The Principle of Equality and the Criterion of Quantity, 241
- C. The Individual and Society, 244
- D. The Problem of Objective Ethical Knowledge, 248
- E. The Real Meaning of Freedom, 252
- F. Summary: The Nature and Scope of a Theory of Value, 258
- G. Moral Value and Aesthetic Judgment, 260

X PROBLEMS OF THE PHILOSOPHY OF RELIGION 264

- A. Ludwig Feuerbach and the Problem of Belief, 264
- B. The Idea of God, 267
- C. The Leading Attempts to Prove God's Existence, 270
- D. Consequences of Disbelief in God, 281
- E. The Meaning of Immortality, 282

Index

Preface

The theme of the present book is the nature of philosophy as a historically conditioned mode of thought. It undertakes to reexamine and to clarify the nature of philosophy and its basic issues from a science-oriented point of view. The concept of science is extended to include philosophical knowledge in its reflective as well as objective forms. This point of view has been set forth in earlier publications by the present writer, including *Naturalism and Subjectivism* (Springfield, Illinois; Charles C. Thomas, 1959) and *Phenomenology and Existence* (New York: Harper & Row, 1967). The present book is concerned with the total philosophic enterprise, and combines features of an independent treatise with those of an introduction to philosophic thought. It may also aid in the understanding and evaluation of recent trends in the literature.

Parts of an essay contributed to a volume in honor of Henry M. Sheffer (*Structure, Method, and Meaning*, ed. P. Henle, H. M. Kallen, and S. K. Langer, New York: The Liberal Arts Press, 1951) have been included in the first chapter with changes; and parts of the ninth chapter appeared in the Proceedings of the XIth International Congress of Philosophy (Amsterdam: North-Holland Publishing Co., 1953) and in the Unesco-sponsored publication *Enquête sur la Liberté* (Paris: Hermann et Cie, 1953). The writer also acknowledges grateful indebtedness to his wife for her help in preparing the text for publication.

MARVIN FARBER

Buffalo, New York
January, 1967

CHAPTER I

The Nature and Function of Philosophy

A. *Philosophy and the Natural View of the World*

Taken literally, the term philosophy means "love of wisdom." That does not tell us much about the nature of philosophy. There is no generally accepted usage, and there are numerous versions of the meaning and function of philosophy. (In the words of Plato, the philosopher was the spectator of all time and all existence.) For the Cynics, the philosopher exhibited a way of life, featuring self-restraint and freedom from illusions. In the Middle Ages philosophy became the handmaid of theology. The mystic theologian Bernard of Clairvaux was quite outspoken: it was not his purpose to condemn the philosophers, or to suppress scholarship, because he well knew how philosophy served the Church. Philosophy was in the service of science early in the modern period, and was conspicuously devoted to social progress in the eighteenth century. It has responded to a diversity of motives in its long history, with philosophers serving rival causes in the same period. To assign one type of motivation to philosophy generally would be to oversimplify.

The fact that conflict is characteristic of the world of philosophy is shown by such persistent issues as materialism versus spiritualism, naturalism versus supernaturalism, realism versus idealism, empiricism versus rationalism, intellectualism versus anti-intellectualism, temporalism versus eternalism, and pantheism versus theism. It may be tempting to argue that some points of view are unphilosophical, and to lay down the one and only correct point of view. But there is no justifiable way to limit the usage in view of the many conflicting types in the history of philosophy. From the point of view of the spiritualist, the materialist may not be a philosopher; and in the opinion of recent positivists, both spiritualists and materialists are wasting their time.[1] Historically viewed, all these types are members of one big, if not happy, family. That the conflicts are usually not total, that there is a constructive core in the development of philosophy historically, and that the opposing standpoints may themselves be better understood in terms of cultural history, will be amply borne out by a careful study of the facts.

As commonly understood today, the term philosophy signifies sustained reflection on fundamental questions of existence and experience. Beliefs about the nature of reality, man's place in the universe, immortality, and the existence of a Supreme Being are regarded as philosophical, even though they are rarely organized in the form of a coherent logical system. Such beliefs are most frequently accepted uncritically from the tradition because of early training and influences, or because of emotional preference.

The standpoint of common sense may be said to be philosophical insofar as common sense provides a comprehensive view of the world and man. The common-sense view includes ideas derived from the cultural tradition as well as elements of scientific thought which have become well established. It is variable in both respects. The culturally transmitted ideas differ in some respects from time to time and from place to place. It is sufficient to refer to ideas bearing upon the alleged inequality of women, or upon the nature and justice of property relations, as examples. Just as religious and moral, political and economic ideas change, so there are always changes in scientific thought. The scientific picture of the world to which we have become accustomed comes to be regarded as a matter of common sense. This has been true of the Newtonian view of the physical world. The ideas of recent physics are gradually becoming "obvious," so that another stage of the common-sense view of the world is in the making. That is not to suggest, however, that the new physical theories completely invalidate the older theories and the world view associated with them. Any stage in the history of the variable common-sense view can be expected to have a fundamental element of correctness, because there is so much evidence to support it; and there are basic beliefs about the world and society which are supported by ordinary experience. Professor Whitehead went so far as to declare that he seriously doubted

---

[1] Cf. for example, A. J. Ayer, *Language, Truth, and Logic* (New York: Oxford University Press, 1936).

the sincerity of anyone who flagrantly violated common sense. This remark was directed against the defense of solipsism, according to which a person is limited to the contents of his own mind, so that the world and fellow human beings are merely ideas in his own mind. In other words, Whitehead expressed his trust in the evidence of ordinary experience as a final test of absurdity.

The expression "natural attitude," or "natural point of view," was used by Professor Edmund Husserl in his description of our attitude in ordinary experience. This attitude (*Einstellung*) was contrasted with other attitudes, notably the thoroughly "questioning" attitude of reflection. Although Husserl conceded that the natural attitude had its rights, he regarded it as naïve and dogmatic from the point of view of critical reflection.

In "natural" experience, man regards himself as part of a world infinitely extended in space and time, which determines a fixed structure or absolute framework of experience. This world of existence is immediately given, and is the field of our thought and activity. As apprehended through sense perception, bodily things are "simply there," located in space and time; and they are there whether they are perceived or not. The world of experience is regarded as independent of one's experience and knowledge. Other men are included in the immediately given field of existence, and one understands what they think and wish. They too are there as realities, and their being does not depend upon their being known.

Throughout all conscious life one naturally believes himself to be in relationship to the same world, although the events and things which make it up are continually changing. Objects are regarded as being immediately given, not only as physical facts, but as values and goods, or as objects of practical interest. Things are there as beautiful and ugly, and as useful objects. This world, including in its scope physical nature and human society, constitutes the natural basis of our experience and scientific thinking. With this attitude we "live in" the experiencing and all the activities which are undertaken, and do not reflect critically about them. With the natural view, then, the world of natural existence is all-inclusive, and comprises the given world of culture.

Nature as the field of the natural sciences is narrower in its scope, however, since it excludes the realm of values. Values enter into the subject matter of the social sciences and philosophy.

The field of investigation is enlarged in philosophy by considering both realms and attempting to set up a critically founded theory of all existence. It is important to note whether the independent existence of other human beings, and of the world, are taken to be matters of belief, just as they were for David Hume; or whether they are regarded as statements of basic facts, as verified knowledge. "Living in" the process of natural experience, one simply takes such things for granted. In order to establish a critically justified view of the world and man, it is appropriate to place the initial confidence in independent existence in question, along with all other beliefs and judgments.

One should however be careful to guard against any tendency to disparage the natural view of the world by calling it naïve. There should be no suggestion that it is a fundamentally incorrect view, or that it must yield in all respects to a view which is advanced as inherently superior. The natural view is sustained in its major beliefs by the evidence of experience, and by the sciences; and since it is based upon perceptual experience, it constitutes the starting point for all reflection. It is true that significant facts about experience are first brought to light by critical reflection. But the understanding which results should be regarded as an extension of the natural view, rather than as superseding it.

A never-ending process of revision of the views of common sense and natural experience results from the achievements of the special sciences. Ideas which are used uncritically in the natural view of the world, such as time, space, matter, infinity, purpose, cause, value, etc., are subjected to analysis by a group of sciences, and this process is continued by philosophy. In the place of uncritically accepted beliefs comes the ideal of a logically justified set of beliefs. A necessary preparatory step that must be decisively undertaken is to place all past beliefs and uncritically accepted views in question. This procedure is often very difficult to institute at all, and is in fact seldom accomplished, which is why it is all the more necessary to emphasize its importance. Ideally, it may be expressed negatively as freedom from prejudgments, or unfounded beliefs of any kind; and positively, as the construction of a theory of man and the cosmos on the basis of experience and scientific knowledge.

The generalization of the findings of the special sciences provides the basis for philosophy in its strictest sense. The term philosophy does not signify universal and complete knowledge, which would be impossible because of the infinitude of reality, and the limitations and difficulties faced by men as finite beings. One of its tasks is the attempt to construct a unified world view on the basis of the scientific achievement of a given period. As a theory of the real world it must always be tentative, for an absolute system of philosophy would presuppose finished knowledge and a closed universe.

B. *The Origin of Western Philosophy and its Critical Function*

The known history of philosophy in the Western world begins with the Greek philosopher Thales (born about 625 B.C.), who is credited with first formulating the problem of the unity of the cosmic process. The answer given by Thales, that the unifying stuff of the cosmos is "water," is far less important than the formulation of the problem itself: Is the world process a unity, and if so, what is the nature of that unity? The thesis that there is a basic unity in all things thus presented a program for future scientific and philosophic analysis. For Thales' younger contemporary and follower, Anaximander, the cosmic process (the "physis") was the "unlimited." The history of the concept of infinity in the Western world begins with Anaximander. In addition to his mechanical view that the earth holds its place because of a balance of strains, Anaximander is remembered for his inference that life originated in the sea, and that man's ancestors had a fishlike form. For Anaximenes, the third figure in the cosmological tradition stemming from Thales, the unifying cosmical stuff is "air" and all things are to be explained in terms of condensation or rarefaction of the "air."

Such monistic attempts were quickly followed by pluralism. Thus, Empedocles supposed that there are four "roots"—earth, air, fire, and water (the four "elements" of Greek antiquity)—which were attracted by a force called "Love" and repelled by a force called "Strife." In this way he sought to give an account of the mixtures and processes of the world. More subtle and helpful was the view of Anaxagoras, who called the units of matter "seeds." The "seeds" were small particles of a great cosmic dough, in which all qualities were mixed; and the seeds represented that mixture. The source of motion was called

"Reason" (the *Nous*). It was a kind of God, introduced from the outside. Anaxagoras was the real founder of theism in the Western tradition; and, as Nietzsche has remarked, it is an ironical fact that he was persecuted for atheism.

This cosmological tradition culminated in the remarkable atomic theory of Leucippus and Democritus. The atomic theory represents the high point of all Greek speculation about the nature of matter and the cosmos. Its authors attempted a quantitative and mechanical explanation of all the qualities of experience. Their theory was a thoroughgoing materialism: in truth, they taught, there are only atoms (invisible particles, varying in size, shape, and motion) and the void.

Philosophy progressed rapidly from the speculative formulations of Thales and his followers to the great systems of Plato and Aristotle, who developed its various divisions to the form in which we know them today—to logic, metaphysics, ethics, etc. Not only did they deepen the field of philosophical thinking; they also added to the knowledge of facts. Thus, Aristotle contributed to psychology and comparative anatomy. The history of modern philosophy registers an equally fruitful development in both respects, Descartes and Leibniz being examples of thinkers who made important contributions to mathematics as well as philosophy.

Originally the philosopher included all learning within his sphere of interests, but as knowledge accumulated it was necessary to separate out the special sciences, both mathematical and empirical. Natural and social scientists now carry on investigations separately that were once provided for in the one field of philosophy, when knowledge was less expansive and specialized. The departure of a special science from the field of philosophy was at times marked by a display of feeling. That may well have been unavoidable in view of the necessity of combating the dogmatic beliefs of traditional philosophers about the nature of the physical universe, or about the nature of organisms, including man. Thus the "Naturphilosophie" of the speculative German idealists came into disrepute among scientists of the nineteenth century. The most recent science to depart from the field of philosophy was psychology; and symbolic logic may be regarded as essentially a department of mathematics.

It was supposed by some thinkers that the development of

psychology to the status of a special science (or a group of special sciences) marked the end of philosophy as such. But such judgments ignored the nature of the province covered by philosophers in their technical studies, just as they failed to do justice to the important historical function of philosophy. Philosophy still retains and no doubt always will retain its autonomy as an independent discipline; and it will continue to investigate and clarify the fundamental ideas of the special sciences.

Whitehead has emphasized the role of philosophy as a critic of fundamental ideas.[2] In his view, "philosophy is the critic of abstractions"; and its function is the double one of harmonizing them as abstractions, and of completing them by direct comparison with more concrete intuitions of the universe. Thus, it involves the survey of the sciences, "with the special objects of their harmony, and of their completion." To the evidence of the separate sciences it adds its own appeal to concrete experience. The sciences are therewith confronted with concrete fact. As expressed in a later work,[3] the true method of philosophical construction is to frame a scheme of ideas and to explore the interpretation of experience in terms of that scheme. He writes: "All constructive thought, on the various special topics of scientific interest, is dominated by some such scheme, unacknowledged, but no less influential in guiding the imagination. The importance of philosophy lies in its sustained effort to make such schemes explicit, and thereby capable of criticism and improvement."

Is it necessary to refer this function to a special discipline? May not the special scientist exercise it? He may, but he then becomes what is historically known as a philosopher. The important thing is the exercise of the function, and not a patent signifying exclusive rights. The need for mastering the history of philosophy, as well as special competence in logic, theory of value, theory of knowledge, and a group of supporting sciences, makes it practically necessary to have philosophical specialists. But they must not operate *in vacuo*, without training in various fields of learning.

[2] Cf. *Science and the Modern World* (New York: The Macmillan Co., 1925), pp. 126 f.
[3] A. N. Whitehead, *Process and Reality* (New York: The Macmillan Co., 1929), p. x.

C. The Divisions of Philosophy

Contemporary philosophy would not be depicted truly if there were any suggestion of a thoroughgoing and systematic unity in its various fields of inquiry. That has been and still is an ideal. In its special sense, philosophy is the title of a group of disciplines, which may be classified broadly as *theoretical* and *valuational* in character. Logic, metaphysics, and the theory of knowledge belong to the first class; and such disciplines as ethics, aesthetics, and the philosophy of history belong to the second class.

Logic is often defined as the science of valid thought. But it should not be limited to formal thought, as though it were independent of all considerations of truth. Wherever there is order, whether in thought or in things, there is material for logic, and logic is thus essential to all science. Each science carries a certain amount of logic with itself, or its logic. All questions of method are proper to logic, which renders it a fundamental study with universal application. In short, logic is primarily the study of the methods for solving problems or answering questions, and it aids in building the ordered structure of knowledge. The central theme of metaphysics is reality, in a peculiarly fundamental and general sense, expressed traditionally as the study of being as being (Aristotle), or the theory of existence in general. As illustrated in the science-oriented literature of recent philosophy, it contributes to the clarification of such concepts as objects, events, process, existence, and causality. In addition to the clarification of basic ideas relating to being and existence, there is the added function of synthesis, which must be undertaken anew in each scientific generation. A reasonably successful attempt at synthesis is a rare event in intellectual history. The ideal of a purely descriptive system of metaphysics has been set up, but never realized. Traditionally metaphysics has been speculative to a large extent; and whether it will always require speculative assumptions could only be decided by the progress of science. Mediating between logic and metaphysics is the theory of knowledge, the central theme of which is the study of the relationship between knowledge and reality. Typical problems of the theory of knowledge include the nature and tests of truth, the descriptive analysis of meaning and judgment, and the question of certainty in relationship to empirical and formal knowledge.

The valuational ("axiological") disciplines may be described as specifically anthropocentric studies. They are characterized by the values and norms that are peculiar to them, as well as by their selected subject matter. The separation of the valuational from the theoretical divisions of philosophy is not absolute, for they are essentially related to one another, the theoretical studies being guided also by practical interests. The natural sciences in turn contribute to the theory of man and his needs. Valuational inquiry is to be distinguished primarily by its distinctive values, not by any basic difference in method. Ethics may be defined as the normative science of conduct, whether individual or social, its positive value being goodness and its goal happiness. It is the primary task of a logical philosophy of values to investigate the descriptive, factual basis of such values and the principles determining them. Just as the principles of logic and metaphysics must be ultimately justified by a descriptive method, so must the principles of the philosophy of values be founded on facts. Ethics must be based directly on psychology and other special sciences, which furnish data on desire, emotion, and human needs in general, and which thus constitute an essential part of its foundation. If the norms of ethics are to be binding on life, they must be derived from life. Ethics must also make use of logic for the justification and systemization of its norms. The primary goal, and in fact the essence of ethics, consists in the formation of a system of desires within the life-span of an individual or group of individuals. Everything that appeals to an interest or desire is relevant to ethics. In this sense, all theoretical disciplines, no matter how abstract and removed from sensory experience they may be, are related to ethics. It is sufficient that they aim at truth and understanding, to be of practical value. The philosophy of history is concerned with the positive value of progress, which must be derived from ethical concepts; and it must be founded on the facts of history and culture.

Many attempts at the elaboration of a system of philosophy have been made—such a system would comprise both the theoretical and valuational disciplines, and it would imply a universal grasp of knowledge—but they have met with failure, for various reasons. Although philosophy is autonomous as a division of learning, it must, as has been pointed out, also depend upon the progress of the special sciences. That part of philosophy which generalizes on the basis of the findings of the special sciences must be regarded as essentially tentative, and must always be dated. This difficulty presents a standing obstacle in the way of a philosophy which is intended to be complete and descriptively founded. Traditional philosophy has also been greatly influenced by uncritically accepted ideas and influences, whether economic, political, or religious in nature. If philosophy is to rise above the perpetual standpoint alignments and share the dignity of scientific knowledge, it is essential that all traditional ideas be critically examined and compelled to justify themselves logically.

D. *The Ideal of a Rigorous Science of Philosophy*

If we may speak of a scientific limitation of philosophy, it is also true that there are factual and methodological limitations to science, since each science must inevitably face problems relating to its basic ideas and assumptions, and the validity of its methods. Husserl, in an eloquent plea for a rigorous science of philosophy,[4] has pictured the state of recent philosophy and science. As he views it, scientific learning never implies a passive reception of strange materials; it depends upon an inner creative repetition of the rational insights gained by creative minds, according to grounds and consequences. It can be said that one cannot learn philosophy because there are no objectively conceived and founded insights, and, what amounts to the same thing, because sharply defined and adequately clarified problems, methods, and theories are still lacking. He does not say that philosophy is an incomplete science, but merely that it is not yet a science, that it has not yet begun as a science. All sciences are incomplete, even the most admired exact sciences. On the one hand they are incomplete in that they have before them a horizon of open problems, which will never permit the quest for knowledge to rest; and on the other hand they have various defects in the doctrines already elaborated; here and there traces of unclearness or incompleteness are displayed in the systematic ordering of proofs and theories. But the objective truth or probability of the theories of mathematics and the natural sciences will not be doubted. There is here, on the whole, no

[4] *Logos*, Vol. I, 1910–1911.

room for private opinions or standpoints. So long as there are such private views, science has to that extent not become science but is in the stage of becoming, and is judged so generally. Husserl suggests that the word philosophy perhaps means, in relation to the sciences, a set of investigations which furnishes them with a new dimension and therewith a final completion. But the word dimension indicates at the same time that rigorous science remains science and that doctrine remains doctrine, even if the transition to this new dimension is not made. As for the system which is desired, and intended to serve as an ideal for inquiry, a decisive choice must be made. There is on the one hand a philosophical system in the traditional sense, which arises like a Minerva from the head of a creative genius, and is to be preserved in later times along with other such Minervas in the quiet museum of history. And on the other hand, there is the ideal of a scientific philosophical system, which after the mighty preparatory work of generations really begins at the bottom with a certain foundation, and grows upwards as does every good structure, in that brick upon brick is added as a firm form, in accordance with leading insights. It is Husserl's contention that thinkers and methods must part on this question. He recognizes elsewhere, however, that important contributions to a rigorous science of philosophy have been made, even by the authors of the systems which he rejects.

The lack of general agreement among philosophers, whether in different historical periods or at a given time, has been the cause of much criticism. Many of the differences in philosophical views may be attributed to the diversity of motives which lead thinkers to more ultimate speculation or inquiry. The attainment of a unified and comprehensive world view is the truly philosophical motive for theoretical philosophy, just as the definition and attainment of happiness is the leading motive for practical or valuational philosophy. The basic problems of the special sciences often lead to philosophical reflection and analysis. Mechanism and vitalism are conflicting answers to the question whether biological phenomena (or "life") can be explained in terms of physics and chemistry. The question of the relationship of the physical and mathematical analysis of reality to the world of perceptual experience has had a long history. The science progressing most rapidly at any given time tends to become the model for other sciences, and for philosophy as well. The question of the mutual relationships of the various fields of learning, or in fact the adequate definition of any one science, are specifically logical problems, which the thoroughgoing investigator must find unavoidable. No attempt at a final classification of the sciences could be expected to stand the test of scientific progress. On the other hand, some philosophers have been led by a search for absolute certainty in knowledge, or for a basis for faith beyond the domain of reason. Considerations of an irrational nature may also enter in. Ideas that are emotionally agreeable tend to persist and to influence the choice of a world view. Even so eminent a thinker as Lotze was inclined to attach value to the "heart's desires," which were supposed to make demands after the day of science had come to an end. The quest for a theoretical justification of traditional beliefs that fulfill such "heart's desires" is merely one expression of an irrational motive prominent in philosophical literature.

That beliefs are often accepted in practice because they are agreeable is true as a matter of fact. This tendency has been justified by one variety of pragmatism by formulating it as a test of beliefs: one has the right to believe when reason is unable to prove or disprove a given proposition, the test being emotional congruity.[5] This test would apply notably to faith in the existence of God and personal immortality. But it may be argued that if certain beliefs are entertained merely because they make life appear more worthwhile, the consciousness that there are no supporting rational grounds will undermine one's faith in them. That is to say, such pragmatic faith, to be effective, must be supported by nonpragmatic grounds. The attitude of otherworldliness must be examined in the light of the scientific interpretation of the once mysterious forces of nature. It is necessary to account for our temporary abode on an earth abounding in evil, if it is believed that we owe our existence to a beneficent absolute being. If philosophy is to become an independent and rigorous science, and if it is to be useful as a critic of the fundamental ideas of the special sciences, its construction must be independent of misleading and irrelevant motives. A rigorous science of philosophy is irrelevant in principle to temperament and unfounded traditional beliefs. That would mean the elimina-

[5] Cf. W. James, *The Will To Believe and Other Essays* (New York: Longmans, Green, and Co., 1897).

tion of much standpoint philosophizing, i.e., philosophizing on the basis of a previously accepted point of view, with a set of traditional commitments.

Practical considerations should not be permitted to decide our interpretation of reality, although they are of basic importance in any program to change the social reality, or the environment itself, in conformity with human interests. Such considerations enter into the subject matter of philosophy, particularly in the field of ethics. As a matter of fact, a large part of the history of philosophy has been concerned with such problems as the nature of goodness, the tests of right conduct, and the attainment of happiness, which often involved the theory of knowledge and metaphysics. That is to say, such a question as "How shall I act?" naturally involved the question "How shall I know how to act, and what are the criteria of such knowledge?" Or take, for example, the question engrossing both to the ancients and moderns, "Is the nature of the world such that happiness is attainable?" This raises the problem of man's place in the cosmos, and of the nature of existence.

But the influence of an individual's personal interests is negligible when compared to the dominating interests of the age in which he lives. It is of the greatest importance to recognize that the problems of philosophy arise in a given social context. A survey of such connections would account in large measure for the changes in the history of ideas, and would explain why some problems become more important in one period than in another. Such a study (often referred to as the sociology of knowledge) belongs to what the present writer calls social-historical analysis, which holds great promise for scholarship. Here sociology, economics, history, and psychology are combined with philosophy.

The determination of the provinces of faith and reason, and the justification (or apology) for authority were prominent in the Middle Ages, when philosophy was used to attempt to justify by rational means what had already been accepted on faith. The reaction against authority and the emphasis upon the rights of the individual, which occur early in modern philosophy, are to be explained in the light of the disintegration of feudalism and its supporting institutions, together with the first awakening of our commercial and industrial system. Again, the conflict between religion and science, as well as social conflicts, led numerous thinkers to attempt to conciliate the opposing factions by allowing each to have its region of justification. This could be done by exploiting the division of reality into two parts, such as mind and matter, or the knowable and the unknowable. Such dualistic constructions have always been found unsatisfactory theoretically, and have brought on much patchwork in the way of monistic theories. The leading interpretations of reality through one principle of existence have been made in terms of spirit by the idealists or upholders of traditional religion, and in terms of matter (or energy) by the exponents of the claims of science. It might be suggested that much trouble could have been avoided if reality had not been divided into two mutually exclusive compartments. But that would be to overlook the historical nature of the distinction.

In the final analysis, one must look to history itself for the nature and functions of philosophy. No one can legislate at any prior time and place for the whole field of philosophy. Neither is it possible to make one's own conception of philosophy retroactive. Economic, social, and religious influences must be examined, as well as the scientific thought of the time, in order to understand the difference between such philosophical attempts as those of Plato and Kant, or St. Thomas and Hobbes, or Spencer and Marx. The problems of philosophy must be viewed in their social and historical setting. Insofar as they are also real problems, however, they may be viewed systematically, and the intellectual progress of man seen to exhibit a cumulative set of methods and a growing technique to meet difficulties of a more permanent nature. Thus philosophy, like science, displays a cumulative growth, even if to a lesser degree. The interplay of the historical and the systematic views adds to the richness and complexity of philosophic study. Both must be allowed for in a comprehensive account, if we are to avoid narrowness.

The field of philosophy is characterized by its universality of application and by its interest in the ultimate concepts of knowledge. Bearing in mind the best examples of the tradition of philosophy, it may be said that the true philosophic spirit requires that one strive to be free from prejudice and bias of any kind, and that the philosopher must be a disinterested investigator in following wherever an argument or the facts may lead. He must not distort the facts to suit a preconceived view, nor should he either consciously or unconsciously permit himself to predetermine his conclusions by a biased selection of facts or reasons. His procedures must be the logical procedures of reason and experience. This is an ideal, deduced from one important section of intellectual history. It might easily have been lost many centuries ago if not for the practical need for the exact methods of science. The philosopher may be expected to set an example of devotion to objective truth in all regions of experience and knowledge. How seldom this ideal is realized is a disillusioning lesson learned from the tradition of philosophy, as well as from the present.

E. *The Philosopher in the Human City*

In 1947, a Round Table discussion was held in Mexico City on the general theme, "The Philosopher in the Human City." It was planned as part of a UNESCO meeting in which representative philosophers from a number of countries were invited to participate. Believing that conflicts originate in the ideas of men, the UNESCO officials attached much importance to the role of the philosopher. A carefully prepared outline[6] was intended to direct the discussion. No one questioned the ideal of peace; but it was evident that a general agreement on numerous basic principles could not be expected in Mexico City, any more than it could have been expected at any other time in the tradition of philosophy. The reasons for disagreement among philosophers are not to be removed at a Round Table, or any other kind of table. Fideists remain fideists, and scientifically minded philosophers hold to their commitments; while no philosophers ever forget their own cultural setting or the social interests they represent.

It is pertinent at this point to examine the various questions raised by the UNESCO outline on the basis of what has been said about the nature and function of philosophy. The UNESCO questions will be quoted at the beginning of each of the four following sections.

(1) THE ESSENCE OF PHILOSOPHY

"*Is philosophy pure speculation independent of the state of society (especially of its material state and the actual conditions*

---

[6] Prepared by the philosophical department of UNESCO in Paris, under the direction of Jacques Havet, for the Round Table discussion in Mexico City, November 5–8, 1947.

of its existence); or is it in a sense the expression of that society, and if the latter, how does it express it?"

Philosophy can never be independent of the state of society in which it arises and is sustained. The "material state and the actual conditions of its existence" are mentioned here. It is always possible to trace out some connections with the basic factors of social existence. Even the most highly speculative philosophy has its material conditions and social motivation. There is no such thing as completely pure speculation. Speculation depends upon facts; no one can construct a cosmic view out of pure thought. It is asked whether philosophy is "in a sense the expression of society?" The term expression is an apt one. It recalls the term reflection, so much used by Marxist writers, and no doubt means much the same thing. There are numerous modes of expression or of response to motivations, needs, interests, and problems.

(2) THE PHILOSOPHER'S EXISTING FUNCTION

"Is the philosopher (in his own view and also in that of nonphilosophers) a specialist concerned with abstract matters having no direct influence upon the concrete preoccupations of men? Or is it also his duty to enlighten and guide his fellowmen? Is it his duty to enter the arena of concrete discussions and is he responsible for shaping the opinions of his fellowmen?"

Is the philosopher's function limited to abstract matters? Certainly some philosophers have no direct influence upon "the concrete preoccupations of man." The question talks of "the philosopher," but, strictly speaking, there is no such being. There are philosophers, and some of them deal only in abstractions, or assert propositions that are neither true nor false; whereas others have a direct influence on human affairs—for better or worse. To speak of a direct influence is not necessarily to mean a good influence.

It is indeed "also his duty to enlighten and guide his fellowmen." The philosopher is a citizen too, and not exempt from the obligations of citizenship. Neither is he exempt from the moral obligation to apply whatever benefits may result from his intellectual activities. In practice, this means being a partisan under conditions that make partisanship necessary. The example of Hobbes and his stand on the problem of the supremacy of State or Church comes to mind. Hobbes has long been stereotyped as a child of fear, but it is fair to recognize that he was courageous enough to maintain that the State must control religion. Few philosophers today would be likely to do anything so daring.

It is also the philosopher's duty "to enter the arena of concrete discussions." The philosopher of values has the task of determining the criteria of conduct. As a philosopher, he is not responsible for their realization, nor for their application in practice. As a philosopher-citizen, however, he is interested in political action, and in the educational process necessary for progress.

The responsibility of the philosopher for shaping the opinions of people is thus a double one. As a philosopher, he must show how an objective and logically cogent philosophy of values can be constructed, a philosophy which, while developed in abstraction from particular conditions, is nevertheless capable of application to the social problems of our time. Again, as a citizen, he must strive to realize the defined ideals in practice.

All of this seems true enough. But who is "the philosopher"? Is he an idealist, a materialist, a neo-Thomist, or a mystic? Or, again, is he a totalitarian apologist? Obviously we have been emphasizing the function of the philosopher as a constructive thinker.

He cannot be unmotivated, however, for there can be no wholly unmotivated thinker. There are various types of motive, theoretical and practical. The youthful Marx protested that philosophers had merely interpreted the world differently, whereas the real point is to change it. That statement certainly expresses a truth, but it is not the whole truth. What about Plato, Aristotle, the Church philosophers, Locke, and the eighteenth-century French philosophers? They not only interpreted the world differently; they also endeavored to change it according to their ideals and motivation. Marx's tersely expressed thesis left a great deal unsaid, although one cannot fail to understand his own intention, oriented toward the working class.

(3) THE PHILOSOPHER'S PROPER FUNCTION

"Is it to be desired that the philosopher should play a direct part in the affairs of the human city and engage fully in contemporary controversies? In order to exert a really philosophic influence, is it necessary that he should to some extent withdraw

from present-day preoccupations in order to preserve his freedom of thought and clarity of judgment? Or is it desirable that he should be as far as possible detached from time and place and concern himself exclusively with pure ideas?"

Understanding now by the expression "the philosopher" the constructive thinker indicated above, the first question here must be answered in the affirmative.

What are the characteristics of such a philosopher? Plato's portrayal of a philosopher may be recalled: his status was supremely important, and there were exacting requirements for the life of a philosopher. But how could such ideally superior beings be developed in reasonable numbers? Plato's proposed process of education was carefully considered; and he was shrewd enough to forbid them to have private property, as guardians of the ideal society, "lest the watchdogs become wolves."

The requirements of a philosopher in the present constructive sense are as follows: (a) the performance of a universal suspension of beliefs of all kinds, so that prejudices and unclarified motives may be brought to light and reflectively examined; (b) the relentless use of logic in all departments of thought, with opposition to anti-intellectualism and irrationalism; (c) a competent grasp of the scientific achievements of the time, and an understanding of social problems; (d) a full sense of responsibility for theory and practice—or, in other words, a steadfast devotion to truth and its realization. The threefold function of philosophy depends upon the observance of these requirements. Thus (1) methodology, including clarification and criticism of basic ideas, requires (a) and (b). It is a convenient term, and is to be construed very broadly to include universal criticism, with clarification of basic ideas common to all types of inquiry, and also those peculiar to a given field of scholarship, together with an attempt at an evaluation of them. The exposure of motives and all causal factors involved in making judgments, in a given cultural system, requires the initial suspension of beliefs referred to in (a). The problems must be analyzed and appraised, as also the methods used to solve them. The danger of using one method exclusively, or of making it official, must be avoided; there must be a plurality of methods to deal with a plurality of problems. A good example of methodological criticism is provided by the critique of the appeal to authority. (2)

Synthesis is another important function of philosophy. Its aim is the elaboration of a tentative world view, on the level of the scientific achievement at a given time. (3) The elaboration of an objectively valid theory of values is an especially important function of philosophy. It is in the field of values that the practical function of the philosopher is (or may be) most prominently featured.

The question whether it is desirable that "the philosopher" should play a part in the affairs of the "human city" may be answered in the affirmative in the light of the threefold function of philosophy just sketched. The social conditions requisite for such a philosophical role must include intellectual freedom, or freedom of thought and expression. It must be made possible, as a matter of fact, for philosophers to exercise the desired universal criticism, and to attempt a constructive philosophy of values without pressure from any type of vested interest. The situation is fundamentally different in the case of a religious philosophy, for example. The role of philosophy in that case is ancillary, and faith, as interpreted by the religious institution involved, is primary.

The philosopher (in a good, i.e., constructive, logical sense) may and should enter into controversies by criticizing the bad use of philosophy (or philosophies), and by discussing philosophically relevant aspects of controversial questions.

As for the question of the philosopher's need to withdraw to some extent from present-day preoccupations in order to preserve his freedom of thought and clarity of judgment, the meaning is not entirely clear. All that a philosopher has to do is to meet the conditions of critical reflection already indicated. If he earns his livelihood under restrictive conditions, he cannot express his reflective criticism except by personal sacrifice, which might well make further activity impossible. This problem should be faced frankly and in detail. It applies to professors of philosophy as well as to many others; and in some countries freedom of expression in general is involved.

To detach himself as far as possible from time and place, and to devote himself exclusively to pure ideas, on the plane of the eternal, as asked in the alternative question, would be to surrender the real social world to the dominant interests. This would be simply a mode of escape, and such a philosophy may be properly called a philosophy of *renunciation*. It is in effect a means of rationalization, for a philosopher to say proudly that he prefers to retire to the realm of the pure, eternal, or timeless ideas, rather than to deal with the sordid world. The result would be a surrender to existing social relations, which must be condemned if the goal is the maximum achievement of human values. There are, to be sure, still other modes of renunciation: by restricting philosophical activity to logical analysis (thus there were "grammarians" of philosophy who interpreted logic narrowly); by otherworldliness, with a resultant depreciation of this world; and by various kinds of irrationalism.

In opposition to these, a philosophy of *participation* is urged —but not participation with unclarified motives, or with antecedent motives rooted in traditional institutions and vested interests. We must be on our guard against misleading generalities. Nothing much is said if one merely endorses participation; the kind of participation must be named and justified.

(4) CONCRETE QUESTIONS

"*Should it be thought that the philosopher's part in human affairs needs to be expanded, what kind of influence is it supposed that he will exert, and what sort of influence is it desirable that he should exert (e.g., appeasement of minds)? How should we regard the relations between the different philosophic trends in the search for an organic influence by philosophy as such, one that, transcending the plane of disputes between different schools of thought, shall serve the gradual enlightenment of the minds of all men, but without any arbitrary indoctrination?*"

It is clearly pertinent to consider the sort of influence the philosopher may in fact exert, if his part in human affairs is expanded; and also the sort of influence it is desirable that he should exert. The question suggests, in parentheses, "the appeasement of minds" as a possibility. What does that mean? If it means neutralizing the thoughts of war, or aiding in critically disposing of them, that is very good. Any contribution toward that end can only be lauded. If, however, it is taken to mean appeasement under social conditions where acquiescence is undesirable, and where human values are at stake, that is another matter.

The last question requires careful consideration, since it involves "the different philosophic trends," and their possible unification. It speaks of "transcending the plane of disputes between different schools of thought." How can that be done? It may be achieved by detached individuals, or by unencumbered individuals, but it cannot be true of the members of the various traditions, with their commitments to basic assumptions, aims, and even articles of faith. On the other hand, one should not assume simply that all the traditional movements are wrong, as a whole or in part. The traditional movements are in part concerned with actual problems, some of them important social problems. It is simply pointless to speak of "transcending" them so long as the problems and conflicts that motivated them still exist.

F. Historical Aspects of Philosophy

An understanding of the historical influences upon philosophy may help avoid the danger of conceiving it artificially. The diversity of traditional views has already been noted. They range all the way from the conception of an eternal philosophy, a *philosophia perennis*, to the view that the reflections of philosophers represent the thoughts of the ruling class in a given period on life and the world in general.

Despite Marx's rejection of speculative philosophy, it was one of his unfulfilled aims to write a treatise on "Dialectic," in which he would have conceived philosophy as an instrument of social change. Joseph Dietzgen, called by Marx "the philosopher of the proletariat," maintained that the natural science of the human mind was the positive outcome of philosophy.[7] The continued interest in philosophy in socialistic or communistic countries is, however, evidence of its broader significance.[8] John Dewey protested in his way against the type of traditional philosophy which had no social and scientific relevance except to signify a retreat from the perils of life.

It is characteristic of the great philosophers to have little regard for rival philosophies. To be sure, the fact of rivalry often leads to an exaggeration of differences, and to an excessive depreciation of one's adversaries. Kant, the transcendental ideal-

---

[7] Cf. Joseph Dietzgen, *The Position Outcome of Philosophy* (Chicago: Charles H. Kerr and Co., 1906). In Dietzgen's view, the positive outcome of philosophy shows the mind to be a part of nature; it is "the knowledge of the monistic way in which the seeming duality of the universe is active in the human understanding" (p. 342).
[8] Cf. John Somerville, *Soviet Philosophy* (New York: Philosophical Library, 1946), Chap. VIII.

ist, wrote a "refutation of idealism." The severity with which Schopenhauer, Nietzsche, Lenin, and Husserl spoke of other philosophers is unsurpassed. In contrast to poets, philosophers do not co-exist like flowers in the fields.

Admonishing his readers that the philosopher must be completely devoted to his investigation and must not be distracted by other purposes, Schopenhauer remarks that philosophy professors are led by their personal advantages, so that they do not see many things, and even miss the problems of philosophy.[9] True philosophers, like poets, he held, are born, but are much more rare. For Schopenhauer, the object of philosophy is experience —not as it is for the other sciences, this or that definite experience, but just experience itself, with its possibility, its domain, its essential content, its inner and outer elements, its form and matter.[10] When Schopenhauer goes on to speak of beginning philosophy with the investigation of the faculty of knowledge, its forms and laws as well as their validity and limits, he does so as a member of the idealistic tradition stemming from Kant. Although he advises his readers to view the "self-evident" as a problem, he is unable to question his own conception of the understanding, with its alleged forms and limits. This shows how difficult it is for a philosopher to be aware of his own premises and assumed entities, and how he may fail to see what a later generation comes to see clearly.

Not everything called philosophy in history is really philosophical, just as one would hardly honor every philosophical claim at the present time. Thus, devotees of the occult are not philosophers. But certainly everything that has been well established in the tradition with the label of philosophy must be regarded as such. The traditional differentiation of the sciences from philosophy meant that in the early stages of knowledge there was less need, or no need, for specialization. It did not mean that mathematics, physics, or psychology were once parts of a well-defined field of philosophy. The physical views of the ancient Greeks were largely prescientific in character. One man often represented and developed what turned out in later centuries to be philosophical as well as scientific departments of learning. It is usually thought that the field of philosophy has

---

[9] Cf. Arthur Schopenhauer, *Sämmtliche Werke, Vol. VI* (Leipzig: F. A. Brockhaus, 1922), pp. 4f.
[10] *Ibid.*, p. 18.

become progressively smaller through the centuries. In one sense that is true, for the special sciences have been taken over and developed by the nonphilosophers. It may be observed, however, that the field for philosophic inquiry has not contracted. It has been extended with the growth of the sciences, and the requirements for productive work in philosophy are today greater than ever before. As to the actual and varied role philosophy has played historically, and its general dependence on the achievements of the scientists, it is clear that philosophy in the traditional sense is always dated, and that it is old, rather than young, as suggested by Hodgson,[11] in whose view philosophy is still in its infancy. A new philosophy is emerging; and that should always be the case, if synthesis is to continue to be an important function of philosophy.

The view that philosophy is primarily or essentially an activity has been frequently maintained. Thus, Wittgenstein wrote: "The object of philosophy is the clarification of thoughts. Philosophy is not a theory but an activity. The result of philosophy is not a number of 'philosophical propositions,' but to make propositions clear."[12] Schlick interpreted Wittgenstein as maintaining (1) that philosophy is not a science, and (2) that it is the mental activity of clarifying ideas; and he expressed appreciation of Wittgenstein's statements, asserting that they "can do more towards the elucidation of difficult problems than many a book on metaphysics." One must point out the respect in which philosophy clarifies thoughts, as distinguished from the way in which clarification is provided by the special sciences. To say that philosophy is not a theory is not correct in every sense, for there are philosophical theories, and there is a theory of philosophy—a number of theories, in fact. Moreover, philosophy is also an activity, just as every science is also an activity. There are certainly a number of "philosophical propositions" established by the great (and less great) philosophers.

The contention that one can only show a person how to philosophize, rather than teach him philosophy as a body of doctrines, cannot be wholly true. There is a large body of knowledge properly called philosophy, including logic and the

---

[11] S. H. Hodgson, *The Philosophy of Reflection* (London: Longmans, Green, and Co., 1878), Vol. I, p. 31.
[12] L. Wittgenstein, *Tractatus Logico-Philosophicus*. Quoted by M. Schlick, in "The Future of Philosophy," *Proceedings of the Seventh International Congress of Philosophy* (London: Oxford University Press, 1931), pp. 112–116.

logically established portions of the other departments of philosophy. One learns to philosophize best by studying the great examples of the tradition, just as one does well, in learning how to compose music, to study the works of the great composers. This was well illustrated by Beethoven himself in his study of his predecessors. The content of the tradition of philosophy includes an impressive cumulative core of systematized knowledge, and one is by no means empty-handed if he today undertakes a systematic inquiry in philosophy and begins "at the beginning," as every philosopher should.

G. The "Great Tradition" of the History of Philosophy

The study of the great philosophers, in relation to their cultural conditions and historical backgrounds, as well as with respect to the logical worth of their ideas, is the theme of the history of philosophy. Unfortunately, the available literature leaves much to be desired, despite the marked excellence of many specialized studies. Books on the history of philosophy have frequently been surveys, mostly based on primary sources, but with little attention to cultural influences; and there have been numerous abridged and selected versions of such surveys.

Always noteworthy are the efforts of distinguished philosophers to interpret the philosophic past. Philosophers are usually given credit for shedding new light on the "great tradition." What frequently transpires is that such illumination reveals the rather familiar features of the writer himself. This has resulted in some interesting falsifications. Forces which had a reality in the classroom have been imaged to be historical realities. Husserl was vulnerable in this respect; and even Whitehead and Dewey were by no means immune to the tendency. It may also be recalled that Bergson interpreted French and German philosophic thought in terms of his distinction between intuition (which he favored as leading directly to the experience of reality) and intellect (a falsifying agent, so far as true knowledge of reality is concerned). By good luck, France and its allies were on the side of intuition. But it was also fortunate that the Germans did not have a monopoly on intellect.

The history of philosophy has become largely stereotyped. There is a conventional alignment of schools and individual philosophers, with the headliners and the minor figures largely remaining the same, regardless of changing historical perspectives. Berkeley rates as a headliner and Feuerbach as a minor figure, while Marx and Engels have been noticed only recently. The German historian of philosophy Wilhelm Windelband speaks contemptuously of Feuerbach as "the lost son of German idealism, who must end in the most sensuous materialism" and of "the tragedy of his development."[13] Prevented in his time, because of his religious criticism, from enjoying the academic career to which his ability fully entitled him, Feuerbach has continued to linger in the purgatory of the reigning historians of philosophy. Marx and Engels have had far more against them. It is because of their growing historical influence that the professional historians of philosophy have begun to take notice of them. But the old alignment of headliners still persists. Plato and Aristotle are usually allowed to eclipse Democritus completely, despite the scientific interest which attaches to the latter's cosmology. Much attention is accorded to idealists, including even a man of such modest achievement as Fichte, while the French materialists of the eighteenth century are grossly neglected.

In some respects, the history of philosophy must be rewritten in each cultural generation. For one thing, it has been added to, and recency should be no reason for neglect. The lasting power and the degree of influence of past historical figures must always be reassessed. Plato and Aristotle will no doubt retain their standing as founding philosophers by merit of their contributions. At the same time, their respective defenses of the institution of slavery mark them as sons of their time, as persons who accepted the privileges of the economic class into which they were born. Plato was quite as down to earth as Aristotle, and perhaps even more so, as shown by his frank recognition of the effect of economic factors on human conduct.

Both Plato and Aristotle were such richly seminal minds that all subsequent intellectual history is bound to show their influence. Their historical significance, while still considerable, is not as great as it was in past centuries, especially the medieval period. But even so noted a philosopher of science as Whitehead could still exclaim fervently, "Plato had the greatest brain that ever existed." He was himself close to Plato in important aspects, particularly in his conception of objects. It is a curious fact that

[13] *Die Geschichte der neueren Philosophie* (Leipzig: Breitkopf und Härtel, 1919), Vol. II, pp. 392 f.

a well-informed thinker in the twentieth century could look at a patch of color in his seminar room, and opine that the patch, as an event, would pass away, but that the "patchiness of the patch," as an object, would not. That kind of Platonic influence may persist endlessly and may live on despite all protest as a two-worlds theory of reality ("dualism," "bifurcation"), in response to conflicting motives. Some admirers of Plato find his greatest depth in his myths, to which Plato resorts so fancifully at times. If there is any pattern of thought which anticipates contemporary ideas, that is evidence of his imaginative powers. In no sense, however, does this have anything more to do with guiding modern scientific thought than ancient—or modern— poetry. The Church still finds Aristotle useful, although it may be surmised that he is, for scientific and logical reasons, a growing liability, and that a more tenable philosophical support may be sought for its purposes.

Bertrand Russell has not hesitated to speak his mind on the merits of the various philosophers. But his judgment of Kant reveals a lack of proper historical evaluation. Thus he wrote:[14] "Kant deluged the philosophic world with muddle and mystery, from which it is only now beginning to emerge. Kant has the reputation of being the greatest of modern philosophers, but to my mind he was a mere misfortune." It is not enough to find a traditional thinker wanting, or largely devoid of logical merit, or scientifically obsolete. A philosopher must be viewed as a product of his age, and his historical influence must be traced out and appraised, no matter what the merit of the ideas may be held to be in our own day, by persons abreast of our scholarly achievements. In fact, however, the study of Kant, like that of Spinoza, may well be indispensable in the study of philosophy in a constructive sense. There is real merit as well as historical significance in the writings of Kant. One of his achievements was to recognize the active role played by the knower in the world of experience.

In his *History of Medieval Philosophy* De Wulf at times reveals a distinctive tendency. When he speaks of Abelard, who was an early defender of the rights of reason in the medieval period, he shows the spirit of the churchmen who condemned him. Abelard, he states, "allowed his head to be turned by the

---

[14] Cf. B. Russell, *Philosophy* (New York: W. W. Norton and Co., 1927), p. 80.

praises of his enthusiastic hearers"; his "Historia Calamitatis" and letters to Heloise "manifest the sentimentality of their author; he is boastful and bitter in his criticisms of his contemporaries, and his judgments must be received with reserve." As for Roger Bacon, the foremost man of science of the medieval period, who suffered imprisonment for many years following the condemnation of his writings, De Wulf sees fit to continue to prod him: "Roger Bacon was an impulsive man, vain and self-sufficient; he thought the human race was going astray in his time, and he was intended to put things aright." The *Index Librorum Prohibitorum* is evidence of one of the ways in which the history of philosophy has been interpreted and appraised. It is a fitting commentary on the arbitrariness of such authoritarianism to recall that doctrines of St. Thomas Aquinas were condemned by Church authorities in his time, and that they were rendered official at a later date.

It may well be that Catholic historians will in the future attach more importance to "immanence" philosophies, culminating in the philosophy of Edmund Husserl, and that names like those of the existentialists Heidegger, Jaspers, and Marcel will be as important for the Church in the future as some of the philosophers in the thirteenth century have been until now. The fact that no cosmology is preached by such writers is an advantage. "Immanence" combined with a philosophy of life and an effectively conceived irrationalism may turn out to be a more secure philosophical direction.

In striking contrast is the history of philosophy as viewed by Soviet Russian scholars. Materialism here comes into its own, and the tradition of Hegel, Feuerbach, Marx-Engels, and Lenin is of the first importance. There is, however, no tendency in Russia to suppress the reading of nonmaterialistic thinkers. Professor Mitin has indicated, in a survey of "Philosophy in Russia after Twenty-Five Years," the enormous extent to which such thinkers as Plato, Aristotle, Spinoza, and Hegel have been read. Even Husserl's *Logical Investigations* was well known there, although it was held to represent a reactionary philosophy. The critical judgment of phenomenology and immanence philosophies in general was in accordance with the viewpoint of historical or dialectical materialism.

It may be asked whether an objective view of the history of philosophy is at all possible. The adoption of a theory of historical change does not necessarily rule out objectivity. A loss of objectivity is incurred if the theory in question is not treated as subject to the logical requirements of a principle of explanation. One does not have to restrict himself to the tedious process of enumerating facts, with attendant disavowal of generalizations, in order to ensure objectivity. There are also broad objective trends and causal relations to be discerned; and there are general questions on historical change, including intellectual history, to be answered. It is easy to show the inadequacies in an oversimplified monistic interpretation of intellectual history. Something is nevertheless gained by such attempts, whether spiritualistic or materialistic in character. Principles of explanation help us discover connections between facts, and their very inadequacies may assist us in establishing better principles of explanation. Broadly speaking, the following considerations must be borne in mind: the social, economic, and political realities of the period in question; the religious tradition (or traditions); the scientific level; personal facts about the philosophers, including peculiar features which might help to explain intellectual alignments; the relationships of philosophers to existing cultural interests and traditions bearing upon their motivation; the sense in which a given philosopher may be said to be an innovator; and influences of earlier and contemporary philosophers on him. Furthermore, the nature of the dominant questions confronting the philosophers must be carefully understood in terms of the cultural period in which they arose, as well as from the later perspective of our own day. The method of handling these dominant problems should be appraised, again in terms of the techniques available at the time, but also from the later perspective of a superior level of intellectual equipment. Finally, a summary view of a given philosopher, or school of philosophers, should attempt to decide what is living and what is dead in their thought systems—whereby it must be observed that the balance sheet of the living and the dead elements may change with later perspectives.

In ancient Greece, the task of the philosopher was a many-sided one, for the philosopher was also a scientist, as scientists then went. Thales' primary motivation was indicated by the aim to determine "a material first principle as the cause of all things" (as expressed by Aristotle). Plato's motivation was more complex. His thought reflected the existing social structure and also gave evidence of religious influences. At the same time, he was an innovator in social and political thought, as well as in the fields of logic, ethics, and theory of knowledge. Aristotle's thought can also be traced in part to the dominant Athenian social attitudes. He sought to solve the traditional Milesian problem of change, and he succeeded in doing so for the time. The problem of the interweaving of change and changelessness received one possible solution at his hands, just as it did in quite another (but more satisfactory) way at the hands of the atomic philosophers. When Plato and Aristotle examined the claims of hedonism as a philosophy of human values, they were dealing with an issue that was meaningful at the time. In the absence of a formulated body of logical doctrines, it was necessary to develop logic and show how the Sophists could be answered. Alternative social philosophies, including communism, were weighed by both Plato and Aristotle. The leading problems confronting philosophers in ancient Greece were varied and important. From the point of view of problems and cultural motivation, it may always remain the golden era of Western philosophy.

In the Middle Ages, the philosophers' motivation is even more clearly outlined. In addition to being a means of defense of theology, philosophy was also an instrument of criticism and intellectual progress. Because of the strong position of the Church in the feudal system, scientific inquiry was inhibited. Innovation was unavoidably restricted, and when it did occur, as in the case of Roger Bacon, it was at great personal hazard. The complete subordination of the intellect was challenged nevertheless. Roscellinus, Abelard, Roger Bacon, and William of Occam are outstanding examples of a trend which increasingly undermined the supremacy of the Church. The practical, social significance of the issue between realists and nominalists, and between rationalism and fideism, is unmistakable. The need to prove logically the existence of a Supreme Being was a constant source of philosophical concern. The much-discussed problem of individuation presented a difficulty to a realistic theory. If universals alone are truly real, what status can be assigned to an individual, and how is it possible to account for individuals? This is an example of a question resulting from the adoption of a preconceived standpoint, in this case, the standpoint of realism.

In the beginning of the modern period, the leading problems

and cultural motivation can again be clearly recognized. Francis Bacon and Thomas Hobbes are best chosen as the inaugurators of modern philosophy, because of their reaction against the authoritarian tradition and their recognition of the true role of science in serving man and achieving truth. Philosophy is now effective in combating the Church, and in lending support to the new society in the process of development. This motive comes to fuller expression in the thought of Locke, whose famous *Essay* of 1690 has been called "the first formal declaration of the intellectual rights of the individual." That Locke was a son of his time (in the same sense that Plato and Aristotle were ancient Athenians) is shown by his imposing a restriction on tolerance through his view that atheists should not be tolerated. Although Descartes appears to be more conciliatory toward the medieval tradition, his thought nevertheless contains progressive elements. His dualism, which provided for two kinds of substance, mental and physical, enabled him to solve the problem of finding a *modus vivendi* in the field of science and also in religion. Admittedly a traditionalist in his treatment of the contents of the mind, which included the idea of God, Descartes could argue for a mechanical theory of physical substance. Spinoza more consistently extended the idea of causal determinateness to the mind as well, so that all substance, all reality, is subject to causal law. This pattern of determinism becomes the ideal goal of scientific progress. Spinoza gave the problem of substance a speculative solution, which was a striking achievement of acumen, consistency, and courage for the seventeenth century. For us today it is hardly more than an empty framework, but it must be judged historically, in terms of the cultural conditions at the time. The pantheistic interpretation of Spinoza may have been no more than an element in a new Divine Comedy. It added nothing, and it deceived nobody. He learned through sad experience that too much God was just as unacceptable to adherents of the traditional religions as too little God. The work of Leibniz, too, was connected with scientific progress, particularly in his development of logic; but he was personally a more conciliatory spirit. He not only preserved traditional proofs of a Supreme Being, but added to them. As an innovator in that area, he is not celebrated, however. His spiritualistic metaphysics, although extremely ingenious, was utterly sterile and served only to support the religious tradition.

Kant is a more potent historical influence than Leibniz, even though he may not equal Leibniz in lasting positive contributions. The problem of reconciling science and religion, while providing for complete scientific autonomy in its domain, was solved in a new way by Kant. As in the case of Descartes, it was accomplished by a dualistic theory, only this one was more intricate and searching. His attempt to provide an *a priori* basis for scientific knowledge, on the other hand, was not even a success when judged by the logical standards of his own time—certainly not after the development of British empiricism through Hume. The equalitarian spirit of his ethical principles .is, however, noteworthy as a forward-looking social motive.

The successors of Kant attempted to render his thought consistent, for his dualism was regarded as untenable. Influenced by the religious tradition, they sought a principle of unity in the concept of spirit, which turned out finally to be a derivate of, or a philosophical surrogate for, the idea of God. The rising bourgeois class provided motivation for the idea of freedom, which became a prominent theme for Fichte, Schelling, and Hegel, just as it had been for Kant. It is a far cry, however, from the vacuous type of freedom extolled by the philosophers, to the actual social interests clamoring to be served under the name of freedom. The restrictions of feudalism had to be cleared away. But what else could it mean, positively? It was not necessary at the time to define the concept of freedom concretely. Its social function was felt, if not understood. That the realization of the commercial ideal of freedom could not provide equal freedom for all people was partially shown by the great French Revolution, but it remained for later nineteenth-century thought to make that clear. Hegel's unification of knowledge and his formulation of the dialectic principle as an explanation of change are the most notable results of the post-Kantian period of development. The reconciliation of science and religion, and the union of change and eternity, were undertaken by Hegel for the purposes of his own generation. But even had he lived longer, his continued personal defense of the position would have been inadequate in the face of new conditions. It should be noted that he by no means convinced all his contemporaries in philosophy (as shown by Feuerbach's criticism of Hegel's spiritualism, for example). It was possible for an acute contemporary to see the glaring weaknesses in his system. Indeed, Feuerbach's observation that Hegel had restored the God of Christianity to his post of honor, through his basic principle of spirit, and Marx's early criticism of Hegel, show that he had after all handed down speculative philosophy in a rather pontifical manner.

Schopenhauer thought Hegel "stupid" and "miserable." But Schopenhauer lacked the feeling for historical reality and the encyclopedic grasp of science which Hegel displayed. His "dream idealism" was the expression of a sick person who had somehow survived his proper time. "The world is my idea"—the initial statement of his most important work (*The World as Will and Idea*)—shows how frankly he declares himself. The death of Schopenhauer in 1860 came at a crucial time, just at the point of the emergence of the evolutionary movement. Darwin's *Origin of Species* appeared in 1859, Spencer's *First Principles* in 1862. The old type of idealistic philosophy did not come to an end, but it ceased to be as important historically. It was superseded by other types of philosophy. The evolutionary movement turned out to be conciliatory toward religion, and capable of adaptation even for the glorification of class domination and war. New types of irrationalism, and also of naturalism, arose, and it became increasingly difficult to discern the social alignment of philosophical writers—with the exception of the Catholic and Marxian movements. There have been numerous prominent philosophers in the last hundred years, but it is certain that some of them will settle down before long to their proper stature. This applies particularly to Kierkegaard, at present highly regarded in some quarters as a forerunner of existentialism. His philosophical competence was exceedingly modest, and he rates at best as a minor critic of Hegel, in which respect he does not begin to compare in significance with Feuerbach, Marx, or Engels. These philosophers, along with Brentano and Husserl, Nietzsche, Spencer, James, Dewey, and Whitehead, are among the most probable candidates of the last hundred years for lasting membership in the "great tradition."

H. *The Philosopher and the Choice of a Philosophy*

To what extent is a person a free agent in his choice of a philosophy? The answer depends upon the meaning of the term free. There is never a disengaged spirit. There are always causal conditions—physical, chemical, biological, cultural, psychological. No one is exempt from such conditions.

The question may then be changed to read: Does the choice of a philosophy depend to any extent upon the kind of person one happens to be? The view that the nature of a person determines his choice of a philosophy expresses a limited truth, which is at the same time misleading. It would be convenient, and it is no doubt occasionally justifiable, to ascribe absurdities and extravagances of thought to an individual's perversities. But a general psychologistic interpretation of philosophy would be hopelessly inadequate. Perhaps Herzberg has done a service in unintentionally showing, by his *Psychology of Philosophers*,[15] how fallacious such a treatment of philosophy can be. The number of marriages per philosopher, the degree to which philosophers are able, or unable, to be active socially, etc., represent factors no more significant for philosophy than for science. This is not to say that psychological analysis is never helpful. In some cases it is pertinent and illuminating to inspect personal facts about philosophers more closely. Figures such as St. Bernard, Eckhart, Schelling, Kierkegaard, and recent existentialists are among those requiring the element of psychological analysis for their total understanding. But Herzberg goes much further than that and, with questionable logic, makes a show of an inductive, statistical study of the philosophers. His case is decidedly vulnerable, and he merely succeeds in discrediting the limited truth that can be achieved by methods of psychological analysis. For example, the "asocial" traits of philosophers are just as much in evidence among scientists and artists, and in short are unavoidable for all men of achievement. The fact to be emphasized is that even when correctly applied, the psychological approach cannot be a self-sufficient or even a predominant explanatory method in the interpretation of the history of philosophy.

There are in fact different psychological types. James had a measure of justification in distinguishing between tenderminded and tough-minded varieties.[16] The former are characterized by their preference for a safe and smug view of the world,

---

[15] Cf. A. Herzberg, *The Psychology of Philosophers* (New York: Harcourt, Brace and Co., 1929).
[16] Cf. William James, *Pragmatism* (New York: Longmans, Green, and Co., 1907).

and the latter by their firm insistence upon building their beliefs on the basis of experience, even though one may be faced with an open and incomplete world, and no certainty of solace. The influence of temperament in the choice of a philosophy cannot be ignored. It is possible that temperament played a role in the ancient Greek discussion of being and becoming, for people react differently to motion. It is also true that some persons are attracted to an authoritarian or absolutist philosophy, because all things are firmly decided, whereas others rebel temperamentally against the rigidity of authoritarianism or absolutism, and are disposed to favor a view which allows for openness and adventure. But the social-historical perspective is more important, in pointing out the interests served by a philosophy of change, for example, or by a philosophy designed to perpetuate the existing order of society.

There is no fixed ontology of man. What a person is can only be determined in terms of what he does. One is nothing in himself, except an organic being, or a complex physicochemical structure, which is dynamic in character. The patterns of behavior which a person may exhibit, whether more or less regular, are culturally conditioned. Conscience and the self are variables. The occurrence of types of men, and their individual differences, can be accounted for causally.

Individual psychical traits are sometimes important contributing factors in the formation of a point of view, although—as in the case of Schopenhauer's pessimism and Nietzsche's extravagant intensity—the state of health and other relevant biographical facts must be considered. Attending to "the heart's desires" is also of psychological interest. It is not possible to generalize, however, or to set up hard and fast criteria. Temperament may be of deciding importance in a given case; psychological factors may be prominent, or merely incidental. It seems safe to state that they are never wholly absent, even where purely theoretical issues are at stake. Neither are social-historical motives and influences ever wholly absent, even though the position taken by a philosopher appears to be reactionary, as in the case of philosophers who oppose scientific progress in the name of an authoritarian tradition.

It may well be that the consequences of a psychologistic

theory of philosophers have not been appreciated by its proponents. Certainly the psychical differences must be due to definite causes, with at least in part a physical and organic basis, and in part a cultural one. The theory of philosophers then takes the form of a physicalistic and evolutionary explanation. But that means an explanation on a naturalistic basis, which is not what is wanted by those who hopefully look to such factors as temperament as a speedy justification for a "will to believe."

Nietzsche, in his characteristically outspoken manner, takes a firm stand here.[17] Every great philosophy, he declares, is "the confession of its originator, and a species of involuntary and unconscious autobiography."[18] He looks to the "moral purpose" of a philosopher to explain how he arrived at even the most abstruse metaphysical assertions, and he observes that the actual interests of the scholar are generally in the family, in moneymaking, or in politics. There is nothing impersonal in the philosopher, his morality indicating "who he is."

Although there is a limited measure of truth in this portrayal of the philosophers, it does not do justice to most of the facts. It simply cannot be said that every great philosophy is an autobiography when it is so demonstrable a fact that a great philosophy reflects the dominant interests and scientific achievements of an entire epoch or of a cultural generation. What follows from the element of truth in Nietzsche's polished assertions is not the condemnation of philosophy, but the need for all the more care in delineating the field of philosophical inquiry and in defining and controlling its procedures logically. It is not admitted thereby that it is wrong to be impelled by ethical motives. Ethical motives can be regarded as fundamental in the elaboration of a general philosophy. They should not be derived uncritically in a sectarian manner, however, and must be treated logically on the basis of objective facts about man as an individual and as a social being. Such facts provide direction and justification for the theoretical enterprise of the special sciences and philosophy. In that case, there turns out to be a factual basis for ethics and philosophy in general.

[17] *Beyond Good and Evil* (New York: Russell & Russell, Inc., 1964), pp. 10 ff.
[18] Santayana makes a similar observation on Husserl's method of transcendental reduction.

1. The Alleged Crisis in Philosophy

The diversity of viewpoints and the prevailing spirit of freedom of inventiveness have led some writers to speak of a current crisis in philosophy. Thus R. G. Collingwood[19] has spoken of a general condition of crisis and chaos in philosophy. For others, there is a great danger of the triumph of "anti-philosophy," meaning all types of philosophy which would undermine the philosophical tradition maintained by the person warning against "anti-philosophy." It is always pertinent to question the viewpoint of the person issuing such warnings, and to determine whether his statements are objectively true.

To some extent the disagreement among philosophers may be due to a lack of understanding of logic, theoretical as well as applied. But that is only a part of the explanation of the continued strife among philosophers, and their failure to understand one another adequately. Because there are important historical and cultural reasons for the differences among philosophers, general agreement would be unlikely to result from a more thoroughgoing study of the principles of method alone.

There may be grounds for maintaining that the present discord among philosophers is more serious than it has been in the past. There has never been a time at which greater criticism of the very justification of philosophy has been exercised. The doom of philosophy has been announced in the past, to be sure. But the challenge has never been as pointed, nor so well defined. The striking development of logic had its impact on philosophy, as illustrated by the writings of Russell and Whitehead.[20] It was a development from Russell's contention that logic is the essence of philosophy to the logical empiricists (Carnap and others), for whom the function of philosophy must be restricted to logical analysis. According to the logical empiricists, such fields as metaphysics, ethics, and the philosophy of religion "do not say anything." The challenge was presented more clearly than ever before: Does philosophy have anything of its own to say? It is understandable that traditional philosophers

---

[19] In *An Essay on Philosophical Method* (Oxford: The Clarendon Press, 1933).
[20] Bertrand Russell, *Scientific Method in Philosophy* and *Mysticism and Logic;* A. N. Whitehead, *The Concept of Nature* and *Process and Reality;* Whitehead and Russell, *Principia Mathematica.*

who operated with inherited absolutes and constructions could only be distressed when faced with that question. Predictably, there was a crisis in philosophy for them.

But this was nothing new for the traditional idealists and fideists, who found it necessary to combat the growing scientific philosophy made possible by modern scientific progress. With the rise of the evolutionary movement and the various sciences contributing to it, the idealistic philosophers and fideists were deprived of their concepts of soul, mind, consciousness, will, and other traditional props. The further development of logic left them with outmoded instruments and patterns of reasoning. With fixed standpoints to defend, they were unable to change their view that there are "necessary" principles at the basis of thought. Their chief line of defense could only be carrying the fight to the enemy, and pointing to present difficulties and obstacles in the way of scientific progress. If they do not retire to "immanent" conscious experience entirely, they may base their hopes on "the moral law within." It should be noted that the moral law in question supposedly cannot be touched by psychological or anthropological inquiry. It is a different anthropology which is invoked—in name alone, for there is no new content—a philosophical anthropology, long familiar in the religious-philosophical tradition.

It does not follow, however, that philosophy has nothing to say. In its long history, it has repeatedly tried to define the good life. Some philosophers endeavored to justify a privileged class, and others have challenged the very existence of privileged classes. Both conservative and revolutionary philosophers have had something to say about living issues, from ancient Greek to the various conflicting social philosophies of the present century. The question is, then, not whether such philosophers have anything to say, but, rather, whether what they say is defensible.

If the formulation of a method for philosophy omits this historical function and significance, a one-sided method results, or at best an incomplete method. A complete logic, inductive and explanatory as well as deductive, is required for the methodology of philosophy; but not a narrow logic, concerned primarily with the formation and transformation of sentences.[21] Apart from the deserved criticism of narrowness, however, the

---

[21] Cp. R. Carnap, *Philosophy and Logic Syntax* (London: Routledge & Kegan Paul, 1935).

logical empiricists have rightly placed emphasis upon the importance of logical method in philosophy. It is necessary to apply the concept of logical method so broadly that no well-defined procedure is ruled out. In the broad sense here intended such procedures as the dialectic method and the phenomenological method are to be grouped under the general heading of logic as methodology, with the requirement that they be subject to the canons of logical method.

CHAPTER II

Philosophy and the Methods of Inquiry

A. Knowledge and Methods

The occurrence of problems is a pervasive feature of experience, leading to methods of inquiry. It may well be said of the process of experience and knowledge: "In the beginning, there were problems." A method is a device, or a procedure, to solve a problem or answer a question. The primary aim of a method is the solution of a problem; and this includes the purpose of establishing knowledge by answering questions.

Three perspectives must be borne in mind in the general consideration of methods: the biological, the social, and the individual. (1) From the biological perspective, man is viewed as an organism, asserting himself in a precarious environment. The problems which arise concern his survival, or the furtherance of his interests. A functional logic and theory of knowledge can be worked out from this perspective. Dewey has illustrated it in his "instrumental" conception of knowledge. There was also an initial biological perspective in James's thought, the recognition of the fact of man's existence as an organism and his primitive problems. There is always a concrete, experienced problem, involving sense perception; and also past experience, of the individual and of the group, if only on a rudimentary level. (2) The social perspective presupposes and includes the organic level, but introduces its own modifications. The development of language and rational functions, and therewith all strictly logical methods, are results of group activities. (3) The individual perspective presupposes both the biological and the social elements. An individual may develop types of method in accordance with his particular capacity.

When there is disagreement among philosophical investigators, it is essential to examine the methods which have been employed. In general, methodology is as important in the field of philosophy as in any other field of scholarship. There are problems to be solved, questions to be answered, standpoints to be defended or attacked, and theses to be justified or challenged.

As already pointed out, the tradition of philosophy displays a diversity of viewpoints and varied motivations. It is entirely in order at any given time to define the field of philosophical inquiry, but it may be doubted whether that could be done successfully once and for all time, or whether one should even attempt to do so. The very distinctions among the various fields of scholarship cannot be regarded as fixed. The questions to which a philosopher reacts may involve the special sciences as well. Unfortunately, his scientific equipment is frequently inadequate. But it is also true that special scientists are often one-sided and myopic.

It is characteristic of the philosophical investigator that he feels free to operate in a universal field of scholarship. If standards of competence are met, there can be no objection to such freedom; but it may not be taken to be the reign of license, or a means of justifying each individual philosopher to go his own way as a seer. Freedom in inquiry must go along with the careful observance of the canons of method. Numerous illustrations of this need, which led to the development of a science of method, can be found in the philosophical tradition. Thus one may recall the difficulties of the prelogical period of ancient Greece, and the speculative excesses in the period of Romantic idealism in modern philosophy.

Logically supported knowledge is gained by the use of inductive and deductive modes of procedure, with the aid of explanatory devices. But what is termed knowledge in more general usage may prove to be questionable. Although everyone has amassed a certain amount of information, it often turns out that instances of alleged knowledge are merely unfounded beliefs. Not many people trace beliefs back to their sources, and few examine the foundations of their knowledge. Every judgment that is presumptive of truth may be challenged to justify itself by indicating the method by which it was obtained. *That all judgments be referred back to the methods by which they were instated or obtained in order to test their validity* may be set up as a general precept for our thinking, and may be called the rule of method. This holds for all types of knowledge, from those dependent upon a direct pointing at an object, to those derived by complex reasoning. Much useless wrangling can be eliminated in this way. An individual is not a seat of authority for his opinions, any more than he constitutes a world in himself. General agreement can only be reached by logical, objective methods. If truth were allowed to be relative to different people, there could be no science, nor social organization for that matter. Hence logical methods must be adopted for practical as well as theoretical reasons. Elementary though the distinction between objective-logical and subjective-individual methods may appear, it turns out to be of decisive importance.

This distinction may be illustrated by examining typical items of knowledge. The resident of Buffalo knows that new buildings have been constructed on the university campus. He also knows that in the 1930s there were many unemployed workers; or he may claim to know (i.e., believe) that "prosperity" has never left us. Again, he may have religious beliefs, and views about past events or the orderliness of nature. If he has had scientific training, especially in mathematics, his knowledge includes much that would not be questioned. But if he is a superstitious or mystical person, his presumed knowledge will contain beliefs all the way from "Friday the thirteenth" as an ill-fated day to the possibility of an ecstatic union with a supreme reality. It should be suggested to everyone undertaking the serious study of philosophy that he make an outline of his leading beliefs, ranging from ordinary experience to organized knowledge, and that he then proceed to examine the methods by which they were obtained or established. The difference between knowledge in a strict logical sense, and opinions, dogmas, and unfounded beliefs derived from social as well as individual sources will be emphatically brought to mind.

No one could make a list of all possible methods. If methods are devices for answering questions or solving problems, it would first be necessary to have a complete list of all possible questions and problems. It is unlikely that anyone will ever even pretend to be in possession of such knowledge. But even if a complete catalogue of questions and problems could be provided, there would still be alternative methods of meeting them. Hence, methodology may well be an endless study. One is guilty either of pedantic narrowness, or of serving dominant interests, if he sets up one type of method as official, or as the only correct method. The world of experience and knowledge is forever open, and there must always be freedom in the formulation of methods and devices for solving problems.

B. *Direct Observation and Induction*

The knowledge that there are new buildings on the university campus is established by the first and most fundamental of all methods, direct observation. It is the primary method of experience and constitutes the starting point for all other methods by furnishing them with a basis of facts. Simple observation, however, would not have enabled us to construct much science. It is only one among a number of methods of arriving at knowledge. The method of simple or direct observation yields perceptual truth and is limited to what is actually observed. The adequate explanation of what is observed is ultimately the goal of all knowledge, for what we desire most is the explanation and control of the world of experience, not an imaginary world. That there may be errors in simple observation is suggested by the conflicting beliefs about prosperity, unemployment, the varying size of the middle class, and other matters presumably before our eyes. There are reasons for that. People often see just what they wish to see, ignoring the rest; or one's observations may be merely one-sided and partial. Furthermore, that the senses often deceive us, and that they are inadequate in any case, has long been the theme of skepticism, which in its extreme form went so far as to reject the evidence of the senses completely. Such criticism should not lead to the rejection of simple observation, but to its correction.

There is another form of skepticism, more limited but far more serious and cogent than the extreme skepticism of ancient times, the form which holds that knowledge can never be absolutely certain, but only more or less probable. Since this point of view does not deny the evidence of the senses, and is essentially a challenge to dogmatism, the name skepticism is perhaps an unfortunate one.

Observation controlled by experiment eliminates the common errors of sense perception; and the logical analysis of other disturbing factors such as the biased selection of facts exposes one-sided or fallacious inquiry. Much that passes for knowledge is accepted uncritically on the testimony of others. The criticism of historical evidence often holds long-cherished beliefs in question. In the field of religious history, the criticism of evidence has been more damaging and striking than in intellectual or even political history. The unreliability of eyewitnesses—who often observe events through the spectacles of preconceived ideas and opinions—as well as the incompleteness of the evidence that has come down to us, have led us to be very cautious in entertaining beliefs pertaining to the past. Seeing may be believing, but a person may also see just what he believes.

The method of induction is an extension of the method of simple observation. It is based on description, or on the observed, but it aims to include an account of the not-yet-observed. The procedure from the observed to the unobserved involves what has been called the "inductive leap." Belief in the regularity of the happenings of nature is at the basis of the prediction of future events. Continued experience of the sun's rising each day has led us to form the habit of expecting it to rise each day in the future. However, such observations do not suffice to establish the necessity of the sun's rising, unless it is proved that nature is uniform, i.e., unless the solar system and the laws of physics will be in the future what they were in the past. But surely the uniformity of nature—past, present, and future—is not capable of verification by observation. Instead of regarding the uniformity of nature as a foundation for inductive generalization, it should be viewed as the ideal goal of scientific progress. The determination of an ordered domain of objects, or of regularity in the occurrence and succession of the events of nature, becomes an ideal that is progressively realized. A uniform system is the goal, rather than a uniformity of discrete atomic facts. It has been held that inductive principles are more or less probable; but the concept of probability does not provide an answer where the domain for inquiry is infinite, as in the field of nature. Furthermore, the method of probability involves special assumptions which are at best approximated by the facts of experience. The method of experiment (including "crucial" experiments which determine the truth of hypotheses) involves the special assumption of the uniformity of conditions, the assumption that under similar conditions similar results always follow. Principles referring to all events of an unlimited domain are incapable of verification by observation. To make use of an assumption of uniformity is to introduce a principle which observation could only partially justify.

It is easy to state the problem of induction in an unanswerable form. On the other hand, it may be presented as a psychological problem, as illustrated in Hume's philosophy. Thus one may try to account for the habit of expecting regularities to occur. But that is to avoid the real problem, which involves the events themselves. Whitehead has sought to justify our belief in induction by the rational insight that any given occasion of experience involves more than itself, and exhibits universal characteristics. He also felt secure in his belief in what he termed "the decency of the universe." That such characteristics and insights have no adequate inductive foundation shows how far removed this approach is from the solution of the problem.

We are vitally interested in the future, and in the establishment of a secure basis for prediction. In practice, we succeed very well, with the help of statistical methods and other types of method, inductive and formal. It would be well for the person first feeling the impact of skeptical doubts to reflect upon the practical success of mortality and longevity tables, for example. There, questions that can be answered are substituted for problems with no apparent solution.

C. *Hypothesis and Speculation*

The descriptive method may well be the first and final method of thought, but it must be augmented by other methods. Among these is the use of hypotheses. One does not depend upon the mere compilation of observed data to establish general principles; the enumeration of cases is not sufficient. Hypotheses are added to the description of facts; and they serve to suggest new directions for inquiry, and possible solutions of problems.

A hypothesis is essentially an explanation that serves to unite a set of facts and that may help us to find new facts. Not all hypotheses can be verified by evidence derived from direct observation. That is shown by hypotheses pertaining to the remote past, for example. Unverified and even false hypotheses may nevertheless be valuable because of their fruitfulness in leading to new knowledge. Frequently the same set of facts may admit of more than one possible explanation, in which case the logically simpler explanation (i.e., the one assuming less) is adopted. Science aims at the utmost possible simplicity in explanation. The rejection of the concept of substance, and later of the ether hypothesis in physics and the soul in psychology, may serve as traditional examples.

There is another kind of hypothesis which is not verifiable, and which does not possess any of the values of the usual scientific hypothesis. This is the merely speculative variety, operating with empty possibilities which may amount to no more than unfounded guesses about such questions as the beginning and end of existence, or its ultimate nature. But speculation also occurs in connection with meaningful questions, and where evidence can be adduced. One can speak of speculation in a good sense when explanatory devices are employed. As an aid to thought, and in calling attention to alternative possibilities in an investigation, it has been and will continue to be useful. There is often a large measure of speculation involved in setting up hypotheses. The so-called scientific imagination is really the gift of speculation at its best.

It should always be borne in mind that a hypothesis is advanced as a tentative explanation. It is a natural human weakness to become enamored of a hypothesis with which one has been long familiar. Nowhere is this more in evidence than in philosophy, where the choice of one of the metaphysical principles of explanation is so frequently a permanent commitment. One must strive to preserve a flexible attitude and to consider the alternative explanatory views. In addition to raising the question of direct confirmation, the well-known philosophical hypotheses—idealism, realism, materialism, etc.—are to be evaluated on grounds of their fruitfulness, logical simplicity, and general value for thought.

D. Deduction

It has been seen that the method of experiment involves the assumption of a principle of "uniformity of conditions." Thus, there is a deductive element in inductive reasoning; for deduction involves first of all the acceptance of one or more propositions to serve as premises for further reasoning. Mathematical knowledge provides the best examples of deduction. The deductive method is the most advanced and developed method in science, and has long been the ideal of philosophy. But even though it operates on a higher level of knowledge, on which assumptions are made explicitly and reasoning is carried on according to logical principles, there has been no general agreement among scholars as to its nature and function. Basic definitions and premises have been disputed and the very principles of logic questioned. It is by no means a self-sufficient method, since it must of necessity take its departure from the accumulated knowledge of science and ordinary experience and make use ultimately of such notions as truth, meaning, and reality. Such concepts are clarified by the philosophical critique of knowledge and experience. A deductive structure in which a few fundamental definitions and assumptions are explicitly formulated, and from which all other propositions of the science follow logically, as exemplified by Euclidean geometry, is a traditional ideal of completion for philosophy. In the seventeenth century, Spinoza made a premature attempt (in his *Ethics*) to present the field of philosophy after the pattern of geometry. The realization of such an ideal would have not only logical value, but also practical and aesthetic value.

The results of deduction cannot be guaranteed as true unless the premises are known to be true and the process of reasoning has been carried through validly. Let us take as a simple example of a deductive form the following syllogism, consisting of two premises and a conclusion: No men live more than one hundred and fifty years, and Mr. X is a man; therefore Mr. X will not live more than one hundred and fifty years. The truth of the conclusion depends upon the truth of the major premise: No men live more than one hundred and fifty years. As a general proposition it could be disproved by experience; but it can only be confirmed for a period up to the present, and never verified completely so far as the future is concerned. In a deductive system, a set of propositions is assumed, which stands for all the propositions of the system. There is a division of the system into P, the premises, and Q, the derived statements; and the deductive power of P is equal to the entire system.[1] The assumed propositions are not established inductively, any more than the proposition $2 + 2 = 4$ is proved inductively. The proposi-

---

[1] Cf. M. Farber, "The Method of Deduction and its Limitations," *Journal of Philosophy*, XXVII, 1930, 506 ff., for a discussion of whether every system may be represented by a postulate set.

tion that quantities equal to the same or equal quantities are equal to each other, and the parallel postulate, are accepted without proof to enable the geometer to deduce theorems. It is a further question to determine their truth, or their application to reality.

It was formerly believed that the premises of such systems were axioms in the sense of self-evident principles. This obsolete view was extended to include the principles and precepts of ethics. The alleged self-evidence of axioms must meet the requirement of universal acceptance. But even the principle of noncontradiction—that a thing cannot both be and not be at the same time, or, expressed logically, that a proposition cannot both be true and false at the same time and under the same conditions—was readily shown to lack self-evidence in this sense; for it was unknown to many people, and was denied or qualified by some thinkers. The English philosopher Locke[2] effectively disposed of that claim by pointing out the lack of universal acceptance of any principle, whether theoretical or moral. Any restricted form of self-evidence must also face a critical examination of its special claims in each case—for example, a special faculty, a peculiar power in experience, or some other shortcut to truth.

The results of deduction must be *valid*, the specific objective being not truth but correctness of reasoning. If deductive reasoning is considered by itself, the only query to be raised is whether the reasoning is valid, whether the rules of logic and of the system in question have been observed. Every deduced (or "proved") proposition is valid, then, with respect to the assumptions of the system. In general, a proposition which is deduced from a set of premises may be said to be valid with respect to those premises. Just as inductive knowledge is probable, with respect to the evidence, so deductive knowledge is relative, with respect to the premises. The premises themselves may be examined for their truth, when they are empirical propositions; or for their adequacy in representing an entire system of propositions, as illustrated by mathematical knowledge. The system itself will then have to be judged as true or false, mean-

---

[2] Cf. J. Locke, *Essay Concerning the Human Understanding* (New York: Dover Publications, 1959), Book I, for his refutation of "innate" ideas and principles.

ing by that the possibility or impossibility of making application to experience and its world.

In its deductive form, logic has been well described as lower mathematics, and mathematics as higher logic. Descartes' discovery that mathematics is logic, and Leibniz's anticipation of the development of a theory of deduction, have been enormously extended and realized in recent developments in formal or symbolic logic. Formal logic is an independent deductive science, but, as the theory of deduction, its applications are potentially universal. The limitations of the deductive method will prevent it from becoming the sole method of philosophy. The question of truth must always be answered; and a group of prelogical notions, such as meaning, judgment, objects, etc., must be assumed before one can begin in deduction, as has been indicated. That is to say, ontology (as the theory of existence or reality) and the theory of knowledge, which treats of truth, meaning, and judgment, are fundamental to logic. Logic must, however, be developed in as complete autonomy as possible, even though it is an instrumental science—just as all science is instrumental in the fulfillment of our interests.

We order the results of thought deductively for practical as well as theoretical reasons. The only way in which we can deal with an infinite number of propositions is by representing them through a finite (usually very small) number of assumptions which act as representatives of the system.

Let us suppose that all sciences were ordered deductively. They would have to be stated in terms of a few fundamental concepts, definitions, and assumptions. This is of course an ideal program. It would be the purpose of philosophy to determine a subset of concepts and assumptions which would be invariant to the various systems. The question of the status of the assumptions of the subsystem would then arise. Are they arbitrary in any sense? It is maintained by most logicians that a small number of primitive or undefined ideas and unproved propositions must be assumed as the basis of logic. Either these must be established as necessary by some method, or the basis of the system is to a certain extent arbitrary, i.e., it can be determined in various equivalent ways, by different groups of primitive ideas and assumptions. These considerations present the philosopher with a group of questions, some of which are still undecided.

E. The Reflexive Method

Philosophers have attempted to determine a certain or absolute beginning of knowledge by the reflexive method, which is popularly known as the method of presupposition through denial. For example, he who denies that there may be truth denies his denial; or, the proposition "All propositions are false" either suspends itself or is self-contradictory. Descartes attempted to establish certainty in knowledge by means of the reflexive method. One can doubt the existence of the external world and even of his own body. They may be objects of an illusion or of a dream, or appearances produced by an evil spirit. But one cannot doubt that he doubts (and therefore that he thinks) without contradiction. The proposition "I think" is supposed to be undeniable on principle, since it is apparently presupposed through its denial. It may be observed that the Cartesian argument presupposes the validity of memory, so that it cannot lay claim to absolute certainty. One can always doubt that he doubted. If it is not possible to doubt that one is doubting at a given moment, as a matter of psychological fact, it is also true that it is not possible to affirm the doubting process at the same time. Once the doubting experience is over, it is possible to doubt that it ever happened. Hence Descartes' procedure would seem to be nugatory. No wonder, then, that he found it necessary to attempt to prove God's existence: he could then appeal to God's goodness to validate the human mind and its experience, and so set us free from doubts.

The attempt has been made to establish the fundamental principles of logic reflexively. It has been argued that the principle of noncontradiction, which states that a proposition and its negation may not both be true, cannot be denied except by assuming the principle of noncontradiction. That is to say, the denial of the principle of noncontradiction would be equivalent to stating that "a proposition and its negation may both be true." Granting the latter, it would follow that its negation may be equally true, so that one could not be persuaded to accept it solely. The point is whether all (or any) of the basic principles of logic can be established reflexively. The proof of the procedure of presupposition through denial is not as obvious as might at first appear. In the words of Russell, "the proof that the contradictory of some proposition is self-contradictory is likely to require other principles of deduction besides the law of contradiction."[3] In any case, the reflexive method is intended to present us with a number of principles which must be accepted in some form as unavoidable presuppositions in any system of rational discourse.

F. The Descriptive Procedure of Phenomenology

Husserl, the founder of modern phenomenology, proposed that philosophy make an absolute beginning, i.e., that it make no use initially of the materials of the sciences, or of any of the assumptions of the natural view of the world. It should in his view attempt to begin without presuppositions. The method must be descriptive, but not in the sense of simple observation or induction. It must be the reflective description of essential structures and connections found in experience. Phenomenology represents a systematic and thoroughgoing attempt to elaborate a strict philosophy of experience. By presupposition is meant positing as true or as real in advance of an inquiry; this may be either the formal assumption of certain propositions, or the material assumption of a domain of objects as a field of reality. Is it possible to begin philosophy without any positing in advance whatsoever? That would be required for an absolute beginning. The natural sciences assume the field of nature, and all fields of learning assume an existent universe. Furthermore, all sciences assume the principles of logic. The descriptions of the facts of reality are expressed in propositions, which are arranged logically. Can philosophy be said to escape both kinds of assumptions?

The starting point of phenomenology is pure consciousness, the stream of experiences of an individual knowing being, with the world of objects as the correlate of his experiences. The region of pure consciousness is attained by a procedure roughly anticipated by Descartes' method of systematic doubt. Thus use is made of the reflexive method in order to define the materials of philosophy. The admittance of some kind of thought as undeniable has been seen to be unavoidable. Indubitability

[3] Cf. B. Russell, *Introduction to Mathematical Philosophy* (New York: The Macmillan Co., 1919).

is, then, a characteristic of the absolute beginning which is proposed. That is a form of conceivability, which thus becomes the basic notion of the procedure. The phenomenological method is professedly radical, in that it proceeds from pure consciousness without presupposing an existent world; and after describing the essential structure of pure consciousness, its ultimate task is to found the sciences on that basis, and to restore to us the apparent stability of nature—the task of "constitutive" phenomenology. This method, which purports to be purely descriptive, must nevertheless make use of logical principles. The clarification of the principles of logic which is accomplished by an examination of their origin and use in experience rules out contradictory observations, and thus presupposes the validity of the principle of noncontradiction. There is admittedly a gain in generality which the phenomenologist effects by considering consciousness with its correlates, without regard to independent existence. All beliefs about existence are suspended and held in abeyance ("placed in brackets"). The delimitation of a universal, inclusive realm of experience is thus made possible.

Husserl's descriptive studies of time-consciousness, of the nature of perception and other types of experience, and of the origin of logical forms and concepts in experience, are particularly noteworthy. It was also very important to carry on the tradition of "inner" description which had been abandoned by the scientific psychology of the time. Phenomenological ("purely reflective") description was intended to avoid the errors of the old method of introspection.[4] Its goal was a complete eidetic psychology and theory of knowledge, free from all metaphysical, epistemological, and scientific assumptions.

If one really means to suspend all metaphysical beliefs and to keep the procedure descriptive, he is not justified in concluding that he has thereby gained a clue to the nature of reality. The methodological procedure (the "reduction to pure consciousness") which Husserl used for the descriptive analysis of the stream of consciousness turned out to be the source of reality itself in his system of transcendental phenomenology. The concealed assumption of the dependence of existence upon a knowing mind need only be pointed out in order to align this philosophy with the idealistic tradition, of which phenom-

[4] Cf. W. Koehler, *Gestalt Psychology* (New York: Horace Liveright, 1929).

enology may perhaps be the last representative.[5] This promising descriptive method has been harmed by the metaphysical use to which it has been put, and also by its unfounded claim to absoluteness. No method has been devised which can obviate the recognition of an independent realm of existence (independent of our process of experience) and the use of logical principles of procedure.[6]

G. *Subjectivism and Objectivism as Methods of Approach*

Phenomenology represents a subjective approach to the problems of philosophy. A subjective procedure is one which treats all things as objects of experience, and only as viewed in the context of experience. It is therefore reflective in character. This is to define it nonmetaphysically.

A subjective procedure is not necessarily idealistic. Idealism requires special assumptions in order to appear at all plausible. The dependence of being upon being known has been called the cardinal principle of idealism. An idealistic procedure may be reflective. But it need not be, for after having transformed things into ideas, it may undertake to describe objects directly or "objectively." The "objectivity" of an idealist is however the result of interpretation, no matter what the particular line of argument in a given case happens to be.

In the present discussion, the dogma of idealism is disregarded. It is possible, and desirable for the well-defined purposes of the theory of knowledge, to examine experience in the context of an individual's conscious processes. When objects are viewed as correlates of these conscious processes, in reflection, the procedure is said to be subjective.

The antithesis of subjectivism in this purely methodological sense is objectivism, which is defined by the following conditions: (a) negatively, there is no "reduction" to an individual's conscious processes; (b) positively, the world and society are taken as the basis of reasoning, i.e., existence is treated as independent of its being experienced, and the individual is a mere incident in the field of existence.

---

[5] Cf. M. Farber, *The Aims of Phenomenology* (New York: Harper & Row, 1966).
[6] Cf. M. Farber, *Phenomenology and Existence* (New York: Harper & Row, 1967).

Objectivism has several varieties, only one of which will be considered as the counterpart of subjectivism in the sense here preferred. It may take the form of so-called objective idealism, which is sheer dogmatism or a mere hypothesis unless supported by epistemological arguments, all of which have been extensively criticized.[7] It has also taken the form of a materialistic theory, with mechanistic and nonmechanistic varieties. In the present discussion, objectivism is conceived broadly as a critical, reflective method of approach which conforms to the standards of scientific method.

Each procedure is able to handle certain types of question. Were it not for the purpose of answering questions which cannot (at least at present, if not on principle) be handled by objective methods, the subjective procedure would be a waste of time. It is important to bear in mind the different types of problem, as well as the technical difficulties restricting the use of the objective and subjective methods. There are problems which are (a) exclusively subjective—the analysis and the clarification of the structures of reflective experience, for example; (b) exclusively objective—induction, for example; or (c) both subjective and objective—truth and verification, the testing of cognitive constructions by reality, the unity of knowledge and experience.

Whether all problems can on principle be treated by objective means must be decided. There is still no known method of supplanting the reflective analysis of meaning, remembrance, etc., by objective procedures. Subjective ("inner") analyses may always be necessary. The claim to superiority has been made on both sides, the objectivist pointing to the greater reliability of his procedures, and the subjectivist maintaining the perfection and certainty of his method. The possibility of error exists for both types. Error is more easily seen and corrected with objective methods. It must be admitted that mistakes may be made in the description of subjective facts, apart from the differences among subjectivists which occur because of preconceived affiliations. Although there is a large degree of agreement among subjective investigators over the findings of their de-

---

[7] Cf. R. B. Perry, *Present Philosophical Tendencies* (New York: Longmans, Green, and Co., 1912); G. E. Moore, "The Refutation of Idealism," *Mind*, XII (1903); V. I. Lenin, *Materialism and Empirio-Criticism* (New York: International Publishers, 1927); and M. Farber, *Naturalism and Subjectivism* (Springfield, Ill.: Charles C. Thomas, 1959).

scriptive analyses, the claim to certainty of subjectivism is not borne out by the facts.

There can be no hope of achieving an absolute method in philosophy, in the sense that it could not be applied wrongly. Direct observation, whether in the subjective context of reflection or in normal experience, is not infallible; one can only say that *if* he has the evidence, *if* what is meant is actually there, *then* he has achieved certainty. But such a statement has only the truth of a tautology. If one uses the method of essential intuition (observation of essences and essential structures), then his statements about essences and their relations must be tested for their correspondence to the facts involved, just as with other types of knowledge and fact. The question of our knowing rational or essential truths is thus a factual question.

There is another point to be noted. The subjective investigator is not interested in his own intellectual or experiential biography per se. He is interested in establishing structural relationships. What he ascertains can be (or will not be) verified by others, for themselves. Certainly it would be desirable to treat all problems by objective (intersubjective) means, if that were possible, in the interest of socially controlled conditions of inquiry, which would reduce the region of error. But there can also be no thought of an exclusively subjective procedure, because of the narrow limits to which it is confined. Merely to duplicate subjectively what is established by the various scientific methods would add little to our knowledge.

The use of the term intentional instead of subjective has been suggested.[8] Intentionality names a general characteristic of experience. That experience is experience of something was emphasized by the Brentano-Husserl tradition and by James. This is not where the problem of subjectivity lies. What is at issue is the way in which subjectivity is located in existence, and whether the cardinal principle of idealism (that being depends upon being known) is assumed. It might be well, for the purposes of a general objective procedure in philosophy, to avoid the term subjective. In that case, positive terms devoid of tradition-laden connotations might be used, such as intentional (meaning directedness upon objects of some kind), or reflective.

---

[8] Cf. G. F. Stout, "Are there Different Ways of Existing?" *Proceedings of the Seventh International Congress of Philosophy* (London: Oxford University Press, 1931), p. 123.

For Shadworth Hodgson,[9] "subjective observation with its application to other minds and to the events of history is the whole of the method of metaphysic." He maintains that past states of consciousness are all that can be observed, and that this is done "in memory or reintegration, spontaneous and voluntary." The past states of consciousness recalled in memory are objects to the reflecting consciousness, and are said to be objective. "Whenever memory is employed, in addition to or in combination with direct presentative perception, there you have the method of subjective observation." Hodgson thinks it is the same for purely presentative observations—e.g., when watching the sun rise out of the sea. He writes:

> ... the object consists of feelings of ours; and whenever we hear the words sun, or sunrise, the meaning of the words consists in those same feelings recalled in memory. Would we know what the object seen is, what we really see, and what we infer from, add to, or combine with, what we really see, we must fix our attention on our feelings, the visible light and color and shape; and in doing this we are applying the method of subjective observation. In fact, subjective observation is nothing but objective observation taken subjectively; the same thing is seen or observed, but in the one case as if it were an absolute independent object, part of an absolute, independent external world; in the other, as a complex of feelings belonging to the observer. Both aspects are equally objective to reflection; but the former, the objective, aspect alone is supposed, erroneously, to have been always objective and not subjective to direct perception.

This passage shows how Hodgson operates with the premise of idealism. To refer to color and shape as "feelings" is to betray the use of that premise. When he speaks of the sun, he says that "the object consists of feelings of ours"—which it certainly does not. He therefore does not succeed in reducing the objective and the subjective to the same type.

Hodgson objects to the "alleged" difference between consciousness and the objects of consciousness, as an unjustified theory. In his view, "The two supposed worlds are inextricably interwoven, and are in fact but one world which a subjective

---

[9] Cf. S. H. Hodgson, *The Theory of Practice* (London, 1870), Vol. I, pp. 28 ff.: "The Method of Subjective Observation." Husserl regarded Hodgson as a writer who had independently anticipated the formulation of phenomenology. But it is to Husserl alone that we must look for a clear definition of a method of procedure.

delusion makes us regard as two." Naturally, everything depends upon the kind of world we decide it to be, whether idealistic or nonidealistic. It is Hodgson's thesis that there is one world with two aspects, consciousness the one, and the objects of consciousness the other. He protests righteously against the erroneous "metaphysical theory" which "divorces" science and subjective observation—as though the refusal to make such a separation would imply acceptance of the type of identity he proposes. The separation need only be methodological, which is sufficient. Hodgson does not object to the validity of the objective method, "but only against the notion that it is independent of metaphysic." No doubt it is literally true that the difference between subjective and objective is given only in reflection, as Hodgson maintains. That does not mean, however, that the two are fundamentally identical. They have resemblances, and also differences. If they have a common basis, that must be existential; they must both have a locus in physical reality, and involve a social organization and a cultural tradition. Hodgson's challenge, that something be named "which is an object exclusively of either one or the other of these aspects," and his contention that the two aspects are inseparable and coextensive, imply a subject-object limitation of reality, which is an idealistic dogma. Although it is true that every object which is considered is related to a knowing subject, it does not follow that, in order to exist, an object must be related to a knower.

In order to distinguish the subjective and the objective, Hodgson states that the connection between empirical and complete objects is given by direct observation, whereas the analysis of such objects separately is given by subjective observation. He writes:

> Thus, although everything is inseparably both objective and subjective, the difference between treating things separately by themselves and treating them in connection with other things external to them is a difference between methods which are the one subjective, the other objective; for to treat anything separately is to treat it in its relation to consciousness alone, and to treat anything in connection with other things external to it is to make its relations to other things the predominant object of enquiry.

Hodgson's distinction is both unclear and untenable. To treat something separately is a relative matter. It may be a separation of a region of a domain, or of an individual object—say an apple. But the apple is still no different from what it would be on the ground in an orchard, so far as its dependence on consciousness is concerned. If one's interest is in one's own perception of the apple, the subject-object relationship is essential. The object is then no longer "apple," but, in reflection, what is observed is "one's perceiving the apple."

The functions of subjective observation are said by Hodgson to be provisional definition and verification; and the function of objective observation is measurement or calculation. But Hodgson confuses things again when he holds that there is no object that is not subjective and objective inseparably, that everything alike is the object of provisional definition, measurement, and verification. The fact that the knower is incidental to reality, that there was a time when there was no subjective factor, should have helped to restore the ground under his feet.

One should record Hodgson's remark that "metaphysic, then, digs down deeper into physical phenomena than physical science does." This claim is often made. But it would be pertinent to show just what the "digging" of the metaphysician has done for the scientist. When a scientist "digs," he is frequently able to persuade his colleagues, and to add to the positive accumulation of knowledge. The reverse is mostly the case for the "digging" of the metaphysician, whose production frequently results in exhuming and reviving old fossil remains, which exist solely in the realm of ideas.

H. *Metaphysical Interpretation*

Mention has been made of an often unnamed device, of which philosophers have made liberal use: the "interpretation" of the nature of reality. This is a procedure in which traditional errors and extratheoretical motives often make themselves felt. From the standpoint of systematic philosophy the consideration of method is again primary. Thus, some philosophers choose to begin "naturally," placing "animal faith" in the independent existence of reality; whereas others suspend belief in all existence after the fashion of the phenomenologists, whether sheerly descriptive or idealistic. The field of existence, both known and unknown, has been interpreted historically in the light of idealism, materialism or naturalism, and neutral realism, which represent the most important alternatives in recent philosophy. Philosophical idealists regard existence as dependent upon knowledge and as essentially spiritual in character, a view which is maintained mostly by exponents of traditional religion. Materialists, on the other hand, attempt to explain the facts of knowledge in terms of matter, on the basis of an independently existing world. In the course of scientific progress radical changes have been made in the analysis of physical science, which has changed the form of materialism. Materialism in its traditional form made way for philosophical interpretations based on the concept of energy. Naturalism, or the philosphical generalization of the various sciences, is regarded by many as the historical successor of materialism, although this claim must be carefully examined. It was dominated at first by physical science, but was later influenced by biology and anthropology. Pragmatism is in part one mode of expression of the philosophical claims of biological science. Although the terms naturalism and materialism may be used as synonyms, in general, naturalism often refers to a more cautious and conciliatory philosophy, whereas materialism represents an uncompromising attitude. It is also important to distinguish the mechanistic and reductionistic materialists from the dialectical and historical materialists. Neutral realism is a recent development in systematic philosophy; it aims to do justice to the claims of idealism and materialism while avoiding their ontological commitments. Neutral realism interprets reality as being neither mental nor physical intrinsically: events appear as mental when related to a knower, but they may also exist apart from the context of experience, as physical events.

Several questions may be raised. Is the reality which is interpreted obtained without postulation; or is it assumed as a general domain of objects? Are there different hypothetical elements in each interpretation? Furthermore, is each principle of interpretation possible logically, granting its special assumptions? It may be stated briefly that a general field of existence, which is both distinct from experience and continuously existent, is acknowledged as nature or reality. This is a basic fact which no amount or kind of theorizing can avoid. That there are different hypothetical elements in each interpretation is shown, for example, by the assumption in idealism of a spiritual substance or an absolute spirit, which is held to make up or to be ingredient in all things. There is no empirical evidence for such a principle of philosophical ether, and its chief claims are either its explanatory value or its significance for religion. The principle of parsimony in logical procedure forbids the assumption of any entities or principles unnecessarily, so that if the explanatory value of a spiritual principle is claimed, then the explanation requires an explanation. As for its alleged emotional value in the field of religion, that must yield to the demand for truth in all things. There must be a method of proving the existence of an absolute spiritual substance, or philosophical idealism remains an unfounded speculative hypothesis. Naturalism (or materialism) is a tentative philosophy which changes its form and often its content in accordance with the development of science. The basic principles and chief findings of the special sciences constitute its point of departure. To be satisfactory, the descriptive view of neutral realism would have to include the truth of naturalism and do justice to all fields of knowledge. Neutral realism speculatively assumes an unlimited field of events or objects which exist independently of knowledge. Thus, it is not neutral over the claims of idealism.

In answering the final question—whether each interpretation of reality is possible, granting its special assumptions—it will be well to bear in mind the principle of parsimony according to which assumed elements are to be avoided as much as possible. Three points should be considered in appraising a principle of explanation: (1) Is there any evidence for its assumptions; (2) if there is no direct evidence, are the assumptions plausible in the light of our total knowledge; and (3) is it possible to dispense with the assumptions by a more economical interpretation? Naturalism and neutralism are clearly superior to idealism in avoiding the special assumption of spiritual substance.

Whitehead has protested against traditional errors in metaphysics. In his *Concept of Nature*[10] he writes: "Any metaphysical interpretation is an illegitimate importation into the philosophy of natural science. By a metaphysical interpretation I mean any discussion of the how (beyond nature) and of the why (beyond nature) of thought and sense-awareness." Maintaining that the philosophy of science is the philosophy of the things perceived, he states that "it should not be confused with the metaphysics of reality of which the scope embraces both per-

---

[10] Cf. A. N. Whitehead, *The Concept of Nature* (Cambridge: The University Press, 1920), p. 28.

ceiver and perceived. No perplexity concerning the object of knowledge can be solved by saying that there is a mind knowing it." This holds for natural philosophy. But metaphysics may pass beyond natural philosophy in a way analogous to that in which Leibniz's monadology speculated further than the classical atomic theory. In so far as it passes beyond the descriptive field of science it is speculative and makes use of a method of interpretation. The best that one can expect is a provisional principle of interpretation, which will be revised whenever the facts so demand. Were the descriptive field of "neutral" facts extended to comprise all existence, the ideal of an adequate and perceptually founded metaphysical view would be realized. That is an ideal which scientific philosophy sets up. Philosophy must always be based upon the natural sciences, even though some of its problems are such that no amount of scientific progress will completely dispose of them. In addition to recognizing the claims of science, it must take account of considerations of value and culture, and must attempt to construct a comprehensive ontological view which is free from dogmatism. That the literature of philosophy presumably devoted to this ideal has thus far only partially fulfilled its promise is no argument against the soundness of this point of view. Rather, it indicates the diversity of motives which influence philosophers, and which render difficult the realization of the ideal of logical method in philosophy. It is sufficient to mention Whitehead's "eternal objects" and Alexander's "Deity" as examples of the persistence of traditional ideas in a scientific setting.

I. *Other Varieties of Method*

If it is true that method is a fundamental concern of philosophy, it is also true that philosophy must always be subject to all the rules of good behavior which apply to methods.

Thus far we have considered the leading objective or logical methods of arriving at knowledge. It will be sufficient to make brief mention of the other varieties, which may be designated *illogical* and *nonlogical*. Authoritarian methods, and fallacious processes in general, are illustrations of illogical procedures; and nonlogical methods are illustrated by the mystics and the intuitionists.

Much knowledge is accepted on authority. That may be

legitimate if the authority is understood to be an expert representing the evidence. It is not legitimate if the authority is taken to be absolute, the sole guarantee of truth. The existence of a first cause is usually accepted on authority. Social and parental authority are different varieties of the general appeal to authority. In order to be logically acceptable, grounds and evidence must be provided. Every authority may and should be challenged to justify itself, and in justifying itself it must have recourse to other grounds, in the last analysis to evidence. The logically minded person always insists upon proof and evidence; and the mere demand that justification for an alleged absolute authority be given is sufficient to undermine its status as absolute. If the justification is given, the authority becomes relative to the grounds or evidence that may be adduced; and if no justification is given, the alleged authority will be rejected. This may be called *the predicament of absolute authority*.

The nonlogical methods which have been more or less popular are intuition, mystical experience, and revelation. These are individual and subjective, and depend upon the testimony of the person using them. Intuition and mystical experience are not meant to arrive at knowledge in terms of the understanding; therefore it follows that whatever they achieve cannot be understood. Not understanding the efforts of those that engage in intuition or mystical ecstasy, we need not trouble ourselves about them (nor do they understand themselves, for that matter). The experiences that motivated medieval mystics are rarely duplicated in our day; and if they are, we are prone to regard such cases as in need of psychological analysis. They are nonlogical because the facts they claim to represent do not behave uniformly, and hence cannot be tested.

Philosophy is not different from science in insisting upon the exclusive use of logical methods. This is commonly professed in the field of philosophy by movements which are more or less incompatible with one another, and even by strongly opposed tendencies. Thus, idealists as well as materialists, naturalists, positivists, and realists may be found among the upholders of logical method. Unfortunately, however, they do not all mean the same thing by logic, and there are alternative philosophies of logic to contend with. This is a difficulty, quite apart from the fact that so many philosophers are preoccupied with one procedure. The types of problem must be made clear, so that the diversity of procedures will not be misunderstood. The deductive method is not necessarily in conflict with the dialectic method, and both of them may very well go along with the use of a descriptive procedure. Methods must be appraised in connection with the problems they are supposed to solve.

All logically acceptable methods may be used in philosophy. It would be too much to say that experimentation, and a laboratory, have no place in philosophic inquiry. Their role is a minor one, but there is a place for them in the development of logic, for example. The special sciences furnish a large part of the subject matter of philosophy. Philosophy shares with the sciences the use of descriptive analysis, especially in the theory of knowledge. Speculation in philosophy takes the form of hypotheses about the ultimate nature of reality, or the interpretation of existence in terms of one or more basic principles. Finally, the ideal of arranging the body of philosophic knowledge in the form of a deductive system is set up as an ultimate goal. Such a program has the advantage of making clear just what is assumed; and assumptions have been seen to be unavoidable. The general rule of method should be applied to all philosophic knowledge: refer all alleged principles back to the methods by which they were obtained. It then becomes possible to appraise them and to estimate their worth. Dogmatism is ruled out, and the critical function of philosophy, as well as its role of synthesis (specifically, the philosophic synthesis of the sciences), stands out in bold relief.

J. Has Philosophy a Distinctive Method?

The claim that philosophy has a distinctive method has been disputed repeatedly. It has been argued that philosophy has no method apart from the procedures of the natural sciences, or of the special sciences.

There is no exclusive method in the sciences. A method may be used extensively in one field, but it is not restricted thereby in its use. An investigator feels free to apply any type of procedure—deductive, inductive, or explanatory—which may help to solve his problem. It is true that the devices of philosophy are seldom honored in that way, but that testifies more to the empirical barrenness of so many standpoint writers than to their peculiarly philosophical nature.

There is no reason why scholars in the field of philosophy should not enjoy the same freedom as scholars in the special sciences, and employ any procedures that suit their purposes. Restricting philosophy to the methods of the special sciences would exert an unfortunate influence on it, and impede its progress. The very generality of philosophical questions, and the peculiar nature of inquiry in the field of values, make it necessary for the philosopher to devise procedures not already in use elsewhere. It is understandable that all scholars are impressed by the sciences making most progress at a given time, and that mathematics and physics should also serve as models for philosophy. Much of the content of philosophical discussion is derived directly from the sciences. But dependence upon the sciences does not mean slavish adherence or the surrender of autonomy.

If there is no monopoly in the field of methods, is this also true of questions? Are certain questions exclusively philosophical, just as other questions are physical, psychological, etc.? The progress of science moves toward the unification of knowledge. Ideally, all knowledge constitutes one great collective system.[11] This must allow for the specific differences of subsystems if all knowledge is to be comprised, which is indicated by the term collective. Questions can be said to belong to the subject matter of a particular science, or to involve a group of sciences; they may belong to ordinary experience or to philosophy, for historical reasons. Although it may be difficult to decide in some cases, because of the continuous growth of knowledge and the great diversity of questions that can be formulated, it is usually possible to refer a question to a more or less organized system of knowledge. In the field of philosophy there are further difficulties resulting from the numerous standpoints more or less in conflict with one another. From one of these standpoints (e.g., realism, or objectivism) a philosopher may argue that questions meaningful only in terms of another (e.g., idealism, or subjectivism) are not genuine. If it is maintained that no one person or tradition has the authority to decide on the differentia of philosophical questions, it is not implied that

[11] See Chapter VI.

all standpoints are equally justified, for the requirements of logic and of the facts must be met. That such claims may be unwarranted is shown by the analysis of the various types of questions ("methodogenic" and "derived" questions, to be considered in the following chapter). The relatively greater amount of explanatory work in the field of philosophy, and the fact that some of its questions are not capable of being decided with evidence, add to the reasons which make rival views co-exist. Philosophy does not entirely differ from the special sciences in this respect.

There can be no finality to the classification of the sciences once and for all time. It may be that all questions pertaining to reality will someday be physical questions, and also that the language of that future physics will be quite different from the present physical language. It may be expected that the nature of philosophical and psychological questions will be determined differently in different historical periods; there is no sure way of predicting what will be done a generation from now. Will psychology reclaim the "inner" description of the mental processes? That could only be greeted as leading to greater progress, leaving it to philosophy to be interested in methodology, the critical clarification of basic ideas, the logical analysis and instatement of values, and the periodical synthesis of knowledge. Philosophy is conditioned by and evolves along with the rest of knowledge.

The most important methods purporting to be strictly philosophical in recent philosophy are the dialectic,[12] phenomenological, and logical-semantical[13] methods. The question whether philosophy has a distinctive method can only be answered after a careful examination of all these, which would go far beyond

---

[12] Cf. G. W. F. Hegel, *Logic*, trans. W. Wallace (Oxford: The Clarendon Press, 1892), pp. 147 ff.; W. James, *A Pluralistic Universe* (New York: Longmans, Green, and Co., 1909), chapter on "Hegel and his Method"; J. Royce, *Lectures on Modern Idealism* (New Haven: Yale University Press, 1919); J. E. McTaggart, *Studies in the Hegelian Dialectic* (Cambridge: The University Press, 1896), and *A Commentary on Hegel's Logic* (Cambridge: The University Press, 1910). For the Marx-Engels conception of dialectic, cf. F. Engels, *Herr Eugen Dühring's Revolution in Science* (New York: International Publishers, 1939).

[13] Cf. B. Russell, *Our Knowledge of the External World as a Field for Scientific Method in Philosophy* (London: George Allen & Unwin, Ltd., 1914); L. Wittgenstein, *Tractatus Logico-Philosophicus* (London: Routledge & Kegan Paul, 1961; New York: The Humanities Press, 1961); R. Carnap, *Philosophy and Logical Syntax* (London: Routledge & Kegan Paul, 1936), and V. Kraft, *The Vienna Circle: The Origins of Neo-Positivism* (New York: Philosophical Library, 1953).

the scope of the present discussion. We can state now, however, that the dialectic and the logical-semantical methods are closely dependent upon the progress of the sciences, whereas the phenomenological procedure aims to begin with a clean slate, and to "constitute" all items of experience and knowledge out of the most elementary units of experience. Even so, it will be found not to be something *sui generis*, but related to other descriptive methods under the general heading of methodology. This theme will recur in a later chapter.

It is always helpful to consider such methods in relation to the primary tasks of philosophy as it is investigated at present. Philosophy functions as a critic of the fundamental ideas of the sciences; it attempts to contribute to the unification of the sciences; it continues to make further progress in its own proper fields, as in logic, ethics, etc.; and it attempts a tentative elaboration of a world view, a general synthesis of knowledge proposing to be the most adequate at a given time and a given stage of scientific advancement. The only methods which may be recognized logically are those founded upon experience, or which make use of reasonable and explicit assumptions. The central problems of philosophy, both in their origin and in their essence, are problems of method, and their treatment requires the exclusive use of logical methods. It is in this sense that logic may be said to be the essence of philosophy.

CHAPTER III

Experience and the Problems of Philosophy

The chief problems of theoretical philosophy can be divided into two groups: (1) those that are immediately suggested by and originate in ordinary, natural experience, or the perceptually founded problems; and (2) those that arise in conceptual thinking and the use of abstractions, or the conceptually founded problems. It should be noted at once that the two groups are not unrelated, and that the primary function of conceptual thinking is to furnish devices to meet the needs of the first group, problems relating to perceptual experience. The perceptually founded problems may be defined by a reflective analysis of the process of direct observation. The method of direct observation, or simple description, is the basic method of experience. It provides the starting point for all scientific thinking; and the adequate explanation and control of perceptual reality is the end of all inquiry. The method of direct observation may not be applied exclusively, however. For the purposes of inquiry, we cannot limit ourselves to what is actually experienced by human beings, because the diversity of problems requires a diversity of methods. Furthermore, it would be disastrous for ontology if the scope of reality were restricted to what is actually apprehended by individuals. Human beings are of course finite and essentially limited in the extent of their experience. Are we to conclude that the realm of existence is no larger than the field of actual experience? If the mind is called the subject and the things of experience are called objects, then this narrow view of direct observation would limit our consideration of objects to just those that happened to be in a relationship to a subject. Professor R. B. Perry has argued[1]

[1] Cf. *Present Philosophical Tendencies* (New York: Longmans, Green and Co., 1912).

against the use of such a "subject-object limitation" (already referred to in the preceding chapter), an error which has been conspicuously committed by idealists, and is also found in the literature of pragmatism.

It is instructive to examine the perceptual process, in order to determine how problems of philosophy arise out of the consideration of what is apprehended immediately. Some of the most crucial problems at the basis of thought are seen to arise naturally out of the process of experience. The failure of actual experience to solve its problems with its own materials has necessitated the use of abstractions and technical devices, which give rise in turn to new problems.

A. *The Perceptually Founded Problems*

It will be sufficient for the present discussion to consider rapidly some of the principal philosophical questions that are prompted by the course of natural experience.

(1) Natural experience always involves reference to an object which is an ingredient in a process of change. The experience itself is an active process. Every object of perception is experienced through a series of changing appearances. A reflective description of the perceptual process shows clearly that objects are perceived from various perspectives, and that they appear with a changing set of aspects. If that is so, what is the basis for our belief in the identity of objects? This may be called the problem of the unity of a perceptual object. Any object of ordinary experience will serve as an illustration. There is a yellow matchbox before me, of which I have a one-sided view. As the light varies, as I turn my head to gain a more complete view, I receive a series of views of the matchbox, changing from impression to impression. Continual eye movements and changes in me, and continual objective changes of the object and its physical environment, determine different appearances of what I believe to be the same object. What is the justification for speaking of the matchbox as an identity? In other words, the question of the unity of the objects of experience arises: What is the basis in experience for maintaining that each object persists as a unity throughout its changing appearances?

As I perceive the box directly or "naïvely," i.e., when I live in the act of perception, I am not aware of the changing stream of impressions. Knowledge of the nature and structure of the perceptual process is only possible with the aid of reflection. The object of natural perception is always incomplete. An all-sided perception of an object has been said to be unthinkable. But the object of reflection is always complete; the incompleteness of the perceptual object is apprehended completely.

(2) Further consideration of the process of perceptual experience brings to light the distinction between appearance and reality as a general problem. This may be seen more readily with the aid of a threefold distinction in the cognitive situation —the distinction between the act, content, and object of knowledge. Perception, understood here in a very wide sense, is essentially an activity which discerns a certain number of features in an object. The features which are actually discerned, such as color and shape, make up its content; and the totality of its features constitutes the object for perception. Whether the object is something more than or other than the totality of the features which could possibly be discriminated in it need not concern this discussion. The threefold schematism of act-content-object oversimplifies the analysis of cognition, but is useful as an introduction to the problem of the nature of the perceptual object. Each act of perception of the matchbox has its content of discerned features, so that there is a changing set of contents to correspond to a changing series of acts. Nevertheless we say that each act refers to the same object, and each content is a selection from the same object. Is the object nothing more than what is meant as the same throughout a conflux of perceptions? The distinction between what is selected in perception and that from which the selection is made, or the object, may also be made for any quality of the object. Suppose that I attend to the color or shape of the box; then what I perceive is a color aspect or shape aspect, from a certain perspective. Here again we may describe reflectively a series of changing appearances of the qualities of the object. Any given appearance of the color refers to the same color; and any given appearance of the shape, from one side or another, refers to the same shape, or the "real" shape of the object. An accurate description of what occurs in perception must therefore require a distinction between that which is actually discerned in a given act of perception, and that which might be apprehended in a complete perception, if that were possible.

In other words, the distinction between content and object must be drawn.

The distinction between appearance and reality is thus discerned in the analysis of normal perception. It was exploited from an entirely different point of view by the ancient skeptics. The skeptics[2] were well aware of the ways in which the human body conditions experience, as well as the ways in which relationships of external factors in the physical world, or relationships of objects to human knowers, make a difference in experience. Had their motivation been constructive, their efforts would have been much more fruitful. The enumeration of difficulties in the way of knowledge collapses as soon as the difficulties are understood. The mountain appears to be smooth from afar, whereas it is not really so. The straight piece of wood appears bent when immersed in water. To continue with a modern illustration: railroad tracks appear to converge in the distance, whereas they are really parallel. The color-blind person, or the person who is unable to discriminate tone intervals, will perceive different appearances from those of normal persons.

The simple negativism of the skeptic was not present in Kant's thought when he undertook to distinguish between phenomena and "things in themselves." Kant took the appearances very seriously: they were the domain of scientific inquiry. But he argued for another realm apart from human experience, which could never be known.

(3) The world which is discovered through perception is essentially incomplete, and there is a dark horizon of indefinite reality which fringes it. Experience, which is always incomplete, involves more than itself, and it tells us that its object is not an isolated part of existence. The matchbox is in this room, which is in Buffalo, which ultimately involves the whole realm of nature as its environment. There are no isolated facts in experience.

If what is experienced is called the field of the known, then it is clear that the incompleteness of experience indicates a further region of the unknown. The unknown becomes more and more known in the progressive course of experience. The distinction between the known and the unknown is illustrated in every occasion of experience, which is partial and incomplete, and

[2] Cf. C. M. Bakewell, *Source Book in Ancient Philosophy* (New York: Charles Scribner's Sons, 1939).

also by knowledge as a whole. There is always more to be known. This is entirely different from the alleged realm of the unknowable, which has been held by some writers to be something inaccessible on principle to the understanding as such (one thinks of Kant and Spencer in this connection). It will usually be found that there are ulterior reasons for pressing the distinction between what allegedly can and cannot be known. Among other things, the objection must be met that to maintain the existence of an unknowable realm involves a contradiction, for it implies knowledge of the supposed unknowable. In brief: the quantitative incompleteness of experience and knowledge is a simple matter of fact, which does not imply the "qualitative" inaccessibility of any region of reality. The unknown, which must always be admitted, does not imply an unknowable. The issue of rationalism versus agnosticism should be considered in the context of its basis in immediate experience. Carefully viewed, taking into account the nature of experience and the logical processes involved, there is no support for agnosticism. The rationalist takes his stand with the growth of knowledge, holding that every meaningful question can be answered, and that the human understanding is ideally capable of solving all problems.

(4) Experience testifies to the reality of change. The ancient Greek philosopher Heraclitus recognized this general truth when he said, "All things flow, nothing abides," and again, that "one can never step twice in the same river."[3] But he also thought that there is a *logos*, or an order in change, which does not itself change. This led to another fundamental problem, which has been debated through the centuries.[4] The philosophy of change had the support of immediate experience. The opposing philosophy of being, which denied the reality of change, had to support itself by logic. No doubt because his theory violated the evidence of the senses, Parmenides was the first philosopher in the Western tradition to attempt to prove his position by logical means. He defined change as involving the

---

[3] Cf. J. Burnet, *Early Greek Philosophy* (New York: Meridian Books, 1964).
[4] Cf. Plato's *Parmenides*, in *The Dialogues of Plato* (New York: Random House, 1937); W. D. Ross, *Aristotle* (London: Methuen & Co., Ltd., 1964), and St. Thomas Aquinas, *Concerning Being and Essence* (New York: D. Appleton-Century-Croft, 1937). Cf. also W. James, *Some Problems of Philosophy* (New York: Longmans, Green, and Co., 1911), and G. Santayana, *Scepticism and Animal Faith* (New York: Charles Scribner's Sons, 1923).

passage from or to nonbeing; and he assumed that thought must be about something, and that what cannot be thought cannot be. Now, nonbeing is nothing, which cannot be thought, and hence cannot be. Therefore, there can be no change, for change involves nonbeing. It followed that time is merely a trick of the senses, and that there could be no divisions of space. Being is all at once, according to this reasoning.

The interweaving of change and changelessness has proved to be one of the most persistent problems of philosophy; and it is in fact directly suggested by the observation of the facts of experience. One must be very cautious, however, lest he impose a fixed framework of permanence on a world which appears as a world of flux. The change of the world acts differently on different people; some find change exhilarating and welcome, whereas others fear it. This holds for change in society as well as in nature. Nietzsche has aptly said, in his *Birth of Tragedy*, that being is a fiction invented by those who suffer from becoming.

(5) The problem of change and permanence, or the issue of temporalism versus eternalism, has also taken the form of an issue about the status of universals. We make use of concepts in order to name objects that we recognize as being the same. Recognition of sameness in the objects of the world is a simple fact of experience. The red color of bricks is recognized in a red sweater. Is it the same; are both merely instances of redness which may be anywhere and yet nowhere in particular? In other words, is redness a universal which exists independently in a preferred sense of the term existence? We perceive many individual men, and describe them by means of the concept man, or humanity. To believe that universals existed in their own right would be to maintain that "men may come, and men may go, but humanity goes on forever." Triangularity, equality, magnitude, justice, and beauty are common examples of universals.

It was formerly believed that ideas of universals were innate in the mind at birth, a view which was refuted in modern philosophy by Locke.[5] We derive our ideas of universals by a process of abstraction from many individual men.

Two questions arise, which must be sharply distinguished to avoid confusion: (a) Is it necessary to use ideas of universals

[5] Cf. J. Locke, *op. cit.*

in our thought, particularly in science? and (b) Are the universals themselves real, i.e., do they exist? This problem, which was prominent in the philosophy of Plato, was of considerable importance in the Middle Ages as the issue of realism versus nominalism, the realists maintaining that universals were real, and the nominalists holding that they were merely names. This issue has by no means disappeared, and in its further reaches it raises one of the pivotal problems of philosophy. Descriptive psychology will account for the development of our ideas of universals as abstractions from concrete experience. But there still remains the problem of the existence, or "subsistence," of such objects.

The careful thinker will hesitate before claiming permanence or a higher level of existence for any objects of thought or experience, and he will consider the method used to justify that thesis. There is no logical method which can enable us to prove that there are permanent patterns of existence in experience. Essential insight into the nature of things will not suffice, for there is no guarantee that either the alleged essential insight or the nature of things will be uniform and permanently ordered in any respect. Concepts are indispensable in all thinking. No one could deny their theoretical importance or practical necessity. But that does not give ontological status to any conceptual entities, unless it be assumed that the conditions of ordered thought are the conditions of being, and that being depends upon thought. Such a standpoint, however, collapses under critical examination; it is not supported by our knowledge of the facts, which show thought to have a subordinate place in existence.

In the preceding discussion, a distinction between universals and essences was not drawn explicitly. In the philosophy of Plato, universals were found to be puzzling (goodness, magnitude, etc.), and there was a great gap between the superior realm of universals or ideal forms and the changing world of sensory experience. Aristotle sought to bridge the gap and to give a basis for knowledge (as distinguished from sense perception) by means of the concept of essence. The object of knowledge must be general, in Aristotle's view, and it is marked off as the genus plus the differentia, which is the definition of a thing, or the statement of its essence. The essences are somewhere between the universal and the particular, and are, for example, dog, ox, etc. An essence marks what is necessary in a thing; it is the "that without which the thing would not be what it is." Essences are accordingly at least "affairs of knowledge." Are they also "affairs of reality"? Does the essence name what is truly real, as distinguished from the changing world of experience? In view of the facts of the evolution of organic life, it would be simply dogmatic to hold that the essence of any animal persists or is fixed in reality.

One may ask furthermore, whether what has been said about universals and essences has any bearing on the status of universal propositions. Consider a universal proposition of the form "All a are b" or "No a are b." If the universals are judged to be fictions, they are justified by their usefulness. Universal propositions, on the other hand, are assertions which are supposed to be true or false, valid or invalid. The proposition $2 + 2 = 4$ is established deductively, on the basis of defined universals—numbers and their relationships. No series of particular observations could positively establish such a proposition as true universally. The proposition is valid independently of actual experience. What the world will be like tomorrow cannot be known with certainty today. That the proposition $2 + 2 = 4$ may be invalid tomorrow is ruled out, however, by its status as formally valid, in terms of the system of arithmetic.

(6) It may be impossible to justify belief in any permanent features of the world of experience. But all experience, because it is limited, reaches into the future, just as it retains traces of its past. We wish to predict the future; what is the real basis of our ability to do so? Anticipation of the future is an essential characteristic of every occasion of experience, just as much as retention from the past is a fact. Every act of perception has before it the open horizon of the future. In the words of Hegel, "Only the present is, the before and after are not; but the concrete present is the result of the past, and it is big with the future."[6] This is the experiential basis of the problem of the prediction of the future. This apparently meager insight into the structure of experience gives us a measure of confidence in the basis of induction, and is at the root of our belief in the uniformity of things. Nevertheless, as already seen, the logical limitations of the belief in uniformity prove to be the limitations of the inductive method.

[6] G. W. F. Hegel, *Sämtliche Werke* (Stuttgart: Fr. Frommanns Verlag, 1929), Vol. IX, p. 86.

It can be said that in practice we find the predictions made by scientific reasoning work well enough to be satisfactory. This is sufficient for immediate purposes, but does not answer the traditional philosophical interest in determining the essential structure of reality. But the desire to find rest in an eternal and orderly world benevolently oriented toward human beings should not dictate one's view of the world. Some people desire a safe world, in which they can find a place "through all eternity." What the ultimate character of reality is, and whether the remote future will reveal a world of existence anything like the present or not, must remain unanswered so far as the evidence is concerned. It would be immeasurably more fruitful and important for people to focus their attention upon their status in the immediate, present world, and to provide for its greater safety.

(7) Any occasion of ordinary experience may present problems within its own scope. The occurrence of errors in experience is in fact unavoidable. An adequate description of the process of perception, through reflection, must bring to light the distinction between correct and incorrect perceiving; and on a higher level, between correct and incorrect knowing. This gives rise to the problem of truth, and, closely related, to the problem of consistency. Consider, for example, an experience of illusion: at night we may not be certain whether the object before us is a tree or a man. We correct ourselves through a series of perceptions, from different perspectives or by means of different senses, to affirm or deny our original judgment. Such a situation exhibits the rudimentary features of what we later call negation and contradiction. Thus we may live through a conflict, namely, the two opposing judgments: "It is a tree" and "It is not a tree, but a man." The judgment "It is a man" is held to be true if it agrees with the fact "that a man is there." We live in perceptual experience; and in that process we set up the ideal of a harmonious stream of correct perceptions. The possibility of attaining that ideal is virtually posited as a practical postulate. This is one place where the genetic approach merges with the systematic treatment of a problem. The problem involved is obviously that of truth and consistency, and although it is solved readily in practice, it has led to various theories about the nature and tests of truth, and to questions of a purely conceptual character.

The ideal of truth as correct perception arises naturally. In the course of reflection and with the growth of knowledge it becomes necessary to furnish tests for the determination of the truth of a judgment. Various theories have been advanced to provide a test of truth. There is (a) the copy theory, according to which an idea is true if it copies or is similar to its object; but it is not clear in what sense an idea can be like its object. Our account of the incompleteness of perception has shown why such a theory has no basis in experience. In any case, the correctness of the copy would have to be shown by means of another idea, which in turn would have to be shown to be a correct copy of the original idea-object situation; and so on. (b) According to the correspondence theory, an idea is true if it corresponds to its object. But the correspondence of an idea to its object must itself be verified; and the various modes of correspondence must be indicated. It would be better to use the concept of correspondence for the definition of truth in its general meaning, which requires tests for its correctness.

(c) The view that an idea is true if it is consistent with the body of established or accepted ideas is a useful auxiliary test, of considerable value in ordinary experience as well as in scientific thought. We have a certain amount of confidence in the truth or validity of a judgment which is consistent with the system of judgments we have already accepted. But there is danger that such a test, if used excessively, would be an obstacle to intellectual progress. That it could not be the sole test of truth is shown by the fact that it could not be made to apply to the first judgments that have been accepted, which require another foundation. The evolutionary theory did not cohere with traditional beliefs; and the same has been true of new and revolutionary ideas in recent scientific development. The coherence theory might on occasion be conservative and reactionary if it were applied excessively. It is quite different in mathematics and formal thinking, where truth is taken to mean validity. Thus, the Pythagorean theorem is true in the sense that it follows validly (i.e., in accordance with logical procedures) from the assumptions of Euclidean geometry. Coherence then becomes an internal test of truth, and in a limited sense it applies to formal systems of knowledge. We may ask whether a coherent body of knowledge, such as a consistent mathematical system, is true in the sense of external truth. In that case, a further test of truth is required, which will only be possible in terms of the application to or correspondence with reality.

((d) The most significant recent theory of truth has been advanced in the literature of pragmatism, a biological and psychological philosophy with William James, John Dewey, and F. C. S. Schiller as its leading exponents. According to pragmatism, ideas are essentially functional or instrumental. A true idea is therefore one which functions properly, or which works. While admittedly correct in its version of the role of ideas in experience, this theory requires a careful analysis of the ways of verifying ideas, if our knowledge is to be stable. The pragmatic test of truth is one which depends upon actual experience. It is a self-sufficient test—the truth to be determined by a process of verification. If practical success is to be regarded as a test of truth, the concept of success must be clarified. How is one to know when an idea works? Ideas function in many ways, hence there are various kinds of practical utility. An idea may be established as true, first of all, by a direct perceptual test. For example, an idea may lead us directly to a desired object. Again, scientific ideas may be verified by experimental methods. Another kind of verification which has been advocated as a test for ultimate beliefs is emotional agreeableness. It may be observed that a person who understands scientific method will be likely to find the test of agreeableness to be itself disagreeable.

(8) There is still another distinction to be noted in the nature of knowledge. It is an essential feature of knowing that it refers to objects which differ from the contents of the experience of knowing. That is to say, it is essential to an idea that it refer to an object which is different from itself. The transcendent reference of the process of experience has been pointed out repeatedly.[7] One's idea of the public library and the library itself are two different things. The descriptive analysis of the perceptual process establishes this as a basic fact. The much-discussed problem of transcendence has long been prominent, although it has appeared in a number of different forms historically. The question of the possibility of consciousness grasping objects transcendent of itself has been raised at various

---

[7] For example, by W. James in his *Principles of Psychology* (New York: Henry Holt and Co., 1890).

times. The denial that consciousness can apprehend nonspiritual transcendences is necessary for metaphysical idealism. If mind and matter are distinguished on principle, with mind regarded as thinking substance and matter as extended substance, as held by Descartes, the traditional problem of mind and matter (or mind and body) is presented in its most acute and insoluble form. For how can mind then know matter, and how can they react upon one another? Historically the popular solution was to use God as the medium, or else to repudiate the metaphysical distinction in favor of a monistic view.

It is necessary to distinguish three kinds of transcendence—cognitive (epistemological), material (metaphysical), and spatiotemporal transcendence. (a) By cognitive transcendence is meant the essentially dual nature of knowing, which is discerned through the reflective apprehension of any act of perception. This is a statement of fact. The passing contents of successive perceptions are to be distinguished from the object of perception, each act of perception selecting from the totality of features that make up the object. This is emphatically brought before us in false perceptions. For the epistemological monist, idea and object are one, and it is a serious problem to account for error in experience.

The following distinctions may be noted: the numerical distinction between idea and object, referred to when it is said that cognitive dualism is true in fact; there is also the distinction between the actual content of an experience, and the possible content; and there is, furthermore, the difference between actual knowledge, or the known, and additional possible knowledge, or the unknown. Finally, there is the distinction between the realm of the knowable and the alleged realm of the unknowable, which has already been criticized. The first three distinctions can be ascertained descriptively, whereas the fourth is logically untenable.

(b) By material transcendence is meant the distinction in nature between the subject or knower, and the object or known, on metaphysical grounds. There is supposedly a substance beyond mind. As has been indicated, various theories have been advanced to explain the nature and relationships of the two substances, following the unsatisfactory dualistic standpoint of Descartes. A philosophy of monism, which interprets all existence in terms of one principle of being, escapes such difficulties. Monistic theories deny a real distinction in kind between subject and object, but must allow for cognitive transcendence as a fact. Monism may be materialistic, according to which mind is interpreted in terms of matter or "motions within a body" (as in the materialistic philosophy of Hobbes), a view which has been defined more exactly by recent scientific psychology. Opposed to this is the traditional doctrine of spiritualistic monism, which has been defended particularly by exponents of the religious tradition, and has therefore been prominent historically. According to that view, the realm of material nature is construed in terms of a spiritual substance (Leibniz), as the contents of a divine mind (Berkeley), as a domain which is posited by an absolute self (Fichte), or as the self-alienated appearance of spirit (Hegel). If one speaks of a beyond on the basis of an idealistic metaphysics, the beyond could not be a spiritual substance. Could it be a Supreme Being, superior to spiritual substance, or a transcendent cause in any sense? There is no compelling theoretical reason why an idealistic metaphysics must allow for a transcendent cause of being. Without a transcendent cause, however, some form of pantheism would be the theological result.

The term spirit has a vague, emotional significance, and there is no empirical evidence to support belief in its existence. Its continued survival may be regarded as an interesting historical fact, along with the survival of institutions in general. That the supposition of a spiritual substance is unnecessary and unfruitful, and that considerations of economy in thought render it superfluous, will be granted by all who are committed to scientific method. As an absolute spirit it is a metaphysical version of the concept of God. Hegel's "philosophy of spirit" was interpreted thus by Feuerbach, who stated that it signified the restoration of Christianity through philosophy.[8]

The effort to find an alternative to spiritualism and materialism has been a motive in the philosophy of the recent past. The philosophy of neutral monism, as represented by neo-realism, is a prominent example, already mentioned. According to this view, mind and matter are but the expressions in different relationships of truly real entities which are neither mental nor

---

[8] Cf. L. Feuerbach, *Die Philosophie der Zukunft* (Stuttgart: Fr. Frommanns Verlag, 1922), p. 47.

physical.[9] This view is advanced as a principle of explanation and is intended to be free from speculative dogma. That one cannot know neutral entities except in a mental context means no more than that all that one knows is known. But it does not follow that things have to be known in order to exist, as has been argued by idealism. This view makes possible an expression of the critical attitude of the older materialistic and naturalistic philosophies, without any actual commitment to them. Therein lies its immediate utility, or its convenience for the cautious academic mind—but also its historical failure, for it places itself outside the arena of strife between the forces of faith and reason. For the rest, the order of neutral entities is simply so much unnecessary superimposed baggage on the explanatory structure of science.

(c) There remains the third kind of transcendence, spatio-temporal transcendence. By this is meant reaching out beyond the immediate specious present as the direct field of actual experience. The field of immediate experience is all that we really have as a matter of fact, but more is indicated by it. The theory of the infinity of space and time is a further extension of this insight into the boundaries of our limited field of experience. The factual basis for such transcendence is to be found in the essential characters, already noted, of retention (retaining from the past) and protention (anticipating the future)—as well as spatial reference beyond the boundaries of the field of actual experience—which are attached to all experience. We do not know whether there is anything infinite in the nature of things; neither do we know that there is not. The principle of infinity is assumed in order to explain what is actually given in experience.

B. *The Conceptually Founded Problems*

It is thus clear that some of the most important and fundamental problems of philosophy are directly suggested by the process of experience. There can be no sharp cleavage between the problems rooted in natural experience and the conceptually founded problems, for it was necessary throughout to use conceptual devices in making distinctions and formulating problems.

---

[9] Cf. R. B. Perry, *Present Philosophical Tendencies* (New York: Longmans, Green, and Co., 1912), and B. Russell, *Philosophy* (New York: W. W. Norton and Co., 1927).

On the other hand, all conceptual problems may be ultimately referred back to perception for their derivation and criteria of truth and utility. In point of time the perceptual problems are first, and are fundamental in the same way that sense perception is prior to reason. But even an exhaustive survey of the facts of experience would not suffice to solve its own practical problems, not to speak of the theoretical problems of philosophy. A descriptive, genetic approach to philosophy is both useful and instructive, but it will neither solve nor dissolve some of the systematic problems of knowledge. Kant has stated[10] that "our reason has this peculiar fate that, with reference to one class of its knowledge, it is always troubled with questions which cannot be ignored, *because they spring from the very nature of reason,*[11] and which cannot be answered, because they transcend the powers of human reason." This applies especially to problems about reality as a whole, and ultimate questions involving space, time, and causality. His belief that the attempt to answer them involves darkness and contradiction may be shown to be unfounded in the light of the progress of science. Meaningful questions can at least be clarified if not answered with the aid of conceptual devices, as shown by the introduction of such concepts as points and instants, and the principle of infinity. Points, which are supposed to make up space, and instants, the units of time, are abstractions and are nothing in fact. The problem of the relationship between such abstract units and the units of perceptual experience then arises. Zeno, famous for his paradoxes, is credited with the discovery of this problem, which has been finally solved in our own time by Whitehead.[12] The method employed by Whitehead consists of deriving points and instants from concrete stretches or extensions as displayed in experience and reality. Two alternative methods are open to us: we may attempt either to build up time and space out of abstractions; or the abstractions may be derived from real occasions of time and space. The latter method abolishes a puzzling distinction between reality and abstract explanatory units. Real time cannot be constructed out of durationless instants; but an instant may be derived by extensive

---

[10] Cf. Kant, *Critique of Pure Reason*, Preface, trans. F. Max Müller (New York: The Macmillan Co., 1919).
[11] Italics mine.
[12] Cf. A. N. Whitehead, *The Concept of Nature* (Cambridge: The University Press, 1920), in which he offers a "complete solution of the problem."

abstraction from a real duration. Furthermore, the concept of infinity has been at the basis of modern mathematics and science. The mathematician postulates a field of entities, or a universe of discourse, which transcends all possible human experience, and the result is twofold. First, he develops a self-consistent system of thought which at least has value for thought; and second, his discoveries may prove to have explanatory value for the field of experience. Thus, modern geometry has been an important aid to physics; and it was by means of the theory of infinity that the nature of irrationals, which troubled the ancient Greeks, has been clarified. The modern theory of infinity, as developed by Georg Cantor in the 1880s, requires the radical revision of some deeply rooted ideas and prejudices. The principle that the whole is greater than any of its parts is applicable to a finite aggregate, but not to one that is infinite. An infinite aggregate is defined by means of postulates, whose consistency must be tested. All disciplines making use of infinitude deal in concepts that transcend the range of human experience. Thus the principle of infinity serves as a basic assumption of empirical thought. There are many more conceptual problems, both in philosophy and in the various sciences. The ordering of knowledge beyond the immediate present involves such problems. The reflective person can no more avoid them than he can avoid the problems of the perceptual class.

The difference between the perceptual and conceptual problems may be stated otherwise: the first group arises from the consideration of the material of experience, whereas the second group is concerned primarily with explanatory devices and deduction. Descriptive analysis and insight into the essential structure of experience are the primary methods available for the perceptual problems.

If we are modest and practical, we may define the goal of philosophy as the best possible explanation of the world of experience within existing human and cultural limitations. At the present time there is much philosophical ferment, with the issue of religion versus science gradually disappearing from prominence. The newer issues are predominantly scientific and logical. The older dualism of spirit and matter has become obsolete; and whatever motivation for dualistic views of the world remains is kept alive by social conflicts. It does not seem unreasonable to expect the elimination of all important social conflicts in the present century. In general, the solution of all practical social problems may be expected, on the ground that what is made by man may be controlled by man. Here, an objective philosophy of values will be an effective aid. Afterwards, the perennial problem will remain—the further understanding of reality, and its progressive mastery through science.

C. *The Nature of Philosophical Problems*

It has already been indicated that problems or questions are the primary determining conditions of all inquiry, including philosophical inquiry. It would indeed be foolish to adopt a method first, and then set sail hopefully on a voyage of discovery; still less should one proceed without a well-defined method, prompted solely from within.

No question is per se "first." Presupposed by questions are the conditions which give rise to them, and the contexts within which they are meaningful, or in terms of which they are defined. It is not necessary to consider whether the knower, or the questioner, is also presupposed. To be sure, there can be no questioning without existent questioners; but the questions themselves need not (and in most cases do not) depend upon the questioner. Questions may be regarded as "first" in the sense that one begins with them, and then seeks to determine their conditions and significance, and to establish answers by the formulation of procedures.

All the significant historical philosophies were designed to solve important problems of their time. To state that every philosophy is set up in response to a single problem or question would be to oversimplify. Some thinkers are primarily interested in a single central problem; but complex motives operate in most of the great systems of philosophy. Religion, science, and politics are important motivating influences, as may be readily seen in the thought of Plato, Aristotle, Hume, Kant, and Hegel. There is no such thing as an unmotivated thinker.

The words problem and question are being used interchangeably in the present context. Problems may be stated in terms of questions, or sets of questions. A question must always be formulated in terms of a system of knowledge. It is a presentation of alternatives, so that the question "Is a included in b?" stands for "Either a is included in b, or it is not." Not every combination of terms constitutes a legitimate and meaningful question. Thus a distinction must be drawn between system-proper and system-strange questions.[13] It is always easy to distinguish such questions in a logically constructed system of knowledge. In the system of arithmetic, for example, any question that can be formulated in terms of the basic concepts and relations is "proper." It is not permissible to introduce a predicate that is "strange" to the system, and to ask, for example, "Is the number 3 green?" System-strange propositions belong to the order of nonsense. A contradictory question is said to be absurd, and it belongs to the order of countersense. Such an error is incurred if one asks about the existence of something outside the domain of nature, so that one asks, in effect, for the location of something outside space. In a system of knowledge which is not well defined it is sometimes difficult to decide on the relevance of a predicate. This difficulty is understandably increased in the field of philosophy as a whole.

It is not enough to consider the problems of philosophy from the point of view of their perceptual and conceptual bases. That may be useful as a first approach to the problems, especially to the more lasting problems, often called the perennial problems of philosophy. The terms empiriogenic and methodogenic correspond in part to the distinction between perceptually founded and conceptually founded problems. Empiriogenic means "originating in experience," and methodogenic refers to problems which arise because of the method in use. On further analysis it is also wise to separate problems due to the use of a method from those due to the adoption of a standpoint, such as idealism or materialism.

Empiriogenic problems arise in ordinary, natural experience, and also in reflective experience. All the forms of experience must be included—not only perception, but remembrance, imagination, conception, etc. The reflective examination of experience shows that it is normal and natural to make use of idealizations. In other words, the use of conceptual devices is rooted in experience itself. There is in experience what Husserl has called a synthesis of identification. What would otherwise be an unrecognizable flux is organized, held together, and ideal-

---

[13] Cf. M. Farber, "Theses Concerning the Foundations of Logic," *The Philosophical Review*, XXXVIII, 1929, and "Logical Systems and the Principles of Logic," *Philosophy of Science*, IX, 1942.

ized in our experience. This may be illustrated in the ordinary perceptual experience of things apprehended as unities (chairs, trees, etc.), and also on the level of scientific experience and conceptual thinking (straight lines, imaginary numbers, chemical elements, etc.). Thus, the basis for the conceptually founded problems is empiriogenic. On the other hand, there are also methodogenic problems on the level of perceptual experience— e.g., the inductive problems resulting from the method of direct observation.

The two classifications of problems overlap, but they are not identical. The second classification, involving empiriogenic and methodogenic problems, is more far-reaching and satisfactory, because it refers to experience in its universal sense, including conceptual processes; and the concept of method is similarly universal. The discussion of perceptually founded problems has shown how problems arise directly out of ordinary, everyday experience. No account was taken, however, of the historical character of experience.

The methods which are devised to solve basic problems of experience may in turn lead to further problems. The subjective method, when conceived in a thoroughgoing sense, is "egological" in character, i.e., the sphere of inquiry is restricted to one's own ego, to one's own conscious processes and the objects to which they refer. Adopting it, the problem of the existence of another knower is unavoidably incurred. That problem is methodogenic. Could it be said to be a real problem, which requires the "reduction" to an individual knower's conscious processes? It is not a real problem, because an individual knower is really the result of group life. If the existence of another knower is a problem for "egological" subjectivism, there are still further problems, equally serious, when the existence of other knowers is established. From the intersubjective point of view, involving the conscious processes of a society of knowers, the existence and independence of what appears to be an external world presents a problem. Thus, one form of the problem of transcendence is unavoidable if a general subjectivistic procedure is adopted. If one begins with the realm of conscious experiences, then what is beyond consciousness—the realm of transcendence—becomes in turn a problem. Such methodogenic problems do not arise for naturalists or materialists, with their objectivistic procedures. The crucial problem of induction (the problem of generalizing from some to all) has no meaning for a subjectivistic procedure, at least of the type illustrated in phenomenology. But for a naturalistic, empirical method, there is an enumerative problem of induction; and the existential status of thought and its abstractions is a problem.

For an authoritarian theological standpoint there is a problem of evil; so too for pantheism. For Platonic realism, the individual is a problem, because if universals alone are truly real, the status of an individual must be determined. Spinoza faced a similar difficulty. The derivation of the finite from the one infinite substance is clearly an example of a methodogenic problem. His failure to solve it was due to the limitations of his own system of thought. Since the infinite and finite excluded one another by definition, the finite could not be obtained from the infinite. On the other hand, an absolutely infinite substance could not be obtained from finite things. Furthermore, the universal is a problem for the nominalist, although it turns out to be one which can be treated satisfactorily, unlike the converse problem resulting from Platonic realism. In other words, beginning with individual events, or particulars, it is possible to provide for the function of universals, without metaphysical hypostasis. But if one begins with a metaphysical theory of universals, the problem of accounting for particulars, and getting into relationship with particulars, may well be insoluble.

Allowance must thus be made for a group of problems associated with the methodogenic type, which result from the adoption of a particular standpoint (authoritarianism, spiritualism, or moral idealism, for example). Such problems may be said to be secondary or derived. They may occur because of ulterior social or religious reasons. The traditional mind-body problem and the problem of immortality serve as further examples. They are due to an antecedently accepted set of beliefs, rather than a well-defined procedure. In this respect the advance of science may present a problem, or a whole set of problems.

It is frequently difficult to distinguish a methodogenic from a standpoint problem because there may be elements of both involved. For the mystic, for example, the existence of matter is a problem; so too is the existence of his own body.

The so-called problem of knowledge has been used as a wheel-horse for idealism. With idealism antecedently adopted, the problem is so defined that it appears to lead necessarily to the acceptance of the idealistic principle of explanation. C. A. Richardson[14] illustrates such a biased statement of the problem when he speaks of a dilemma faced by a realism of the type maintained by Russell: "For if we accept the conclusion commonly drawn from the Weber-Fechner law it follows that there must be three classes of sensibilia. Those which do not form part of an object of experience; those which do, but are not perceived; and those which do, and are perceived." He asks for the criterion of difference between members of the first two classes: "What difference *can* there be? And if we admit that there *is* no difference, it follows that all sensibilia which form part of an object of experience must be perceived." It does *not* follow, however, unless one tacitly assumes the cardinal principle of idealism, which declares that being depends upon being experienced.

The confusion incurred in the argument may be traced to the motivation of the standpoint. In general, idealistic thinkers reveal a characteristic haste in their attempts to transform reality into spirituality.

In his discussion of "The New Materialism,"[15] Richardson writes: "I cannot *find* the subject in the content of my experience, for I *am* the subject. Yet why should this preclude me from being aware of my own existence? On the contrary, it seems to me to imply an order of certainty at least equal (though on different grounds) to my certainty of the existence of the sense-data I perceive. I am *acquainted* with sense-data; I *realize* . . . my own existence. This term 'realize' is the nearest I can get to a satisfactory expression of that indubitable awareness of one's own existence which is implied in self-identity." Richardson fails to see the simplest way of treating the problem of the relationship of mind and body—to treat mind as the way the body acts. One does not have to operate with such a mysterious epistemological subject as he "realizes," and speak of "one's own existence" as something one "realizes," leaving the question of existence apart from one's body unclarified. The living body in action includes mental activity in its scope; and nothing is left out. By using assumptive terms, a specious pseudoproblem may be engendered. Turning to "the problems

---

[14] *Spiritual Pluralism and Recent Philosophy* (Cambridge: The University Press, 1919), pp. 108 f.
[15] *Proceedings of the Aristotelian Society*, XXI (London, 1921), 51–70.

of substance, permanence, and change," Richardson asks: "What *is* a substance, and how is its permanence reconciled with the change of its states?" "Sense-data" are ruled out, as not being of help here, for they change, even if gradually. He wishes to use the notion of the subject here: "For the subject would seem to be the very type and pattern of what may be called substantial or concrete existence." "Concrete existence" is construed in such a way that only "the subject" would seem to meet the requirements, as "an entity which is something *in and for* itself, something with a nature which cannot be fully grasped or apprehended by any other entity, but which has to be 'lived' or 'realized' to be understood. . . ." The problem posed is a false one in terms of experience. But even the false problem of "permanence" is not solved by the use of a ready-made set of assumptive concepts, notably the subject. The main target is materialism. Richardson's text is as clear as it is revealing: "Materialism, in its modern form, will receive a shrewd blow if it can be shown that the being of sense-data depends, at least in part, upon their being perceived." To the question whether there are any entities at all which are not perceived, he replies that "there is no reason whatever to suppose that there are no entities of any type which are not perceived." At least one type has been referred to, the subject.

It would seem, then, that important historical problems may have no basis in empirical reality. This leads to still another mode of designation and classification of philosophical problems, into merely historical and real problems (referring to the real world of experience). All problems are historical in the sense that they arise in a definite historical context, at a particular time, and derive their significance from a culture setting, which is historical. To say that a problem is merely historical means that it has no basis in existence, or in empirical reality. The question of the immortality of the soul is a clear example: if there is no empirical evidence for a soul, the problem cannot be said to be a real one. The term real refers to the real world of experience, to the realm of evidence. Every experience is real, in the sense that it is a real psychological event, involving a real nervous system. But not every object of an experience is real. Thus, a dream object (a centaur) is real in a subjective sense, even though it is not an object of our social, factual reality. The traditional mind-body problem is similarly a merely historical problem (of course, this does not apply to the descriptive and causal problems of mental behavior). The belief in such entities as minds (the old-fashioned mental substances, or spiritual containers) as distinguished from extended matter, or in "spirit and flesh," is sufficient to bring about the merely historical problem. It would be hasty and superficial, however, to dismiss such problems as not significant. They may be historically significant, even though they can be dissolved by applying the scientific test of reality.

The following questions should be asked of any philosophical inquiry or reflection: (1) What question is it designed to answer, or what problem is it intended to solve? (2) Is it a real question, in terms of experience, or does it arise from a preconceived standpoint or method? (3) What is the context to which it belongs? That must be determined in order to make sure of its significance. It should be considered in terms of its own context, in which it is directly meaningful; and also its place in history, to determine its social-historical significance. (4) Can it be handled by any of the already defined methods in the natural or special sciences? (5) Can it be said to be a peculiarly philosophical question, and how can that be determined? (6) How can it be answered in philosophy? Before one treats philosophical questions as such, he should have a theory (or logic) of philosophy, in order to settle upon criteria and guiding principles. It must also be considered whether the criteria and principles can be final in any sense.

It followed that every philosophical problem should be examined to begin with in two ways: its source, to decide on its reality; and its place in history, in order to determine its social significance. It must always be ascertained whether a problem can be solved by the accepted procedures of the sciences; or, if it is peculiarly philosophical and not open to scientific treatment, whether a solution can be obtained by philosophical means.

It is often said that there are persistent or perennial problems of philosophy. Is it true that the same problems appear again and again in the history of philosophy? Or is it our interpretation of the problems as perennial which is projected into the history of philosophy? This question must be examined carefully by studying the actual formulation of problems by philosophers in various periods. It will be convenient to discuss the two extreme views which are possible: (a) that problems are always the same, and are interpreted in the same way; (b) that problems are never the same, with that fact merely obscured by the custom of using the same terms, or sufficiently related terms to suggest the identity of the problems.

(a) The evidence is clearly against the view that problems are always the same, and are interpreted in the same way. When the problem is the same, for instance the truth problem, it may be understood differently in different periods, or by different thinkers. Gorgias has been credited with the discovery of the problem of transcendence. But it would be presuming a great deal to read such a methodogenic problem into the thought of that sophist, who could hardly be regarded as a serious thinker. The truth problem itself is different in the setting of ancient philosophy and in a modern idealistic or pragmatist setting. It is also understood somewhat differently.

The exponent of perennial problems has in mind the problem of a first cause, the existence of God, immortality, freedom, the space and time dimensions of the universe, appearance and reality, the nature and criteria of goodness, beauty, etc. It is sufficient to point out how such problems are affected by the changing level of science and by different social-historical conditions, to show that they could not have been exactly the same throughout all history, and that they could not have been understood as the same.

In a limited tradition, in which there is a great degree of continuity and dependence upon transmitted ideas, one may indeed speak of the persistence of problems. That has been shown by Professor H. A. Wolfson in his monumental historical studies of Philo and Spinoza.

On the other hand, we must be careful to recognize the change in significance of a problem, or of an issue, in different historical periods. A good example is the problem of universals as raised in Greek philosophy, in the medieval period, and in modern philosophy. Consider, for instance, Berkeley's nominalism in its significance for a conservative, religious, and anti-materialistic philosophy, as distinguished from the radical nominalism of the Middle Ages which was anti-religious in effect, if not in intent.

(b) To argue that no problem can ever persist is to violate some obvious facts. The problem of the existence of God appears frequently in the same form. Hence it would be false to state that the same problem never appeared again. On the other hand, to argue that it is not possible to understand the problem in the same way as others have conceived it may mean that identity of (psychological) understanding is impossible or highly improbable. It may also mean that different cultural conditions, with changes in language and accumulated experience, make it impossible ever to grasp the same type of problem. But that is patently false. Even though the actual understanding of problems may differ somewhat from case to case, that does not rule out sameness of the type of problem. Certain general types of problem are recurrent; but there are also many changes in problems, so that sometimes only the same name may persist.

It has not been the fashion to settle philosophical controversies in accordance with a set of logically determined criteria and principles. Some disputes go on endlessly, and acquire the reputation of being perennial problems, or of being insolubilia. Even the logical destruction of an argument does not necessarily bring about its disappearance. Anselm's ontological argument for the existence of God, although invalidated by an obscure contemporary monk and rejected by St. Thomas, has gone on nevertheless. The treatment of traditional theological arguments by Hume and Kant was sufficient, in the words of Whitehead, to "warn theology off the premises of philosophy." But it has not been "warned off" a large section of recent and contemporary philosophy. A philosophical problem which is an expression of historical or deep-seated personal factors is never effectively solved, no matter how acute the logical analysis that is brought to bear upon it. Such problems may be forgotten, by-passed, suppressed, or revived again and again. The most conspicuous traditional problems should be called issues. Here problems are involved, but no settlement occurs because of the influence of conflicting interests and party alignments. Prominent illustrations are provided by spiritualism versus materialism, supernaturalism versus naturalism, rationalism versus authoritarianism, and realism versus nominalism.

It is a striking fact that a controversy may be kept alive under what would seem to be the most discouraging logical conditions. The parties apparently do not need to speak the same language, or even really to understand one another. They may even seem to be talking about different things, if one presses for exact definitions. But—and this is where some linguistic analysts miss an important point—they really may be opposing one another, even though the questions at issue may not be in the foreground. The fact that the opposition is felt strongly is sufficient evidence that a cause of some kind is at stake, no matter how indirectly or obscurely the issue may show itself.

An analogy may be helpful. It has been said that religion and science cannot conflict because they can never meet. And yet, theories like Spencer's notwithstanding, religion and science have met repeatedly. No plan for a "peace without victory," no dualistic arrangement, from Descartes to Spencer and beyond, has prevented the opposition from appearing in an acute form. The reason can only be that everyone is talking about the same thing sufficiently to keep the opposition alive. The exponents of the traditional party of religion are not deceived by a subtle division of reality into the knowable or phenomenal, which is to fall to science, and the unknowable or noumenal, designed to be the last resting place for religion (if it can be called a place). Neither will a logical empiricist be more acceptable to the party of religion when he points out that his analysis of religion as "saying nothing," as virtually nonsense, is distinct from atheism.[16] Such a disclaimer of atheism is still in effect a disclaimer of religion, which aligns him against it.

The issue of spiritualism versus materialism is particularly instructive. It would be convenient to find, as Sheldon does,[17] that they just belong together as a polar unity, and in that way dispose of both as errant members of what is at bottom an indissoluble unity. The reasons for the opposition go far beyond the speculative attempts to solve the mind-body problem in the modern period. The mind-body problem—the problem based upon the supposition that there are two kinds of substance, mental and material—was solved speculatively in a number of ways, among them the theories of materialism and spiritualism. Contributions toward the real scientific solution of the mind-body problem have been progressively made through the cooperation of the sciences, especially philosophy and psychology, physiology, and physical science. Yet the issue persists, and it may be expected that spiritualism in some form will remain opposed to materialism and its historical derivates, whether

---

[16] Cf. A. J. Ayer, *Language, Truth, and Logic* (New York: Oxford University Press, 1936).
[17] Cf. W. Sheldon, *Process and Polarity* (New York: Columbia University Press, 1944).

for personal or social reasons. So long as there is organized interest in a supernatural realm, there will be a lively motivation toward spiritualism, irrationalism, or agnosticism. In addition to such personal factors as temperament, spiritualism in one form or another tends to be perpetuated by schools, and a position once taken by a member of a school is apt to be preserved, if not out of loyalty to a beloved master, then perhaps out of sheer inertia.

It has become tempting to scholars recently to dispose of materialism as an obsolete doctrine. Among others, Bertrand Russell has referred to changes in the conception of matter in physical science as a source of difficulty. Certainly the older types of materialism are obsolete in important respects. Philipp Frank has similarly characterized materialism:[18] "If . . . one understands by materialism the opinion that all processes of nature can be reduced to the laws of Newtonian mechanics, then this is not a philosophical principle but a physical hypothesis," a hypothesis which has been shown to be wrong. It must be borne in mind that the nature and content of materialism changes historically, and that it has to be reformulated in each scientific generation. Furthermore, it may be predominantly physical, or biological, or historical, in its emphasis. That Frank ignores the historical meaning of the issue of spiritualism versus materialism is shown by the following statement:[19] "But this antithesis that according to traditional philosophy exists between materialism and idealism is not, according to Mach, a scientific antithesis . . . they can be neither proved nor refuted by experience." The historical opposition was nevertheless a significant one.

It is very easy—and convenient—to dismiss materialism as metaphysical, or as a vague term. One may then exercise the critical function of materialism as opposed to spiritualism, and take over its constructive scientific function, without having to bear the stigma of "crass materialism." Frank treats the realist, as opposed to the idealist, in the same way on the question of whether the outer world really exists.[20] Speaking of the Kantian

---

[18] *Between Physics and Philosophy* (Cambridge, Mass.: Harvard University Press, 1941), p. 153.
[19] Pp. 220 f. Cp. *Philosophy for the Future*, ed. R. W. Sellars, V. J. McGill, and M. Farber (New York: The Macmillan Co., 1949) for an account of the significance of materialism in history and in relation to modern science.
[20] Pp. 63, 88 f.

view that scientific truth is truth only in relation to the human mind, Frank observes that this conception permits every type of question, but makes it difficult to distinguish between sensible and meaningless formulations or problems. "With this conception, one can ask whether the outer world really exists, and whether we can know the world in its true properties. To these questions the realist replies in the affirmative, the idealist in the negative. Neither can adduce any concrete experience as decisive for his answer. Both agree, however, that such a question is a sensible problem." But Frank is wrong in maintaining that the realist cannot adduce any concrete experience as decisive for his answer, for all experience, individual and social, overwhelmingly speaks for the realist, and against the idealist, here. All natural experience and much scientific knowledge testify to the independent existence of an outer world. Frank and his colleagues go too far in their criticism of metaphysical questions as devoid of meaning. Their adoption of a syntactic-logical method does not compel them to treat both realism and idealism as nonsensical in the question of the existence of the outer world. Frank cites the view of Carnap and Wittgenstein, that "the questions beloved by the school philosophy, such as whether the outer world really exists, not only cannot be answered, but cannot even be expressed, because neither the positive assertion, falsely called the realistic 'hypothesis,' nor the negative idealistic assertion can be expressed through constituted concepts." But why may they not be expressed as methodogenic or derived questions? To hold that both realist and idealist are guilty of a question without sense is to operate with a narrow conception of the sense of a question. The historical significance must be established and care taken to distinguish the real from the merely historical, as well as the empiriogenic from the methodogenic.

The traditional problem of knowledge has undergone similar modes of treatment. Like materialism, the problem of knowledge has appeared in numerous forms, and in different historical contexts. The very possibility of knowledge has been challenged, and its limitations have been outlined in different ways at various times in the history of philosophy. Conflicting theories of knowledge are still with us, some of them rooted in remote traditions.

Montague has offered a solution of one problem of knowledge in his *Ways of Knowing*.[21] The three schools of theory of knowledge which he considers—objectivism, subjectivism, and dualism—are opposed to one another in important respects. To illustrate their concordance, however, he shows how the concept of truth can be stated adequately in terms of each theory and translated from one to the other without essential change of meaning. For the objectivist, the true is "the real considered as the object of a possible conscious belief or judgment"; for the subjectivist, it is "whatever would be confirmed by an all-comprehending or absolute experience"; and for the dualist it is "whatever in the individual corresponds to what exists outside the individual." Montague reasons that if any of these three theories is valid, the other two must be equally valid. The claims of the idealist and the realist with respect to one part of the problem of knowledge can be disposed of in this way without affecting the issue as a whole. The metaphysical and factual differences remain: what status is to be assigned to the alleged "all-comprehending or absolute experience"? Is it a hypothesis, or merely a voice, an auditory phenomenon? The general alignment of viewpoints will continue despite the key of translation provided. The problem is not intellectual only. It is the spearhead of a set of motivations, which may be reorganized in order to form a somewhat different spearhead. Montague has merely reconciled restricted aspects of a problem which derives from standpoints that have been adopted for antecedent reasons. The recurrent historical problem of knowledge is not disposed of thereby.

Had it been so vulnerable to logical analysis, this problem would never have survived Dewey's earlier treatment of it in a memorable paper[22] first presented in 1901. Dewey asks "what this interest, prolonged over three centuries, in the possibility and nature of knowledge, stands for; what the conviction as to the necessity of the union of sensation and thought, together with the inability to reach conclusions regarding the nature of the union, signifies" (p. 273). Asking for the meaning of the problem of knowledge, Dewey does not want it answered "simply for reflective philosophy or in terms of epistemology itself";

---

[21] W. P. Montague, *The Ways of Knowing* (New York: The Macmillan Co., 1925), pp. 311 ff.
[22] "The Significance of the Problem of Knowledge," in *The Influence of Darwin on Philosophy and Other Essays in Contemporary Thought* (New York: Henry Holt and Co., 1910), pp. 271-304.

he wants its meaning "in the historical movement of humanity and as a part of a larger and more comprehensive experience." It may be observed that reflective philosophy does not have to be conceived as narrowly as is here implied. Dewey himself is really resorting to a more comprehensive reflection in insisting upon the historical perspective. From his point of view, "the abstractness of the discussion of knowledge, its remoteness from everyday experience, is one of form, rather than of substance"; and he holds that "the problem of knowledge is not a problem that has its origin, its value, or its destiny within itself." He sees the problem as one which social life has had to face, whereas philosophers have formulated the question in a technical and abstruse manner.

For Dewey, "the possibility of knowledge is but an aspect of the relation of knowing to acting, of theory to practice" (p. 273 f.). The distinctions and oppositions made by philosophers, such as sensation and thought, subject and object, mind and matter, are formulations of "points of view and practical conflicts having their source in the very nature of modern life, conflicts which must be met and solved if modern life is to go on its way untroubled, with clear consciousness of what it is about. As the philosopher has received his problem from the world of action, so he must return his account there for auditing and liquidation." Whether the account may be liquidated so long as there are social causes for the conflicting views is something Dewey has not considered. These passages indicate the importance of the social factors which motivate philosophers. The unusual amount of emphasis placed upon them by Dewey was due to their gross neglect at the hands of professional philosophers. The "abstruse and technical" formulations of the problem are, however, not without their social connections and significance, at least in the historically prominent cases.

Continuing his social-historical interpretation, Dewey suggests "that the tendency of all the points at issue to precipitate in the opposition of sensationalism and rationalism is due to the fact that sensation and reason stand for the two forces contending for mastery in social life: the radical and the conservative. The reason that the contest does not end, the reason for the necessity of the combination of the two in the resultant statement, is that both factors are necessary in action; one stands for stimulus, for initiative; the other for control, for direction." Whether this is a correct explanation of the traditional opposition between sensation and reason (or between empiricism and rationalism) will be questioned. What were the actual historical alignments of empiricism and rationalism? Empiricism reflected the interests of the rising commercial and industrial class, whereas rationalism retained some intellectual elements from the feudal-ecclesiastical tradition. But rationalism also contained revolutionary elements, and its progress toward a genuinely logical method, its broader conception of deduction, superseded the narrower type of syllogistic deduction which had been made to serve an authoritarian theological tradition. The interesting thesis advanced by Dewey does not entirely fit the facts.

The outcome of the problem of knowledge is for Dewey the recognition of the instrumental function of knowledge. "There must come a time when we have so much knowledge in detail, and understand so well its method in general, that it ceases to be a problem. It becomes a tool. If the problem of knowledge is not intrinsically meaningless and absurd it must in course of time be solved. Then the dominant interest becomes the *use* of knowledge. . . ." (p. 300). By "becoming a tool" Dewey obviously means that it becomes recognized as a tool, for it was always instrumental in its function, as a matter of fact. That a meaningful problem must eventually be solved would have to be shown, in any sphere of problems. In the present case, as Dewey himself recognizes, the historical basis for conflicts among philosophical theories of knowledge may be used to account for their long-continued existence. Granting that the known historical conflicts will some day end, is it not possible that they will be succeeded by different types of conflict which will keep alive interest in the theories of knowledge? But even if that should not prove to be so, is there not real meaning in the (empiriogenic) problem of knowledge, or better still, problems of knowledge? The problems of the determination of objective truth and of the analysis of experience are endless, opening up unlimited horizons of future examination. In that sense there is a constructive problem of knowledge. This is in fact a fundamental agreement with Dewey's conclusion: "Philosophy is henceforth a method, and not an original fountainhead of truth, nor an ultimate standard of reference." For the actual development of philosophy, as well as Dewey's own later development, this statement should read: Philosophy is methodological in character, in two senses: (1) it institutes special procedures; and (2) it is concerned with establishing criteria for methods.

CHAPTER IV

Questions and Methods in Philosophy

A. *The Method of Knowledge in Philosophy*

In his discussion of "The Method of Knowledge in Philosophy,"[1] Professor C. J. Ducasse maintains that some of the problems metaphysicians have discussed are pseudoproblems, that some others, although genuine, do not belong to philosophy, and that still others are or contain genuine problems that are philosophical and are capable of solution. When he criticizes philosophers for not testing their hypotheses, either at all, or adequately, he treats philosophy as a free inquiry, untrammeled by vested interests—in short, like a science. He speaks of a "knowledge-yielding method in philosophy." Two methodological maxims are formulated: (1) When a question is to be investigated, one should not only ask oneself just which facts it is about, but also state them explicitly. (2) Do not merely name or allude to the question about the facts one has listed; it should be stated as explicitly and unambiguously as possible. Thus, one will separate a complex question into the several questions of which it is composed, and so clear away confusions.

In handling the problem of the nature of reality, Ducasse's method requires that statements be chosen as the data, statements showing the use of the term real. Then the question at issue is, what does the term real mean in such examples? This is in keeping with his general view, expressed in his important book on *Philosophy as a Science*,[2] that philosophy deals with appraisals. This method is valuable in that it helps to make meanings precise and rules out unnecessary quarrels, especially

---
[1] *University of California Publications in Philosophy*, Vol. XVI, No. 7, 1945, 143–158.
[2] New York: Oskar Piest, 1941.

when the same term is used in different senses and in different contexts. It is certainly necessary to take into account the context in which a term is used, in order to make possible the completeness and thoroughness of understanding that philosophy aims to achieve.

We should by all means have careful definitions and distinctions of meaning, and a careful examination of the question under consideration. These are initial stages in the method. There are additional preconditions of philosophical reflection to be noted, including freedom from prejudgments, at least provisional freedom from assumptions, the procedure of descriptive analysis, and the determination of social-historical significance. Ducasse restricts himself in the present context to a version of the treatment of philosophy made familiar by logical and linguistic writers, and he does not include other aspects of the method of philosophy which Husserl, Dewey, and Whitehead have emphasized.

Ducasse's notion of an ontological position must be examined carefully. An ontological position cannot be true or false, nor can it be refuted or proved; it cannot even be shown to be more or less probably true than another ontological position. There would accordingly be nothing to prevent idealists, materialists, and others from taking their favorite ontological positions, with no fear of being challenged. This recalls the "principle of tolerance," which was featured at one time in the literature of logical positivism. It is also reminiscent of C. I. Lewis's notion of a "quale" (in his *Mind and the World-Order*), even though the latter is described as ineffable. As Ducasse puts it, "ontological positions may only be occupied or not occupied, be embraced or abandoned." What leads one to embrace or to abandon such a position is not stated. That one may do so for reasons, or even after much reflection and inquiry, must also be considered. Ducasse is inclined to take standpoints or attitudes as finalities, just as he treats appraisals elsewhere. Another line of inquiry is then called for, to explain and appraise the different standpoints themselves. The philosopher cannot afford to be less demanding than the special scientist, and that may be suggested if an initial point of view is not examined critically. A social scientist would want to know, in the light of the sociology of knowledge, what conditions a given ontological position. Were a mere commonplace expression used, it might appear far less plausible to place it beyond reproach, as neither provable nor disprovable.

Ducasse describes the ontological position of the idealist as declaring for the primacy of minds and their ideas, intending to construe everything in these terms. It is pertinent, however, to recall the elaborate arguments and fallacies employed to demonstrate or justify idealism. Moreover, the usual idealist goes further than merely declaring for the primacy of minds and their ideas. To personal idealism, for example, the world is a collection of selves.

Both idealism and materialism are dismissed by Ducasse, since both cannot be true. But if they represent ontological positions, why should they not co-exist peacefully? Perhaps because it is obvious that they do not get along so well, their incompatibility must be recognized despite the freedom of ontological positions. Ducasse is careful, however, to have the idealist say that all reality is exclusively mental (which some idealists do say, of course), and have the materialist say it is material; and, furthermore, to insist on the customary meaning. But if one dealt with customary meanings (whereby it should be considered whether they are customary for idealists or for materialists), there would be no problem, and philosophers would merely be guilty of abuses of language. In terms of which ontological position does he judge idealism and materialism to be incompatible? That assumed position would itself then be beyond reproach, one would suppose. If one talks about reality as a whole in its terms, then one either has to appeal to customary meanings again, or else turn to a justification of a new ontological position. The latter was not provided for, however. Finally, on Ducasse's ground, still another ontological position would have to be resorted to for the appraisal of this one; and so on. How problematical it can be to allow the same status, beyond proof or disproof, to traditional commitments and a position based upon scientific knowledge, may now be seen.

According to Ducasse, appraisals constitute the subject matter of philosophy. They distinguish philosophy, and not any method per se. For example, there is the appraisal "It is wrong to kill," which can be studied by various scientists—the historian, the statistical sociologist, the psychologist, and the philosopher. How does the philosopher's interest in it differ from the others? Appraisals could not be said to constitute the peculiar subject matter of the philosopher if other scientists are interested in them. It follows, then, that they must be conceived differently by philosophers; and that must be clarified.

Philosophically, the reliance upon appraisals and ordinary meanings raises further methodological questions. Philosophy should indeed "follow" the sciences and the facts. On the other hand, it has a great constructive task, which also involves the reconstruction of what has been established by other disciplines and by general experience.

B. *The Question of the Autonomy of Philosophy*

Let us return to the question raised at the close of the second chapter of the autonomy of philosophy. It is of paramount importance in justifying philosophy to determine whether it has a separate subject matter, or whether it raises distinctive questions and introduces special procedures.

If it is maintained that philosophy is not distinct in subject matter from the special sciences, does it then follow that its methods are not different from the methods of the sciences? In other words, would the alleged coincidence of subject matter imply sameness of methods, so that all procedures used in philosophy would either be already in use in the sciences, or would be capable of such use? A philosopher's ingenuity may result in the formulation of a new procedure. Assuming the same subject matter, can we expect that the procedures devised in philosophy will in turn be applied to and in some cases found fruitful in the sciences, just as the methods of the sciences may be adopted (or adapted) in philosophy? An affirmative answer is unavoidable if the same subject matter is meant literally. The situation is changed, however, if one means that the domain of the sciences is also the domain of philosophy, but that philosophic inquiry deals with different aspects of that domain. In that case, distinctive procedures may be expected in philosophy; and it is true in effect that the subject matter of philosophy is distinctive, even if it belongs to the same domain as the subject matter of the sciences.

What is the domain of the sciences (i.e., sciences of existence or of reality)? It comprises all that is in space and time, including human experience. All that is physically real, or everything that has a locus in space and time, makes up the universal domain of science. Is there anything outside that domain? The term *is*, if it means existence, predetermines the answer: there cannot *be* anything apart from *being*. (In the present context, existence, reality, and being will not be distinguished, and will be used interchangeably.) It is quite a different thing to refer to objects which, as objects of thought, are not located in space and time. Such objects are known as intentional objects, or as intentional objectivities. There is a sense in which one may say that thought is bigger than or goes beyond nature, but this must be expressed carefully to avoid dogmatism. By idealization and the construction of conceptual fictions, as well as through actual errors, thought gets away from nature (or away from the field of existence, including cultural existence). Although such thoughts get away from existence in their reference, it cannot be said that they are not conditioned by existence, physical and cultural. The type and style of idealization and the types of error are themselves accounted for causally in terms of real existence. Hence, to say that thought goes beyond nature is not to say that it is not caused, motivated, or reflected by the domain of existence.

The objects of thought include so-called ideal objects, such as triangles, real and complex numbers, etc., and, in general, abstractions, imaginary objects, and even impossible (i.e., contradictory) objects. The designation of existence, being, or reality is simply "strange" to such objects, and it may even be regarded as misleading to call them objects. The temptation is ever present to reify such objects, and so to *misplace* them. If the term object is retained here, this is because it is desirable to introduce as few new terms as possible.

The technical term *noema*, meaning correlate of an act of experience, is useful for the analysis of experience, as illustrated by Husserl's phenomenology. As already indicated, Husserl's method provisionally suspends the framework of natural existence, and undertakes descriptions of the processes and structures of experience which are said to precede the distinction between the real and the unreal, as a matter of method. Instead of beginning with the domain of existence, in which man the organism as well as knower finds his way, the phenomenological procedure begins with the experiences themselves, and proceeds "correlatively," with a dual interest in the experiences as activities and in the objects to which they refer. This mode of reflective analysis does not obliterate the distinction in question between the existent and the nonexistent objects of thought and experience; it can only avoid it temporarily. In fact, it is not meant to show the way to existence, nor to safeguard it in any way. The evidence provided by general experience and the sciences is enough for that. It would be monstrous presumptuousness to seek to found the evidence derived from the sciences and natural experience. And it is simply superfluous to ask for the evidence of the existence of an external world, when all experience testifies to that existence, and the knower as a human being involves not only an external world but a society as well.

The procedure of phenomenology is devoted to the reflective examination of the structure of experience, and thus the question of existence is strange to it. The suspension of beliefs is performed in order to make clear the nature of evidence itself, and its various degrees; and also the nature of the experience of existence, of illusion, etc. A universal treatment of experience, on the basis of an individual's experience, can thus be instituted. But to suspend is not to deny. Never may the subjective analyst deny existence, or even question its validity on principle. In his quest for certainty and fullness of understanding, the philosopher cannot begin with a fraud. He does not have to deny his patrimony or violate his nature as a man to accomplish something that must be utterly meaningless apart from actual human beings. Only one who has been permanently damaged by the tradition of idealism, and who fails to see its assumptive and dogmatic nature, can succeed in forgetting what the most ignorant human being knows—that he is a part of a world which existed before him and which is independent of him.

Man is incidental to existence; he occupies a very minor position in the universe. This basic fact of the nondependence of the field of existence on man, or on any mind, makes philosophical idealism impossible. No suspension of beliefs can eliminate the mountain of evidence which supports that fact. To begin with immediate experience in its extreme form would be to suspend the evidence of memory, and also the past experience of all other persons. A solipsism of the present moment would result, which would be devoid of consequences, except for the special descriptive purposes for which it was originally intended.

On the other hand, there is undeniable merit in the phenomenological procedure, even apart from its being an aid for description and providing a well-defined field for philosophic inquiry. Freed from its idealistic encumbrances, it may assist the examination of theories of existence, and promote a thoroughgoing critical attitude. In this respect it is a helpful auxiliary method, serving scientific method in the broadest sense.

These considerations have bearing on whether philosophy has its own subject matter and a special procedure. The program of universal questioning, or radical analysis, requires two dimensions of investigation: (1) the subjective, involving a reduction to the experiences of an individual; and (2) the objective (temporal, genetic), operating on the basis of the field of existence, which is temporally and spatially unlimited in extent. The field for inquiry of (1) is restricted to primary and secondary evidence. "Primary" refers to direct evidence, of the present moment; and "secondary" to the degrees of evidence, in relation to primary evidence. The field for inquiry of (2) comprises the physical universe, a particular social-historical context, as well as the knower and his body. (1) constitutes a distinctive subject matter and the procedure involved is peculiarly philosophical. (2) does not constitute a distinctive subject matter, but it does involve treatment of existence in its most general and fundamental features. The methods used are not different from those in use elsewhere, however. (1) involves direct apprehension or intuition, led by the ideal of freedom from presuppositions. But it has a limited program, for it can never provide the physical universe nor the evidence of its nondependence upon man. Its proper questions must therefore be carefully pointed out. There are innumerable questions to which it has no approach whatsoever. These are handled by (2), the objective, genetic procedure. Existence becomes an inaccessible problem for (1); it is a basic fact for (2).

The distinctive character of philosophy may now be considered more pointedly. When one speaks of having the same subject matter, does that mean identity of domain, i.e., of objects, or of events; or identity of questions and problems? Identity of domain may go along with difference of questions and problems. This is so for a naturalistic (or materialistic) philosophy of science, which differs from the special sciences in the questions it raises, but refers to the same domain. Is it possible to limit the types of question that may be regarded as exclusively philosophical? Some writers have concluded that logical questions about the use of language, or logical questions in general, may alone be regarded as distinctive of philosophy. Another line is taken by those who see philosophy as dealing with ultimate questions about reality, which is not to be distinguished from the domain of the sciences.

At this point an outline of the possible views at issue should be helpful.

I. Identity of Domain as involving:
   A. The same objects or events
   B. The same questions
   C. The same methods
II. Difference of Questions as involving:
   A. The same objects or events
   B. Different objects or events, and hence a different domain
   C. Different aspects of the same domain, or different selective questioning
   D. The same methods
   E. Different methods, or peculiarly philosophical procedures

Note: Sameness of questions is ruled out, since philosophy would then be indistinguishable from the sciences. Sameness of domain may go along either with sameness or difference of questions. But sameness of questions implies sameness of domain, whereas difference of questions may go along either with sameness or difference of domain.

I,A rules out the supernatural, and such metaphysical entities as life-force and spirit.

I,B rules out philosophy as a distinct discipline, making it pointless and superfluous.

I,C The method of philosophy is simply the method of the sciences, with sameness of domain. Philosophy may then become a science of thought, or of experience.

II,A, like I,A, rules out the supernatural, etc.

II,B may allow for a supernatural realm or agency, or a realm of spirit, a life-force, etc. It may also mean that a nonmetaphysical distinction is drawn between the natural world of existence and a domain of pure reflection, which is purely cognitive in significance and is delineated as the province of philosophy.

II,C That different selective questioning is illustrated in philosophy is maintained by all who are monists, whether materialistic or spiritualistic, in one way or another.

II,D The view that the procedures of philosophy are not different from the methods of the sciences is prominent in the literature of naturalism. The distinctiveness of the questions of philosophy, admitting that it is a specialized type of inquiry, and the sameness of its methods, may go along with sameness of domain or with difference of domain; for sameness of method does not imply sameness of domain. Philosophers may in turn contribute to the common store of methods; their contributions need not be limited to philosophy.

II,E The view that there are special philosophical procedures, or that there is one exclusively philosophical method, such as intuition, or logical analysis, or intentional analysis, etc., may go along with difference of questions and either the same or different domains. With the domain taken to be the same, the questions must be different, if the difference of methods is to be meaningful. If there is to be anything distinctive about philosophy—in this case, methods—there must either be a difference of domain or of questions.

When the three factors of domain, questions, and methods are considered in their possible relationships and combinations, the results may be summed up as follows:

(1) There may be sameness of domain, difference of questions, and difference of methods.

(2) Another combination is sameness of domain, sameness of questions, and difference of methods. This is impossible if philosophy is to be an autonomous discipline. The phenomenological procedure is not an exception, since it does not have sameness of domain. It does not affirm a difference of domain in an ontological sense, although it asks questions beyond the field of interest of the special sciences as such.

(3) The combination of difference of domain, sameness of questions, and difference of methods is a logical impossibility: the same questions cannot be asked about different domains.

(4) Sameness of domain and sameness of methods may go along with difference of questions as a possible combination: the type of questioning of philosophy is sufficient to distinguish it. The sameness of domain may be a restriction, however, unless it is interpreted so as to provide for selectivity of questions.

Questions and Methods

(5) There is also the conjunction of sameness of domain, sameness of questions, and sameness of methods. This would mean the disappearance of philosophy as a separate discipline.
(6) The combination of sameness of questions and of methods with difference of domain is impossible because questions cannot be the same if the domains are different.
(7) Sameness of methods, along with difference of domain and of questions, is a possibility in principle. But the sameness of method should be read both ways, i.e., philosophy may also contribute procedures which are open to the sciences as well.
(8) Finally, there is the combination of difference of domain, of questions, and of methods. It is a possible combination, often defended by philosophers of various schools and traditions.

Thus, sameness of domain may go along with difference of questions; sameness of methods may go along with difference of questions; and difference of domain and of methods may go along with difference of questions. Sameness of questions is ruled out, if philosophy is to be autonomous in any sense. But if there is a difference of questions, it does not matter whether the domain or the methods are the same, so far as the autonomy of philosophy is concerned. Difference of questions is thus necessary for its autonomy.

This calls attention to the fundamental importance of questions. "By their questions shall they be known" is true for all distinct sciences, including philosophy. The first thing to be considered in philosophy, then, is the nature of the questions formulated. The various fields of knowledge are distinguished by their peculiar questions. Not that they are fixed and final in all cases: the sciences are always changing, especially the real (as distinguished from the formal) sciences, and it is not possible to anticipate what the classification of the sciences will be in future periods.

Two distinct sciences or systems of knowledge, S_1 and S_2, must have peculiar questions to distinguish them, which can be guaranteed by the requirement that they each contain at least one peculiar concept or basic principle, or both. The presence either of peculiar concepts or principles is sufficient to determine unique questions. Does this apply to philosophy as well?

C. H. Langford states[3] that "it is difficult to see how there can be any ideas which are peculiar to philosophy or to logic." If there were no peculiar concepts or basic principles, and if it were also true that no method could be restricted to the subject matter for which it is introduced or devised, then how could it be maintained that philosophy is an autonomous discipline?

The term proposition is peculiar to logic, number to arithmetic, point to geometry, etc. There are ordinarily three groups of terms, undefined and defined, which occur in the discussion of a system of knowledge, whether in formal or in real science. There are (1) the terms of ordinary discourse, the common terms; (2) technical terms belonging to other systems of knowledge; (3) technical terms peculiar to the system in question, which may be taken as undefined, or defined. An undefined term is regarded as unique and irreducible, at least for the purposes of the system in question. Thus, point may be taken as an undefined term in geometry, or value in ethics. If these terms are defined in other treatments of these systems of knowledge, do they surrender their status as peculiar terms? A nominal definition of "point" merely consists of a substitution of symbols. It is enough that certain formal properties are retained in the process of definition, so that if point is defined in terms of number, or in terms of logical concepts, nothing is lost thereby. The use to which the defined term is put in the system of geometry shows what is peculiar about it; and that use is indicated by the basic relations and the postulates of the system.

But the situation is different in real science, where real definitions are used.[4] The possibility of reducing objects on "higher levels" (say, organic or cultural objects) to the physical level is then involved. Assuming the complete success of scientific analysis, the uniqueness (and peculiar properties) of the behavioral activities of a human being will remain. The same may be said of the concept of value. Although it is reducible to "lower-level" terms, as will be seen later, it is nevertheless a peculiar concept because of its very complexity. It would be a

[3] Cf. *The Philosophy of G. E. Moore*, ed. P. Schilpp (Evanston and Chicago: Northwestern University, 1942), p. 340.
[4] This subject will be discussed more fully in Chapter VI on "Monism and Pluralism."

mistake to suppose that a complex has no distinctive nature once it is analyzed into its component parts. For the rest, it may be worth noting that the process of analysis can be endless, so that every present level of analysis may face the danger, at some time, of surrendering its autonomy.

Finally, in considering the autonomy of philosophy, one should bear in mind that philosophy is a many-sided discipline, with different stages and types of inquiry. One should be careful to recognize the fundamental distinction between (1) the program of philosophy which assumes the existing sciences, and (2) the program which attempts to begin radically, restricting itself to direct experience. For the first, philosophy is fundamentally a regressive discipline; for the second, it undertakes to be a progressive discipline, a founding science.

The philosopher who undertakes a synthesis of knowledge at a given time proceeds regressively. He accepts the findings of the special sciences, even though he maintains a critical attitude toward their basic ideas and assumptions. There is a world of existence, or a world of events, which he acknowledges as "pregiven." The generality of the questions raised in attempting a synthesis guarantees the occurrence of distinctive propositions. Neither the logician of science nor the philosopher who is interested in questions involving relationships among various special sciences is embarrassed by his dependence upon the existing world, for each has his own questions.

The function of criticism and clarification is treated more radically in the progressive stage of philosophic inquiry. Here the procedures may be descriptive or analytic, but always under carefully defined conditions. Placing all beliefs in abeyance as a matter of method, and suspending assumptions in all existing fields of knowledge, progressive inquiry begins with the immediate stream of experiences in its descriptive stage. The procedure in phenomenology moves from the simple to the complex, and the aim is to trace out the "genesis" of all ideas in experience. Every proposition is peculiarly philosophical, owing to the radical procedure which is involved, and to the special cognitive setting. The process of experience is treated as though it were autonomous and independent, for the purposes of philosophic inquiry. Ideas that are peculiar to logic are clarified in the course of the descriptive analysis of meaning structures, such as negation, relation, etc. The constructive activities of logic justify the use of the term progressive. It is also evident that every proposition formulated within the conditions outlined is peculiarly philosophical.

C. Aporetics as an Alleged Separate Discipline

There has been considerable recognition of the importance of problems for the theory of knowledge and logic, most notably in recent literature by Dewey. In recent German philosophy, Hartmann[5] has outlined his conception of aporetics as a separate discipline in philosophical inquiry. The course of his reasoning is as follows:

The phenomenon of knowledge must be so described that the connection of its essential features as a whole can be seen. The method of such a description of essence is provided in the procedure of phenomenology. Although this young philosophical science has brought many important essential analyses, it has been devoted mainly to the logical and psychological sides of the phenomena. Special attention should be paid to the essential analysis of the metaphysical in the phenomenon of knowledge. The phenomenology of knowledge must constitute a separate science. Proceeding with the natural attitude of the knowing consciousness, the point is to conceive the phenomenon of knowledge as broadly and completely as possible. The preparatory analytic work of phenomenology precedes all standpoints and theories, as well as the genuine formulation of the questions themselves. It is prior to all problem formation, and it treats of a pure *quaestio facti*. The description of a phenomenon is indifferent to the weight of the problems which result from it. The essential features are considered, regardless of the distinction between the metaphysical and the nonmetaphysical. The question whether a fact can also be a metaphysical fact leads to the analysis of problems, and it is in that area that the *quaestio juris* begins.

The analysis of problems constitutes a second preparatory study, with an entirely different task from the descriptive analysis of the phenomenon. The aim is here to work out what may be questioned in the phenomenon, to establish the points which

---

[5] Nicolai Hartmann, *Grundzüge einer Metaphysik der Erkenntnis* (Berlin: Walter de Gruyter and Co., 1921), pp. 28 ff.

first need theory for philosophical understanding. It is here that the metaphysical can be consciously separated from the nonmetaphysical. The problem-analysis of knowledge also constitutes a separate science, which is still in its beginnings. Aristotle can be regarded as a classical representative of aporetics, or the pure science of problems. His method—to investigate problems before their theoretical treatment and independently of all possible attempts at solution, purely in themselves; to separate the conceived from the unconceived; and to work out difficulties and contradictions of the present phenomena for their own sakes—serves as a model for Hartmann. In the latter's view, this almost forgotten method should be restored to its old place of honor. In one point Hartmann hopes to go further than the old aporetics, which he claims was not based upon the analysis of the phenomena and was not supported by preliminary descriptive work; hence it suffered from a certain formlessness. Phenomenology and aporetics are inseparably connected, and together they provide the preparatory work for a treatment of problems. The order is not reversible, however: when problems are formulated, a piece of phenomenological work is already presupposed, and the more consciously such work is performed, the more precisely can the problem be stated. That holds not only for the problem of knowledge, but also for every problem. Like phenomenology, aporetics fundamentally precedes all theory, all standpoints and their metaphysics. The metaphysical as such is first known through its work. But it is no longer descriptive. It compares, tests, separates out the given, establishes the incongruities contained therein, and gives to them the sharpness of the paradox which attaches to all conflict in the factual. It does not have to bother about overcoming contradictions; that is the function of theory. Theory is concerned with the creation of new method. But aporetics merely leads up to this point, never going further. It proceeds from the given to the formulation of tasks which are then assigned to theory.

Hartmann's sketch of aporetics is too vague and general to be satisfactory. In order to do justice to the facts of experience, he would have had to realize that the awareness of problems occurs in most cases on a high level of knowledge. Certainly theory is devised to meet problems; but there are problems which are incidental to theory as well. The Hegelian element worked in with the talk of contradiction and paradox does not help matters. It appears that Hartmann had a limited and formal view of description, problems, and theory. Unlike Dewey, he does not seem to have had actual cases in mind, or a grasp of what the conditions of actual inquiry are like.[6]

Without some experience and knowledge, there can be no awareness of problems in any significant sense. It is impossible to begin a descriptive inquiry without prior experience. One describes because he is led by a question or a problem. Awareness of a difficulty, or of a question, is the psychological starting point. One does not begin as a purely cognitive being, deciding to engage in description "before all theory." Such a being is highly sophisticated theoretically to begin with; and at a later stage of experience he consciously determines to go back to the rudiments of experience, naturally prompted by problems.

D. Classification of Questions and Problems

The various types of questions and problems can now be summed up, together with some further suggestions for classification and terminology.

I. With respect to the status of the knower in reality, questions and problems may be classified as (a) knowledge- (or experience-) bound, and (b) reality-bound. In (a), everything is taken to be for a knower. Reality is regarded as the correlate of thought processes, and even the consideration of history is limited to changes of meanings. Phenomenological questions are formulated here, limited by what appears to a knower, everything else excluded. In (b), the knower is incidental, a very small part of reality. There was a reality for an infinite time before the knower appeared. Things need not appear to a knower in order to exist.

II. With respect to the conception of possibility which is involved, questions may be classified (a) as meaningful in terms of a special system of knowledge (arithmetic, physics, economics, etc.), or a special language, with the range of possibility determined in terms of the subject matter; and (b) as questions limited by general logical forms and principles, the range of possibility determined by noncontradiction. Thus, any-

[6] Cf. John Dewey, *Logic, The Theory of Inquiry* (New York: Henry Holt and Co., 1938).

thing noncontradictory is possible in this broad, logical sense. (c) There is, finally, the "unbound" class, with no restriction of any kind. An unlimited conception of empty possibility applies here, allowing any type of question to be formulated. Even if there should be nothing against some of the questions thus freely formulated, there would also be nothing to speak for them.

III. With respect to their origin, questions and problems may be classified as (a) empiriogenic, with perceptually founded and conceptually founded varieties; (b) methodogenic, with the following varieties: (1) Some problems result from methods involving the natural or naturalistic point of view, such as induction, certainty, and infinitude. For materialists, values present a particular problem; prominent here is the explanation of the mind and the process of knowledge in all its complexity. (2) An unlimited number of problems results from the use of deductive reasoning, so that all formal problems belong here. (1) and (2) comprise objective problems. (3) Another class of problems arises from the use of a subjective procedure, as seen in the phenomenological method: the problem of overcoming solipsism (the "alter ego" problem), the problem of certainty, the problem of the world's independent and continued existence. (c) There is, furthermore, the class of standpoint problems, resulting from the position adopted. For spiritualism, in the form of subjective idealism, the external world is a problem. The existence of God, and of evil, the question of immortality, and the reconciliation of religion and science, all present conspicuous problems for the upholders of this standpoint. The distinction is, broadly, between primary problems with a factual or evidential basis, and secondary problems, arising from the choice of standpoints, the warfare of the schools, or the adoption of special procedures.

IV. With respect to the presuppositions of the philosophical procedure employed, questions and problems may be classified as (a) regressive, with philosophy proceeding on the basis of the existing sciences to the clarification of their fundamental concepts and principles, and also toward a synthesis of knowledge; and (b) progressive, with an attempt at a beginning without presuppositions. Such questions are philosophical throughout, since they are based upon the realm of pure consciousness or pure reflection.

V. As already indicated, philosophical questions and problems may be classified as (a) real and (b) historical.

VI. There is also the division into (a) soluble and (b) insoluble problems. It is important to distinguish whether a given question is insoluble on principle or merely unsolved at a given time. In the last century, it appeared unlikely that the chemistry of the stars would ever be known. Although it may well be impossible actually to go to a distant sun, other methods may render a personal visit unnecessary for any question asked. The list of traditional "insolubles" has tended to be reduced progressively. This applies to the questions listed by Du Bois-Reymond,[7] including "the nature of matter and force," "the origin of life," and "the freedom of the will." Whether all questions which are unanswerable on principle are therefore meaningless should not be decided without careful and full consideration of the nature of meaning.

VII. In terms of their social-historical significance, a broad distinction may be drawn between philosophies of participation and of renunciation. There are diverse examples of each type. Participation may be radical or conservative; and renunciation may take the form of asceticism, mysticism, or a retreat to an external realm through reason, thus actually or in effect disavowing the sensory world. Indeed, the restriction of the program of philosophy to formal-logical and semantical questions may involve the withdrawal of the philosopher from the realm of social change.

E. *The Treatment of Philosophical Questions*

The study of questions and problems in philosophy shows how important it is to avoid two errors: (a) taking them literally, as what they purport to be; (b) reformulating them in contemporary terms without considering their historical significance—as though all past problems had a common denominator and were capable of systematic solution or dismissal.

(a) Questions may merely express more deep-seated or concealed motives. As has been seen, this applies even to so conspicuous and perennial an issue as spiritualism versus materialism;

---

[7] Cf. E. Du Bois-Reymond, *Wissenschaftliche Vorträge*, ed. J. H. Gore (Boston and New York: Ginn & Co., 1896).

and to such questions as the nature and status of universals, which may have social-political and religious significance.

(b) Questions are always related to a system, whether that system be a formal structure, as in arithmetic, or a given social-historical context, say European society in the thirteenth century. A question that is meaningful in terms of the fourteenth century may have a different meaning at another time, say in the eighteenth century, as illustrated by the nominalism of William of Occam and of Berkeley, which represent responses to radically different motives. To attempt to reinterpret all questions in contemporary terms, especially in terms of a narrow philosophy of experience, would be to miss the real nature of many questions. The situation is not improved by ruling out a host of past questions as meaningless (i.e., judged from the assumed point of view). The only defensible common denominator is a procedural principle which takes care to do full justice to the historical and system-bound characteristics of all questions. These remarks apply to systems in the loose sense of a given historical period, as well as in the sense of a special system of knowledge.

No question which has meaning in experience (including historical experience) or meaning in terms of the sciences may be outlawed, even if it fails to fit into any established system of knowledge. Most questions come and go; and systems of knowledge are by no means unchanging. If a meaningful queston (in the empiriogenic sense) arises which does not fit into the collective system of science, conceived broadly as logically systematized or organized knowledge, it should not be refused a hearing. The body of scientific knowledge should be enlarged to include it.

Furthermore, no controversies should be ruled out as meaningless if they have historical significance, or if they follow from the adoption of standpoints which represent responses to social motivations. Neither is it sufficient to invalidate one argument because a new argument is put forward. The analysis must probe to the nature and conditions of the questions that arise, and not only to the worth of the arguments and the evidence. The complete act of reflection which is required in philosophy thus involves nothing less than a comprehensive logical-historical program.

The radical attitude of universal criticism, according to which nothing is taken for granted or declared immune from examination, distinguishes this philosophical approach. In practice it represents an ideal which is rarely approximated. The term radical was a favorite of Husserl's; and its use by James is well known. It is pertinent here to examine it further.

F. *The Meaning of Radicalism in Philosophy*

That a genuinely logical philosophy must be radical will be readily agreed. As to the meaning and application of radicalism, however, there will be doubts, misgivings, and misunderstandings. All who have reservations of faith or of special interests will oppose the ideal of submitting every judgment and belief to a searching examination in terms of actual, direct experience; for that is what is involved in a radical program. All presumed items of knowledge must be examined for their evidence. This does not imply that all who agree to such a program would consider themselves bound by its findings in actual practice. It is one thing to examine the evidence for beliefs, and frequently quite a different thing to act (or to suspend action, as the case may be) in accordance with it. Supposedly radical procedure may turn out to be a means of reinstating a vested tradition of long standing. That positive descriptive findings of real worth may be obtained in the process does not alter the fact that such procedure serves special interests if it finally accords with the party of fideism or of any vested tradition.

Among recent philosophers, Edmund Husserl liked to speak of his method as radical, in the double sense of probing for evidence and undermining dogmatism. But it was William James who popularized the term, through his well-known *Essays in Radical Empiricism*.[8] In one of the essays in the volume, entitled "A World of Pure Experience," James states (p. 42): "To be radical, an empiricism must neither admit into its constructions any element that is not directly experienced, nor exclude from them any element that is directly experienced." He observes later (p. 241) that "this is only a *methodological postulate*, not a conclusion supposed to flow from the intrinsic absurdity of transempirical objects"; and he asserts his willingness (p. 242) "to admit any number of noumenal beings or events into philosophy if only their pragmatic value can be shown."

[8] New York: Longmans, Green, and Co., 1912.

In the modern tradition, Hume is rightly regarded as a critical thinker. But he was not a truly radical thinker, in the sense in which the term is used here. In his attempt to trace out the sources of evidence in experience, he neglected the very first facts about experience. He retired to the stream of impressions and ideas of the knower, and so was led to approach the question of the existence of the external world from the perspective of belief. His seemingly radical procedure incurred fundamental errors in the analysis of experience, errors deriving from the psychological atomism of Locke. This method was not true to experience itself, and failed to recognize what is given to begin with in experience. The initial fact for man is his membership in an independently existing universe and a historically conditioned social group, of which he is a product and upon which he is dependent for his thought processes, his inclinations and aversions, and his interests. Any purported radicalism which violates this basic fact is merely a pretense, at best a mistaken venture with a limited value. In the quest for complete understanding, for an appraisal of all assumptions in terms of evidence, one must not fail to distinguish between assumptions and facts. Reflection must be based upon the primary evidence of natural and social experience.

There are degrees and types of radicalism. Almost all philosophical radicals are opposed to political radicalism. That is understandable enough, for the selection of academic philosophers and the pressures upon teachers are such that only those who support the status quo are able to have such a career. It may be objected that political radicalism is completely different from the ideal of philosophy. Political radicalism involves first the same kind of evidential criticism, applied to political, social, and economic beliefs and theories; and second an alignment with a party, if possible, to carry out a practical program that is supported by facts. Apart from the question whether it is necessary for philosophy to realize itself in practice, it is clear that political radicalism as a form of criticism may be conceived as a continuation of the general program of philosophy. Whether particular groups or parties calling themselves radical are really entitled to the designation in this sense must be decided in each case. Radicalism in politics presupposes a descriptive and analytical understanding of social interests and relations. It presupposes a thoroughly scientific account of production, distribution, and all other important human relations. If basic social conflicts are shown to exist, the radical does not hesitate to advocate and champion the cause of change, aligning himself with the party of progress. Progress is construed in terms of an increase in the realization of ethical value. The point here is that political radicalism is an illustration and further development of the type of analysis required by a radical (meaning thoroughly reflective and critical) philosophy.

In philosophy the questioning of all judgments and beliefs is carried as far as possible. There are no absolutes or untouchables. Locke expressed the challenging, critical spirit very well in one context when he declared that no moral rule may be proposed for which one may not justly demand a reason. The avowal of the program of a critical justification of beliefs did not prevent him from upholding the prevailing religion and condemning atheists, who were not to be tolerated. It is also striking to find philosophers in our own time, who profess to question the very concept of an objective world and the existence of other human beings, to be partisans of vested interests, accepting their special privileges as finalities. "Radicalism" must therefore be treated with all due caution. In the field of philosophy, the effective union of a thoroughgoing, sound theory with practice is as excellent as it is rare.

G. *Philosophical Neutrality*

More widespread among philosophers than any pretense to radicalism is the aim to be neutral, or objective and detached. "Beyond realism and idealism" and "beyond socialism and capitalism" are titles which promise, or presume, neutrality in philosophy as well as in social science. The condemnation of both sides is a familiar formula for the treatment of a deep-seated conflict. Are such pretensions to neutrality made good in actual fact? Can one rise above socialism and liberalism,[9] as well as above capitalistic conservatism?

What usually happens when a philosopher renounces not only realism and idealism, but materialism as well? Does he remain on purely descriptive ground? If so, he consciously restricts

---

[9] Cf. V. I. Lenin's *Selected Works* (London: Lawrence & Wishart, Ltd., 1939), Vol. XI, pp. 369 f., for Lenin's account of how a disciple of Avenarius, a representative of the empiriocriticists, claimed to do so.

himself to painstaking description, refusing resolutely to go beyond what is actually given in experience. That may be fully justified for the particular purposes of a theory of knowledge. But the aim is to include all that is possible in the descriptive field, and undeniably many facts usually unobserved are thereby brought to view. Is it not true, however, that still other facts are not discerned, or are kept from view? Philosophers should be reminded of (or, indeed, acquainted with) the facts of living in an industrial system, as well as the facts of our actual business practices. Perhaps a philosopher disposed to subjectivism might be unaffected by a trip in a crowded New York subway train, if he has gone too far in his ascetic detachment. If one is interested in the descriptive analysis of experience, he has the right to undertake selective and abstractive analyses. But he must never suppose that the doctrine of an abstract ego will absolve him from the responsibility of providing for actual egos in their real social conditions.

Purely reflective inspection of phenomena, or of experiences and their objects, can only be of interest as a matter of essential analysis, where there are general relationships, structures, and laws to be discerned. The knowledge which results is judged according to both its theoretical and practical fruitfulness. It may help to answer questions (especially in clarifying basic structures of experience) which need not involve the issue of materialism (or realism) and idealism.

Those who speak of going beyond the standpoints of materialism (or realism) and idealism frequently express the hope that a complete philosophy can be instated which will avoid the limitations of the opposing positions. The result is often enough a covert form of idealism, or some form of irrationalism, in any case a product which does not disturb the dominant interests of society.

Let us consider the implications more closely. What principle, or principles, are at issue between materialism and idealism? The objective independence of existence, so far as human beings and their experience are concerned, is a cardinal thesis of materialism, and also of realism—the most important thesis which distinguishes them from idealism. One can never abandon that principle in fact. There is no neutrality. Only provisionally, and as a methodological device, can one speak of suspending belief in the independent order of existence; and then for descriptive purposes. If anyone believes he really penetrates beyond the principle of objective existence, he is simply violating a primary fact of all experience.

There are some crucial issues over which one cannot be neutral. At most, one can disregard an issue provisionally, as the sound phenomenologist does. But he can never ignore the historical and social implications of such an issue as materialism versus idealism. A subjective procedure which derives its justification from the aim to deliver a still more complete account of experience fails utterly if in the process it falsifies or ignores the very meaning at issue. The analysis of meaning cannot relinquish meanings. That would reduce philosophy to a set of abstractions devoid of all historical significance, and hence incapable of fulfilling its aim completely. If one is dealing in essential structures, he must be careful to bring all regions of experience into view, so that the stock of essences is not limited to what the prevailing social pattern considers appropriate. Or are there no "bad" essences? But it must not be thought that only angels reside in this realm.

Perhaps "neutrality" should be banished from philosophical usage. If educators have been called "that third sex," some philosophers will be found in the right wing of that diversified class. Less neutrality and more action should be urged upon them.

CHAPTER V

Experience and Knowledge

A. *The Locus of Experience and the Status of the Mind*

All questions of truth and confirmation involve appeals to experience. Experience has become a term with which to conjure, and it is widely used as a eulogistic epithet. Sooner or later the choice between rival philosophies must lead to the inspection of experience. Only that does not necessarily mean much, for everything depends upon the way in which experience is located and construed. It is a striking fact that mutually hostile philosophies have avowedly been philosophies of experience, each claiming to be true to its findings.

Experience may be examined from a subjective point of view, in reflection; or it may be considered as being in nature, with its organic and physical conditions; or, again, it may be viewed as culturally conditioned. The subjective point of view purports to deal with experience purely, i.e., emancipated from all dependence on nature or on anything transcendent of experience itself. The naturalistic conception of experience regards it as presupposing the whole order of nature. That conception of experience is characteristic of the scientific psychologist and the cultural anthropologist.

The following universal characteristics of experience may be noted: (a) Experience is processional, or temporal, in character. (b) There are the elements of organic, physical, and cultural relatedness. Thus, experience is investigated by a group of sciences, including physics, psychology, and physiology. (c) The dimensions of experience are: the now, the no longer now, and the not yet—or the specious present, the ever receding past, and the indicated future. This gives expression to the temporal continuity of experience. (d) Experience exists and consequently has a space-time locus. There is always a *where* and a *when* for an experience. When a person has an idea, there is a transformation of energy in the nervous system, and in this sense an idea has a physical and temporal locus. One might go so far as to say literally that the idea which he has is related to the remote stars in the universe. (e) Experience is always experience *of* something. The scholastic term intentional, which was used by Brentano and Husserl, expresses this relatedness to an object of some kind. The object may be fictive in character, or even absurd. There is always the actual content of an experience, and the object that is indicated. (f) There are various types of experience, for instance, perceptual, imaginative, and conceptual.

Experience is generally recognized as being the result of two factors, the mind and the given objective world. The contributing activity of the mind should not be ignored. But it is also important to determine the nature and extent of its contribution.

Has the mind any status independent of the spatiotemporal order? Not according to the scientific point of view. To be real is to be located in the physical universe, in space and time; this applies to any kind of existent thing. A mind, so-called, is a name for an organic body in action, on a certain level of development. It presupposes group life and the development of language. The mind, or, more exactly, mental behavior, is in nature. Mental behavior is a part of the process of experience, which includes all the feelings as well as perceivings, conceivings, rememberings, and imaginings of organic beings.

This scientific point of view is opposed by the various religious traditions, and by the traditional philosophers who refuse to go along with the development of scientific psychology. Thus, the traditional problem of mind and body tends to live on. Locke, Berkeley, Kant, and a host of lesser figures provided a distinctive ontological place for a mind.

That the traditional problem of mind and body is insoluble on principle is evident from its very statement. If two essentially different kinds of substance are supposed to exist—mind and matter (or body)—then it is impossible to relate them to each other causally. The assumed conditions prevent them from entering into effective relationship, even though we know, as a matter of fact, that mind and body do influence one another. Joy and grief have bodily effects; and, in turn, injury to the body may affect one's thinking. In Descartes' hands, the dualism of mind and matter was thoroughgoing. His attempt to solve the problem of relating the assumed two substances reveals him on a weaker side. It is understandable that he was handicapped by not knowing the nature of the pineal gland, which was supposed to be the seat of the soul. But it should have been evident to him that the problem of mind and body would reappear at that very point. Although much can be said about matter, since it is extended and has mathematical properties, and although much can be said about our thought processes, it is not possible to say anything about the way in which a nonextended substance can be related to an extended substance. The patchwork undertaken in modern philosophy is a well-known chapter in the history of speculative thought.

The conception of mind as mental behavior assimilates the mind to the body and to physical reality. It recognizes that the special sciences descriptively and experimentally undertake the task of explaining mental processes within the framework of nature, without the need for a transcendent, undefined, and essentially mysterious spiritual substance, whether it be called mind, self, consciousness, or soul (in a substantive sense).

As already pointed out, the traditional mind-body problem is a secondary or derived problem, which results from the adoption of a standpoint, or special assumptions. The problem of mind (or mental behavior) as viewed today is not different in principle from the problem of breathing (lung behavior).[1] The structure of the lungs must be understood, and also the mechanism of breathing and the conditions affecting it, both external and internal to the organism. The same holds for mental behavior: the nervous system, the action of stimuli, and internal organic factors must be considered along with all relevant external physical and cultural conditions. Mental behavior and the philosophical problem are very complex, admittedly much more so than the problem of breathing. But there are no insuperable obstacles, and there is no room for standpoint differences aligned with traditional metaphysical beliefs. Differences of opinion

---

[1] It is worth recalling D. W. Prall's discussion of "Knowledge as Aptness of the Body," *The Philosophical Review*, XLVII (March, 1938), pp. 128 ff. Prall states that "if we are to reason about knowledge as we do about other things, it seems necessary to admit that knowledge is inseparable from the body. . . . My knowledge is simply never to be found where my body is not." (p. 139).

should be expressed in terms of the logic of explanation, and all views are subject to the final test of the evidence.

B. The Problem of the Given

The analysis of experience brings to light the distinction between the activity of the knower and what is given to him. Kant made this distinction in his theory of knowledge, and in his hands it led to troublesome consequences. The difficulties were due primarily to the dogmas implicit in his conception of the mind, but also to the assumptive character of the concept of givenness. There is not a fixed structure of the mind, to which a given raw material, without form, must conform. It is an unwarranted dogma that the mind provides all form to the world of experience—space, time, causal connection, etc. Only an absolute mind could be capable of providing the form for an objective world; and there is no evidence for such a mind. Real minds are themselves causally conditioned products of the world of existence. The world of existence is different because of the activities of real minds, but that is not because the minds are at the center of existence in any sense. Man attempts to adapt the world to his needs as much as possible. In his brief period of activity he is able to affect only a very small part of the world. The mind is not central in reality because man is not central.[2]

The Kantian distinction lingers on in the thought of recent and present-day philosophers, such as Husserl and C. I. Lewis. Husserl was greatly interested in the contributive activities of the mind, and he was successful in his attempt to show how much the process of experience owes to the organizing and synthetic activities of the knower. Both Husserl and Lewis attempted to appropriate Kant's insight, that we participate in the formation of our experience. In Lewis's view, the mind constitutes conceptual interpretations such as geometries of different kinds, which are *a priori* because they are brought to experience. Something is given, however, which is called a "quale" and is declared to be ineffable (in Lewis's *Mind and the World-Order*).

In the tradition of British empiricism—in Locke's theory of knowledge, for example—there was a mind (Locke's "empty

[2] Cf. M. Farber, *Naturalism and Subjectivism* (Springfield, Ill.: Charles C. Thomas, 1959).

cabinet," as he referred to the mind in his *Essay Concerning Human Understanding*), into which "simple ideas" could enter. The given element consisted of an unknown substance, and primary qualities, or the physical and mathematical qualities which were supposed to inhere in the supporting substance. Hume was able to dismiss the fiction of a mind-container, but he preserved the dogma of discrete qualities which are known through a series of impressions and ideas. The given in experience was regarded as consisting of atomic units which are fused into compounds through the activities of the knower. The most serious criticism of the traditional empiricism is that it is not true to experience in important respects, even though it professes to be a philosophy of experience. This is strikingly shown by a passage in Berkeley's *Principles of Human Knowledge*:[3]

> Smelling furnishes me with odours: the palate with tastes; and hearing conveys sounds to the mind in all their variety of tone and composition. And as several of these are observed to accompany each other, they come to be marked by one name, and so to be reputed as one thing. Thus, for example, a certain colour, taste, smell, figure and consistence having been observed to go together, are accounted one distinct thing, signified by the name apple. . . .

It is hardly true to experience to picture a small child observing a certain color, figure, etc., as going together repeatedly and then exclaiming, "Lo, an apple!" The elements of Berkeley's traditional empiricistic given are themselves products of a theory; they are the results of an analysis which are read into experience as its primary elements.

What is really given in experience? In reality, things and events come first for us. The apple is experienced as a whole object, with very few of its features discriminated at first. No mental chemistry—or alchemy—is necessary to provide unified things. The world of things and events, with all their forms and relationships, is the primary reality. One entity in the system of reality, the human knower, must reckon with the pre-existence and independent reality of an infinite universe. He is not entitled to the privilege of rubbing his eyes and asking, "Is there a world?" The terms pregiven and independently given

[3] George Berkeley, *Principles of Human Knowledge* (LaSalle, Ill.: The Open Court Publishing Company, 1920), pp. 29 f.

might be used to make clear that only a limited region of activity is possible for the human knower. Certainly he makes a difference, and is able to engage in activities of interpretation and meaning. It would be wrong to state that he is never active. His contributions are sometimes falsifying constructions. No one who is aware of the occurrence of error will deny that the mind can embark on expeditions of its own. It is also fair to recognize its great success in constructing what might be called intellectual pseudopodia, in the explanatory phase of scientific method, when hypotheses are projected, in the hope that they are what is wanted. There is no complete independence of the physical and cultural world, although there is a considerable degree of freedom and inventiveness.

The analysis of experience into the side of the knower and of the sensuously given elements has its limited justification. It is one type of analysis that should in any case be carried through. If one is then led, however, to suppose that there is an unknowable side of experience, he is guilty of confusing the limited analysis with the total reality. No matter what type of analysis is engaged in, there are certain primary facts which must be recognized as such. The philosophical knower is a human being within a space-time locus, and he is a complex physical event, enduring with a certain degree of unity for a short time. He is a member of a society which is the most important element in his given. Strikes, taxes, wars, race hatred, etc. are given to all philosophers in our time. They do not have to be constituted in pure consciousness, or built up out of simple ideas. They are real events, and the subordination of the philosophers to the social system which exhibits them is a simple fact.

The philosophy of experience which derives from the traditional concept of the given is, in short, both assumptive and confusing. It is assumptive because the mind is assumed to have a central and antecedent status, with something given to it, as material which it has to work up or endow with form. It is seen to be confusing when a special limited analysis of experience into the elements of knower and known data is taken to be the complete reality. It may appear that the star-studded sky brings million of stars within the field of vision. As a matter of fact, only a few thousand are actually seen. Direct seeing may not be taken as a defining condition of what is given. The entire sidereal universe is there as an independent fact, unrestricted by the mind.

The emphasis upon the given in experience has been widely regarded as meritorious in itself. In order to avoid errors and implicit dogmas, it is very important that the philosopher remind himself of the basic fact that man has had a long line of progenitors in an evolutionary process. Hence what is pregiven is an infinite process, just as what is given is an infinite physical universe, and a social system which he can hope to change only in part. The more congenial dualistic interpretation of the world and man turns out to be a very flat affair, when one considers the stubborn realities of experience.

C. *The Problem of Certainty*

Reference has already been made to the doubts of the skeptic and the methodological doubt which was supposed to establish certainty. It is a curious fact that this problem should have been so prominent in the philosophical tradition. The pathological doubt of the person who turns away from the evidence of experience is of little interest here. Far more important is the contention that empirical knowledge is never certain.

When Descartes instituted a procedure of systematic doubt, he undertook to doubt everything which could be doubted without contradiction. That an evil demon might possibly be deceiving us, or that we might be dreaming, so that there might not be a world really, could apparently (i.e., in Descartes' view) be said without contradiction. Similarly, there might not really be other human beings. In short, the world, other people, and my own body could be doubted without contradiction. Only my doubting experience itself was certain, because it could not be doubted without doubting. To doubt is to think, and hence "I think" (*cogito*) is the fixed Archimedean point of certainty. The disappointing outcome of Descartes' attempt, and the use to which Husserl put the procedure of doubting, have already been seen. The entire procedure has been found to be nugatory, so far as the actual achievement of certainty is concerned. Only the present doubt is indubitable; but it recedes into the past, the "now" becomes "not now" and a new "now" takes its place. But the former "now," which is "not now," can be doubted without contradiction. Perhaps it is merely a trick of the memory which leads me to think the alleged "not now" was ever a "now." Hence, a restriction to the present (but passing) moment is the outcome. Only the help of a Supreme Being could extricate one from this predicament. Unfortunately, another predicament would then take its place, for the knowledge of the existence of a Supreme Being would have to be rendered certain.

The problem of certainty is frequently raised in connection with beliefs of various kinds. One is allegedly certain of many things, even in the absence of conclusive evidence. Sometimes, as in the case of religious beliefs, it may be impossible on principle to obtain the evidence, and yet certainty may be claimed. The source may be an accepted authority, which is taken to be absolute; or there may be an appeal to an internal source, a feeling, or a power of discerning truths. The lack of general agreement over the authority in question, and the fact that the authority itself must be justified, remove the basis of certainty claimed. It becomes merely a psychological condition which anyone can experience, or challenge. The feeling of certainty is variable, and the alleged power of discovering truths must itself be tested.

In the tradition of the history of philosophy the distinction between empirical and formal mathematical knowledge has long been recognized. Empirical judgments depend upon our knowledge of matters of fact, whereas formal knowledge is regarded as certain. For Hobbes, "experience concludeth nothing universally," while the result of reasoning is "general, eternal, and immutable truth." Leibniz distinguished between truths based on perception and truths based on the understanding. Perceptual truths are such that their opposites are not precluded; whereas truths of the understanding are necessary, for their opposites are inconceivable. Mathematical knowledge was held to be necessary in this sense. Hume also maintained a distinction between matters of fact and relations of ideas. Knowledge of matters of fact can only be probable. Mathematical knowledge can be certain, however, since it is concerned with relations of ideas, and is thus not limited by the process of experience.

When Kant undertook to save mathematics as well as natural science from Hume's skeptical analysis, he really went too far, because Hume's skepticism did not apply to mathematical knowledge. Kant had to formulate his problem in such a way that mathematics was in question. This he did by arguing that mathematical knowledge, like empirical knowledge, is synthetic. A proposition is said to be synthetic if the predicate adds something to the subject and analytic if the predicate is contained in the subject. Thus, "Americans like baseball," is synthetic; whereas "A right triangle is a triangle" is analytic. Analytic propositions are clearly necessary, in the sense that their opposites are impossible (i.e., contradictory). There could be no possibility of ever meeting a right triangle which would not be a triangle. But one might very well be able to modify the proposition "Americans like baseball" by further observations. "Liking baseball" is not included in the content of "being an American." Such propositions are said to be *a posteriori*, as well as synthetic (in Kant's sense of the term). The analytic propositions are said to be *a priori*, in the sense of being independent of experience, and of being universal and necessary. Kant regarded mathematical propositions as being synthetic, although he also held that they are *a priori*, or necessary and universal. In the proposition $7 + 5 = 12$, the predicate is not contained in the subject. Hence it is a synthetic proposition. How, then, can it be said to be *a priori*, or certain? Kant's famous formulation of his problem was expressed as follows: How is *a priori* synthetic knowledge possible? Such knowledge is claimed by mathematics, as well as by natural science. No one would doubt its existence. But how can it be justified?

Kant's answer has proved to be important historically, because of its great influence. His critical, transcendental philosophy, with its elaborate and intricate set of concepts, obsolete psychology, and limited conception of logic, was intended to be the means of solving his problem.

Neither the formulation of the problem nor the proposed solution are of interest today to the validity of mathematics or natural science. The conception of analytic knowledge has been broadened to mean logical-analytic or deductive knowledge. A proposition following deductively from the basic concepts and premises of logic is logical-analytic; and, in a broad sense, any proposition deduced from a given set of premises may be called analytic. The really important question is one of application to reality. A proposition may be valid, or invalid, in terms of a given system of knowledge. The propositions of logic are supposed to be valid in all conceivable systems. Kant took over the logic of Aristotle, and lacked the advantage of the modern logic of deduction, which, although anticipated by Descartes and Leibniz, has been largely developed in the last century. There need be no psychological foundation of arithmetic and geometry. We can operate definitionally and formally with numbers and points of space without considering our psychological equipment. Kant's clue to a solution of his problem of proving mathematical knowledge *a priori* was a false one; it was his aim to determine what the mind brings to experience. In Kant's view, if the mind brings something to experience, the descriptive analysis of its contribution will bring to light an *a priori* foundation of experience and knowledge. This, he thought, was shown on the level of sense perception by the forms of time and space, and on the level of the understanding by the categories, such as causality, unity, etc. It is of course only an absolute mind which could give the desired support and stability to the world of experience. Kant did not justify the acceptance of such a mind, with its fixed forms; and neither does mathematics need that kind of salvation. Even if Kant had been successful in his method, he would have succeeded in saving something that was never lost.

Analytic propositions, including propositions which tell what is involved in the meaning of a term, do not depend upon the evidence of factual events. They are not at the mercy of the facts of experience. The talk of a "formal *a priori*" is really modest.

More pretentious is the conception of a "material *a priori*," which depends upon the theory of essences. Since essences are assigned to a different order than natural facts, truths about them are regarded as nonfactual truths. All that can be said is that if any things illustrate such essences, then they must have certain characters. In other words, this is merely an extension of the realm of analytic knowledge. If it be objected that essences are abstracted from empirical occasions, so that there is a genetic reference to reality, or to real facts, it may be observed that all language has an empirical origin, and so does formal logic. No matter how a given meaning, or proposition, is derived from experience, the question of *a priori* knowledge is merely a hypothetical one: if a figure is a square, it has four sides; if a man is President of the United States, he is elected for a four-year term, beginning at a specified time. There are different kinds of so-called *a priori* knowledge (a questionable term, in any case)—purely formal and material in a host of different ways. With exact concepts one can always assert what is contained in the definition. The example of the square is a clear one. In the case of the President of the United States, the years must be cited because there may be changes instituted by new laws, or by amendments.

If one tries to tell something about a revolution by mere analysis of the meaning, he is obviously limited by a set of historical circumstances, which may change in the future. The concept of a war is another example. There are undeclared wars, and perhaps there is such a condition as perpetual war. Whatever follows from such time-bound empirical concepts could only be said to be *a priori* in the sense that the facts are past and are so to speak stored away. The range of application of propositions with an empirical reference is restricted. In the hypothetical form, such a proposition may read: "If the conditions remain the same, then a President of the United States takes office at such and such a time, and he is elected for a four-year term."

Quite different is such an example as "An organism must be spatially extended." Were there no organisms, this proposition would not have been asserted. But analysis shows this to be a true *a priori* proposition, which holds in the "if, then" form, even if all organisms should disappear.

Mathematical knowledge is certain in the deductive sense of following from premises by logical means. That is to say, it is certain if it is valid. If a mistake is discovered, it was never valid and never certain. Our feeling may be one of certainty, but that is another matter. In other words, mathematical (or formal) knowledge is certain when it is correct. Can one ever be absolutely certain that it is correct? Or should one speak, in the words of the late Professor Felix Kaufmann,[4] of a "principle of permanent control," to the effect that every scientific proposition is subject to the possibility that it may be modified or even repudiated at some future time? Although we usually have

[4] *Methodology of the Social Sciences* (New York: Oxford University Press, 1944).

good reason to be more confident in the realm of formal thought than when we deal with matters of fact, there is still the possibility that there may be future control.

There is a sense in which it can be said that a given factual proposition is always true if it is once really true. Bradley has interpreted the principle of identity as meaning "Once true, always true," or "What is true in one context is true in another."[5] But the range of the proposition in question must be carefully determined. If I say, in a classroom, "There are now thirty persons in the room," and if that is correct, it will always be true "through all eternity," that at such a time and place there were thirty people in the room. This proposition is also subject to future control, and, like the mathematical proposition which is absolutely valid if it is correct (i.e., valid), it is true if it expresses what is actually the case (i.e., if it is true). It would seem that all claims to absolute certainty are hypothetical in character, and are of the nature of tautologies. This should not be taken to deny the difference between formally valid and empirical knowledge, which is important and far-reaching.

Professor C. I. Lewis was a prominent exponent of the view that empirical knowledge is at most highly probable, while formal knowledge is certain.[6] As Lewis expressed it, empirical beliefs are justified or warranted, but are less than certain, i.e., they are probable. In his example of an "objective judgment,"[7] "A piece of white paper is now before me," there is always some theoretical possibility of a mistake; "there will be further consequences which must be thus and so if the judgment is true, and not all of these will have been determined. The possibility that such further tests, if made, might have a negative result, cannot be altogether precluded; and this possibility marks the judgment as, at the time in question, not fully verified and less than absolutely certain." A judgment of this type, which is never completely verified, is said to be nonterminating. On the other hand, a judgment which is describable in "expressive language" is called terminating, because it can be completely verified or falsified. For example, if I say, "I see

---

[5] Cf. Francis Bradley, *The Principles of Logic* (London: William Clowes and Sons, Ltd., 1883; and New York: G. E. Stechert and Co., 1920), p. 133.
[6] Cf. *Mind and the World-Order* (New York: Charles Scribner's Sons, 1929) and Lewis's more recent book, *An Analysis of Knowledge and Valuation* (LaSalle, Ill.: The Open Court Publishing Co., 1946).
[7] *An Analysis of Knowledge and Valuation*, p. 180.

what looks like a flight of granite steps in front of me," I am not saying that the steps *are* granite, but am merely expressing "what I take to be the objective facts this presentation signalizes." This is to restrict oneself "to the fact of presentation itself, as contrasted with the objective state of affairs more usually signified by the rest of my statement."[8] In this way, one may try to express "the direct and indubitable content" of his experience.

The distinction between terminating and nonterminating judgments recalls Husserl's distinction between purely reflective knowledge of conscious processes and the external, natural experience of matters of fact. For Husserl, one can be absolutely certain of one's inner experiences, but can on principle doubt external natural facts, which could also "not be." Lewis is satisfied to distinguish carefully the types of evidence for terminating and nonterminating judgments (i.e., those which express what something "looks like" to me, and those which deal with objective things). But Husserl, as a continuator of the tradition of idealism, has a systematic goal. We are not allowed to remain in a predicament, if certainty is what we want. The subjective, "inner" realm is certain. We cannot legislate for matters of fact, but we can discern essential structures, without which nothing could be what it is. As for the factual world, it "might not be." Having retired to his subjective realm, Husserl undertakes to constitute all being out of pure consciousness. He is careful, at any rate, to recognize it as an endless task.

The claim that the inner experiences are certain has already been criticized in connection with Descartes' method of doubt. Only the immediately present conscious experience is indubitable. Unless the memory can be trusted absolutely, the certainty is limited to the specious present, which is entirely unsatisfactory and unfruitful. Furthermore, the report about what a thing "looks like" may be erroneous. Direct observations are conditioned by one's whole store of experiences, and there may be unconscious as well as conscious influences of interpretation. One need not refer to the complex cases well known to analysts; there are enough examples in normal, everyday experience. Differences in sensory equipment, including deficiencies, the influence of self-feeling or self-interest, errors in observation, faulty inferences: these are factors to be reckoned with in

---

[8] *Ibid.*, p. 173.

appraising the allegedly superior and certain realm of subjective appearance. If outer experience is not certain, then neither is inner experience. To be sure, if one's interest is restricted to the reflectively viewed structure of experience, he does not deal with actual inner experiences. It would not be disturbing that a given observer is color-blind, for example. The relationship between or among colors would be a more appropriate theme for him. One's particular memories would not be a theme of inquiry, but, rather, the essential nature of memory. Is it possible, however, that the nature of memory has been incorrectly reported, or that after many years a modification may be made in the essential analysis of memory?

If the world is constantly changing, and if there is a universal evolutionary process, how can we regard essences or essential laws as exempt from change? In so doing, does one not cut off essences from the order of facts? This question then leads us once more to the distinction between the analytic and the synthetic. It is true and certain analytically that an experience of negation (or denial) refers back essentially to a prior experience of affirmation. That would be the case even if all experiences of negation were to disappear, along with all experiencing beings.

Husserl speaks of essential seeing, or the observation of essences. What guarantee does one have that it is incapable of error, or that later instances of essential seeing will not give us a somewhat different view? May not even the observation of essences be faulty? At one time, Husserl referred to the occurrence of error in the field of subjective inquiry, so that he was aware of that danger. But it appears that it was relatively unimportant in his opinion, for it did not affect his judgment of the merits of subjective analysis.

Viewed practically, one may be led to say that certain means sufficiently certain for our practical needs, or for scientific purposes. There is a methodogenic problem of certainty for a sheer, narrow empiricism, or for a pure phenomenology of experience. The certainty of the *cogito* (i.e., of the "I think" which is indubitable) is prominently assumed in French philosophy. The primary of the *cogito* has been a fundamental article of faith for existentialists as well as idealists. How important is certainty (defined as that which cannot be denied without contradiction) in practice? It is negligible. The claim that absolutely certain knowledge may be a thin truth, but that it is the important truth, is not borne out in practice.

In actual experience, certainty may have other meanings. It may mean "having a probability of 1"; or it may simply be interpreted in terms of verification, as in the case of determining the cause of a given disease, or the cause of the death of a given person. Can it be said that verification is never certain or conclusive? When the cause of a disease has been described, and the disease cured, has there not been an effective verification? The philosopher's further demand for absolute certainty is as empty as it is unwarranted. Would it affect our practical actions if we declared in the 1930s, for example, that "Hitler is evil" was highly probable but never certain? For example, might there have been the possibility that Hitler did not really exist, or that the world did not really exist? Is there no limit to nonsense?

It belongs to the order of factual knowledge that human beings sometimes believe they see things which are not there, and confuse a dream experience with reality. Even if that happened only once out of every billion instances of experience, it could not be said that experience is certain in the sense of being infallible without exception. Such experiences are taken at random. Suppose that socially controlled or experimentally confirmed experiences are considered. It is doubtful whether a single questionable case could be cited. There is therefore no reason for depreciating experience. The problem of certainty is simply the problem of establishing knowledge. Experience and knowledge as a whole are not under indictment.

D. Sameness and the Ideality of Meaning

The cognitive situation is tripartite. There is the experiencing or judging person; judgment-meanings are asserted or denied; and objects are referred to or presupposed. The judgment has been widely regarded as the unit of knowledge. There are other types of experience—wishing, willing, etc.; and there are more complex forms, as seen in processes of reasoning. Broadly defined, a judgment may be said to be a characterization of reality (in its primary sense), or of some subject matter, which may be purely imaginative or artificial. It is the basic function of judgments to express facts, whether they are events in nature or products of abstract thinking. There may be ideal facts, as illustrated in mathematics. It is a fact that 17 is a prime number, and the judgment gives expression to it. When a judgment is expressed in communicable symbols it is called a proposition. Judgments or propositions give expression to the relationships of various kinds of objects, in the form of expressions which are true or false of the indicated objects. Although there are no centaurs in reality, judgments about centaurs may be true or false, according to the domain of fable involved.

The question has been raised, whether the judgment-meanings may be said to exist in a special sense, as distinguished from natural events in space and time. It appears to some philosophers that the locus of judgment-meanings, or the content of what is expressed, is a third thing, distinct from the subject or knower and the object. "The tree is green," "3 is greater than 2," and "Dulduls are gulguls" are examples of different types of judgment-meanings which are expressed in relationship to the domain of natural reality, natural numbers, and nonsensical objects (or objects with nonsensical meaning). "The tree is green" may be judged any number of times, and we say that the same meaning has been expressed. In Frege's view, meaning is not subjective, and yet it is not to be identified with the object.[9] Meinong's "objects of a higher order"[10] and Husserl's "ideal expression-meanings"[11] represent attempts to reconcile the objective nature of meanings with the psychological reality of changing experience. The real physical experiences of thinking beings are different from case to case, and from person to person. One does not experience exactly the same way when he asserts what he intends to be the same judgment-meaning that he had asserted the day before. The judgments "π is a transcendental number" and "That is Beethoven's Fourth Symphony" may be repeated any number of times, and by means of different modes of symbolic expression. We say that the same meaning is asserted, despite variations in the symbolic expression and differences in

[9] Cf. B. Russell, *Principles of Mathematics*, Appendix on Frege (Cambridge: The University Press, 1903).
[10] Cf. A. Meinong, "Über Gegenstände höherer Ordnung und deren Verhältnis zur inneren Wahrnehmung," in *Abhandlungen zur Erkenntnistheorie und Gegenstandstheorie* (Leipzig: Verlag von J. A. Barth, 1913).
[11] Cf. E. Husserl, *Logische Untersuchungen* (Halle: Max Niemeyer, 1922), Vol. II, pp. 42 ff., and M. Farber, *The Foundation of Phenomenology* (Albany: New York State University Press, 1967).

the experiencing persons. There is something different and perhaps unique about the experience of the meaning in each case. Is the meaning the same in an ontological sense?

To speak of a third realm of being (or of a second realm, if physical existence is taken to be all-inclusive, as it must) would be to commit the fallacy of hypostatization. There is no evidence to support such a metaphysical thesis, and it can only be advanced as an assumption. The so-called world of meanings, or of propositions, exists in so far as it is experienced. It would be simply dogmatic to assign a transcendent species of being to those meanings which refer to subjective states of experience. In the first place, all experience is significant in that it is experience of something, whether that something be an external object or a subjective state, as in an experience of remembrance. The significant experiences always exist, regardless of the nature of the things to which they refer. The primary experiences themselves may be called meanings of a first order. Secondly, propositions about primary experiences may be expressed, and such propositional meanings may be said to exist, when they are experienced, as meanings of a second order. It should be borne in mind that existence in a primary sense is physical existence. If the propositional meaning refers to a passing subjective state, such as "I just recalled a pleasant experience," it is not only a remembrance of a particular event; it is also in turn a particular event. But if a propositional meaning expresses a general (essential) fact, such as "Every experience of remembrance refers back to an original experience," that fact exists as a determination of all cases of remembrance whenever they occur. The propositional meaning has no existence of its own apart from the particular meaning in which it is expressed, any more than there can be remembrance apart from actual experiences of remembrance.

What is true of propositions referring to subjective states is equally true of propositions with objective reference. The particular propositional meaning, "That is a red patch," exists as a significant experience, and its symbolic expression exists as an auditory or visual phenomenon. Suppose that one repeats the proposition, "That is a red patch." The repeated experience is not identical with the original experience, and yet we say that the same meaning has been expressed. The ambiguity of the term meaning confuses the meaningful experience with the proposition which is meant (or presumed) as the same, despite differences in the mode of its expression.

Propositions which express general relations illustrate the same distinction. A true general proposition, such as "$2 + 2 = 4$," exists as a meaningful experience as often as it is asserted. Despite the innumerable ways in which it may be expressed symbolically, it is supposed to persist as the same meaning. The possibility of referring to the same meanings is the first condition of ordered thinking and cumulative knowledge. One can never maintain that the objects are the same, as existent entities. Permanent objects which are separable from the particular events of the world have never been proved to exist. In the course of experience we suppose that events exemplify general objects, we recognize events as having features in common, and we construct a world of ideal meanings which helps us to understand and control the world of actual events. There are to be sure important contributions of the understanding, which are indispensable in a practical sense. To ask about the existence of the ideal meanings, however, is to raise a false question. Either a crude fallacy is committed, i.e., meanings of permanence are taken to be permanent meanings, which is the standpoint of those who posit an independent order of subsistent meanings; or the predicate of existence has no application to the ideal meanings. In the second case, meanings may still be said to be either true or false, in the sense that they apply or do not apply to the events of the world, or to some special universe of discourse. Questions of evidence and demonstration (in the case of deductive knowledge) then take the place of ontological questions about the reality of entities which by their very definition have no spatiotemporal locus, and hence no place in reality. The real question is, "What are the facts?"; and ideal meanings are devices used to help in determining facts.

E. *Judgment and Reality*

Although Kant was right in recognizing that we, as knowers, participate in the formation of our experience, the mode of participation was rather different from his account of it. The absolute mind, and the fixed forms provided by the mind to the world of experience, have vanished with the eighteenth-century powdered wig and snuffbox. And yet Kant must be given credit for his insights and achievements. It suited his purposes to regard the judgment as the unit of cognitive experience. In accordance with his idealistic premises, the table of judgments—which in his view summarized the basic ways of knowing—supposedly provided a clue to the ways of being in the world of experience. The evolutionary, historical conception of the mind and its forms superseded Kant's construction. But it remained fashionable to regard the judgment as possessing fundamental significance for the theory of knowledge. The structures exhibited in the analysis of judgment were also seen in the parallel analysis of willing, wishing, etc.

Take, for example, the judgment that $2 + 3 = 5$. The fact *that* $2 + 3 = 5$ is a part of the system of arithmetic. A fact is selected for expression; and this applies generally, either in the unavoidable course of experience, or in response to the voluntary exercise of our theoretical and practical interests.

In mathematics, the whole is prior to its parts. That is not to declare the geometrical axiom stating the relation of a whole to its proper parts absolute. Infinite wholes do not conform to that principle. But all totalities, whether finite or infinite, are prior to their constituent parts in two respects: first, in the case of existing entities, the individual objects are always found to be members of a larger domain; and second, in propositions based upon the objects and their relationships, no single proposition can have significance by itself, but must involve a system of propositions in the light of which it has meaning. For knowledge generally, as well as for logic and mathematics, it can be said that a domain or system is prior to particular events or meanings.

Does this say too much? Is it true to state, for example, that the number 2 cannot be defined by itself? The definition of a cardinal number in terms of classes involves a larger system in turn, namely, the system of classes; and if it is defined as a concept, a system of concepts is involved in order to give significance to the concept of number. Our principle is as inescapable as it is universal. Every item of ordinary experience is interpreted in the light of the larger whole of our past experience in everyday life; and in our scientific thinking, we subsume all real events under the system of physical reality.

In every case of judgment, there is a selection of one or more characters from the collective totality of characters which are basic to and indicated by the judgment. In the judgment "The tree is green" we have a situation similar to that of "$2 + 3 = 5$." The tree is the immediate basis of the judgment, and the character of being green is selected. Other characters, such as its size and color, are not singled out. The tree in turn is part of a larger context, which must ultimately be taken to be nature as a whole.

The judgment-question, "Is the tree green?", is more primitive logically than the judgment-answer, "The tree is green." The judgment-question is neither true nor false. It merely presents a disjunction of the possible judgments, "Either the tree is green" or "It is not green," without making a decision. Nature raises no questions; it gives only answers. The judgment-question, however, is of great importance in the quest for knowledge, and also in the construction of organized knowledge. In the present illustration the tree is abstracted from its environment, and is made the basis for a judgment. What has been said holds equally for the judgment-question, "Does $2 + 3 = 5$?". It is neither true nor false, and it is selected from the totality of propositions making up the system of arithmetic. The differences between the two illustrations are due to the differences in their foundation; the judgment about the tree is empirical in character, whereas the judgment about numbers is a deduction from the postulates of arithmetic. In both cases a larger whole is involved. The empirical judgment involves empirical reality as a whole, which is taken to be an extension of the perceptual world as it is actually known.

The descriptive analysis of judgment, when viewed from the side of the experiencing person, includes judgments in experiences of illusion and hallucination, and also judgments of impossible entities—for example, "That figure is a square triangle." In the interest of a complete account of the modes of experience involved, all the objects referred to may be treated as correlates of judgment. To use Husserl's terminology, judgments are noetic (cognitive), and the objects are noematic (correlates of judgments of all kinds, without any restriction to natural existence). The objects belong to various domains, which may be real, imaginary, or impossible in the sense that they violate the principles of logic.

On the noetic side, the actual experiences of perception, remembrance, etc., exhibit structural features which interest us in the analysis of judgment. In the analysis of experience, the actual processes are regarded as examples of general structural types. But it is not necessary for us to assume that there are general experiences in order to discern general structures in experience. Every experience is a particular event, regardless of the nature of the object involved; and the object may be abstract, concrete, general, or individual.

The extension of the range of the objects of judgment to include all possible objects of possible thought is necessary for the theory of knowledge. Not all experience refers to actual existence. The analysis of judgment must include in its account all types of judgment, whether presumptive of existence or not. The admission of all possible types of judgment with their correlates undoubtedly opens the door for much nonsense; but it also allows free play to the scientific imagination. The explanation of the concrete world of experience has required the use of concepts which appear at first to depart widely from the existing world. This is illustrated by mathematical fictions and the principle of infinity, and in general by scientific explanatory devices. Freedom of construction is required for the unimpeded development of formal reasoning, and for the explanatory purposes of science.

While giving expression to a fact, a true judgment excludes other judgments which are false. The judgment "This tree is green" excludes, for example, the judgment that it is white; "$3>2$" excludes the cases that $2 = 3$ or $2>3$; and "The ghost is white" excludes "The ghost is red." Spinoza's dictum that "*determinatio est negatio*" and Hegel's principle that negation is limitation aptly express important aspects of judgment.

In each of the cases of judgment mentioned, a domain or system of elements is presupposed and a fact is asserted. Objects of any nature whatsoever may be presupposed, and they are taken to be independent of actual experience. This is in opposition to the standpoint of intuitionism, according to which all objects must be brought into view or traced to structures in experience. The consequences of such a view would be undesirable for the principle of infinity, for example, since infinite aggregates cannot be discerned intuitively. The contention that the infinite can be brought to view in the case of the natural number series, in the form of an "and so forth," has extremely limited significance. If a rule of progression is provided, the series is rendered independent of intuitive discernment. In logical thinking, as in mathematics, assumptions are made which transcend the field of actual experience.

It should not be supposed that the traditional analysis of judgment could give a clue to the nature of reality. Reality does not conform to judgment, except in the very special sense in which a part of reality is made to conform to human ends—for example, in reforestation, and in other humanly caused changes in the environment. The real place of man in nature must never be forgotten. Man the knower is still in nature, even though his position is immeasurably more important and effective because of the power of knowing. As already argued, it is a mistaken, sterile dogma to suppose a general mind which gives form to the world. If that is done, it is then a natural step to attempt to grind all of reality out of an absolute spirit, which is believed to be the subject of judgment. The real nature of judgment is recognized when it is seen that a judgment expresses a thesis which must be tested in experience. It is not prescriptive for the world; it is predictive, and in need of verification.

If there is no one subject of judgment, there is also no one domain of reality about which all judgments are asserted. Although physical reality is the primary domain, allowance must be made for a plurality of domains of objects, including artificially defined abstractions and ideal objects. What is the meaning, then, of the claim that knowledge—or at least scientific knowledge—is unified? Are the various formal systems of knowledge capable of being united with the real sciences; and can the real sciences be united in one system of knowledge? These questions, and their relationship to the traditional problem of monism, will be the theme of the next chapter.

F. *Hypothetical Judgments and Conditions Contrary to Fact*

The fact that prediction of the future is a primary function of empirical knowledge explains the importance attached to hypothetical judgments. A plan of action is expressed by a hypothetical condition, which is supposed to bring about a predicted result. For example, if X studies every day, he will pass the examination. Hypothetical judgments play an important role in the structure of knowledge. Propositions of the form, "If p, then q" or "p implies q" abound in our discourse, and they are most prominently illustrated in formal logic and mathematics. Thus, if p (or the set of premises constituting p) is accepted, then theorem q follows. The antecedent condition p must be sufficient for the consequent q; and if the antecedent condition holds, then the consequent follows.

The "if, then" relationship, or the implicative relationship, may be defined differently in different contexts, ranging all the way from the analytic and deductive to merely factual and passing circumstances. One may say that the Euclidean axioms imply the theorem that the sum of the interior angles of a triangle equals 180 degrees. Or one may say that being President of the United States implies being commander-in-chief of the armed forces, or that being a man implies living less than 200 years.

That a hypothetical empirical judgment may express something that is contrary to fact has been the basis of a lively exchange of ideas following C. I. Lewis's discussion of it in his *Analysis of Knowledge and Valuation*.[12] It is a good example of what has been called a methodogenic problem, or a problem which results from the adoption of a particular method and the concepts involved.

The concept of implication is of fundamental importance in deductive reasoning. It has been defined in various ways, and no single version of implication can be declared to be the only correct one. A weak form of implication, known as material implication, has proved useful as well as objectionable. With two propositions, p and q, there are four possible combinations of their truth and falsity: (1) p true and q true, (2) p false and q true, (3) p false and q false, and (4) p true and q false. Material implication allows three of the combinations of truth and falsity out of the four possible combinations. Only (4) is rejected, in the definition of material implication as "not p or q," or "either p is false or q is true." The usefulness of this concept for the purposes of formal logic was shown by Russell and Whitehead. But it was also evident that there were undesirable consequences in the form of paradoxical theorems. It followed from the analysis of material implication that a false proposition implies any proposition, because p false and q

---

[12] *Op. cit.*, pp. 211 ff.

false, and also *p* false and *q* true were possible combinations. Similarly, it also followed that a true proposition is implied by any proposition. It appeared to students of logic a generation ago that the proposition "The law of gravitation is a student" would then imply that "The moon is made of green cheese," etc. With *p* and *q* standing for "any propositions," there was no limit to the mischief.

Making use of what he calls a terminating judgment as his illustration, Lewis is led to conclude that the consequences of a contrary to fact statement cannot be expressed in terms of material implication. His example is[13]

> ... in believing that a piece of real paper is before me, I believe that if I turn my eyes right, the seen paper will be displaced left. But I do not now turn my eyes ... Nevertheless I believe that if I *should* turn my eyes the predicted consequence *would* follow ... And an 'if, then' relation of this sort, which we may express by recourse to the subjunctive mood ... *cannot* be expressed in terms of material implication. Because when the hypothesis '*A*' is contrary to fact, '*A* materially implies *E*' holds regardless of the truth or falsity of '*E*', and regardless of the question whether '*E*' *would be* true if '*A* were* true. For example, since I do not at present turn my eyes, it holds that 'I now turn my eyes' materially implies 'The thing seen is displaced.' But also and for the same reason—namely, that the antecedent in the relation is false—'I turn my eyes' materially implies 'a loud explosion is heard,' or anything else you please to mention as consequent. When '*A*' is *false*, the material implication '*A* implies *X*' holds, *no matter what* statement '*X*' is. Thus the consequences of a contrary to fact statement—in any sense *in which some things are such consequences and others are not*—cannot be expressed in terms of material implication.

Thus, the problem of contrary to fact conditionals appears unavoidable on this basis.

Not only is it important to consider the numerous implicative relationships in various contexts; the judgments must also be examined for their truth and evidence. A proposition such as "If X studies every day, he will pass the examination" is simply a case of probable inference. The question is one of the frequency of persons studying every day who also pass the examinations for which they are preparing. And even though I do not step out of the window, I can say, "If I step out of the

[13] *Ibid.*, pp. 214 f.

window, I shall be injured." That the antecedent condition is contrary to fact presents no problem, because, again, it is a question of the frequency with which people who step out of windows (under defined conditions, of course) are injured. Lewis points out that three logically defined types of implication, including strict implication, cannot be used when the condition is contrary to fact. What follows, then, is their treatment in terms of probability, regardless of their being contrary to fact.

G. *The Social Conditions of Experience and Knowledge*

It is certainly important to establish the locus of experience securely within the world-order. But it is not enough to do so, if one is to understand the influences bearing upon the formation and change of experience. Human experience normally occurs within the limits of a definite social system. Exceptional cases of relatively detached individuals may be disregarded, as being of minor importance. In any case, such individuals are always indebted to a definite cultural system for their language, techniques, and thought processes.

In the usual analysis of experience and knowledge, one takes a knower as such and confronts him with the natural world. Constant patterns result from the analysis of the distinction between act, content, and object. If social relations are considered, they, too, are apt to be of a nonhistorical type. The individual is considered in relationship to society or the social system. The ego, conscience, perception, and the imagination do not have any historical accidents for the systematic analyst. But as a matter of fact they are variable in important respects, and it is necessary to determine the conditions which affect them. The same objects are experienced differently by different people, especially by people representing different cultural groups.[14]

Curiously, it was the anti-naturalistic and anti-Marxist philosopher Max Scheler who directed the interest of professional philosophers toward the development of a sociology of knowledge.[15] Although this was a tribute to his ability to discern an important need for research in social science and philosophy,

[14] Cf. F. Engels, *Dialectics of Nature* (New York: International Publishers, 1940), Chaps. I, IX, and X.
[15] M. Scheler, *Versuche zu einer Soziologie des Wissens* (München und Leipzig: Verlag von Duncker und Humblot, 1924).

his own philosophical commitments inhibited his efforts. It was Karl Mannheim who turned popular attention to the sociology of knowledge, beginning with his *Ideology and Utopia*.[16] As he described it,

> The sociology of knowledge is one of the youngest branches of sociology; as theory it seeks to analyse the relationship between knowledge and existence; as historical-sociological research it seeks to trace the forms which this relationship has taken in the intellectual development of mankind. . . . The sociology of knowledge is concerned not so much with distortions due to a deliberate effort to deceive as with the varying ways in which objects present themselves to the subject according to the differences in social settings.

The total mental structure of the asserting subject, as it appears in different currents of thought and historical-social groups, is of interest to the sociology of knowledge. The question is, "when and where social structures come to express themselves in the structure of assertions, and in what sense the former concretely determine the latter." Avoiding the use of the term ideology, because of its moral connotation, Mannheim speaks instead of the perspective of a thinker. The term perspective refers to a person's "whole mode of conceiving things as determined by his historical and social setting."

It is undeniable that the social setting influences one's mode of conceiving things. The evidence is conclusive. The mine-owner has his perspective; and so has the miner. In outlining the scope and function of the sociology of knowledge, it is necessary to make it clear that ideas are not taken to be due solely to social factors. That this has been misunderstood has already been shown in the controversy which has been developing about the sociology of knowledge. Thus, Northrop wrote:[17] "It is becoming clear . . . that man through knowledge can be something more than a loudspeaker for the particular class or the provincial culture in which circumstances happen to place him. Nature exists one and the same for all men, as well as the many classes and cultures. Hence there is another source

---

[16] K. Mannheim, *Ideology and Utopia: An Introduction to the Sociology of Knowledge* (New York: Harcourt, Brace and Company, 1936), pp. 237 ff. Cf. also K. Mannheim, *Essays on the Sociology of Knowledge* (New York: Oxford University Press, 1952).

[17] F. S. C. Northrop, Preface to J. J. Maquet's *The Sociology of Knowledge* (Boston: Beacon Press, 1951), p. xix.

for the existential validation of philosophical knowledge and its attendant norms than either class or culture."

In truth, it has been clear for a long time that man can be something more than a spokesman for a social class, or for a type of culture. But it has been equally clear that man is also responsive to personal, class, and more general cultural influences; and it is the function of the study of social influences upon ideas to determine the extent to which that is the case, and to evaluate the various causal factors. By no means does that mean ignoring the existence of nature—unless one has lapsed into an effete form of idealism. Nature is always there, but it will give little help in accounting for ideas such as fascism, Nazism, socialism, and democracy; or the equality of women, the rights of labor, freedom of competition; or, again, the belief that some people are naturally slaves. Such variable ideas must be explained by reference to passing historical interests.

Does this imply cultural relativism? How can one speak of objective truth if there is always a historical perspective? The difficulty is hardly more than verbal. The proposition that a given individual, or a social class, is influenced by economic interests, for example, is either true or false objectively. The apparent relativism enters into the content of a new proposition, which asserts the fact that there is a perspective in operation. The American historian Professor Charles Beard was able to establish the fact that the founding fathers responded to economic influences. They had a perspective. Did he have one? Probably a person without a perspective does not exist. However, a statement about relativism is not therefore a relativistic statement. One may describe the value attitudes of primitive peoples without always fearing falsification. If it can be maintained that verified propositions, or highly probable propositions, can be instated in our social sciences, then the question about objective truth is answered therewith.

The very forms of knowledge are historically conditioned. The emphasis upon direct observation and intuitive experience, as contrasted with the interposition of conceptual schematisms, can be explained on the basis of the social conditions in the East as distinguished from the West. The motivation for the development of scientific techniques, and so of the scientific view of the world, can be traced to conditions early in the modern period of western European history. The discovery of the calculus in England and Germany was just such a response to a prime social need. In general, mathematics had to provide essential tools for the theoretical and applied sciences which would make possible the control of nature through industrial development.[18]

It does not follow, however, that past forms of mathematics—classical geometry, for example—are outmoded and no longer valid, as judged from a later perspective. Although there is a unique element in the mathematics of a given historical period, just as there is in its sculpture, music, politics, and philosophy, it is not true that all such cultural products are superseded without residuum. There is a considerable degree of transmittance of techniques and scientific knowledge, so that one can speak of the cumulative side of cultural growth. Spengler's thesis[19] that the West is doomed, for deep-seated organic reasons, is simply a case of false analogy. The organic realm universally registers growth, decline, and death. In the cultural realm there is no necessary cause for total death. A given system of society might go on endlessly; and, along with innovations, there is the element of preserving cultural achievements of the past, while reinterpreting and adapting them to present conditions. Experience is indeed a changing process of reaction to a changing world.

---

[18] Cf. D. J. Struik on "Mathematics" and J. D. Bernal on "Science, Invention, and Social Applications of Technology," in *Philosophy for the Future*, ed. R. W. Sellars, V. J. McGill, and M. Farber (New York: The Macmillan Co., 1949); and also J. D. Bernal, *The Social Function of Science* (London: Routledge & Kegan Paul, Ltd., 1939).
[19] Cf. O. Spengler, *The Decline of the West*, Vol. I (New York: Alfred A. Knopf, Inc., 1926).

CHAPTER VI

Monism and Pluralism

A. *The Historical Problem of Monism*

It has been pointed out that all philosophical problems are historical, although not all of them are real problems. If a problem is meaningful in the sense that it deals with entities which have status in the world of experience, it is empirically real; and if it is meaningful in a well-defined system of knowledge it is formally real. It is possible to say the last word about merely historical problems as such, once their motivation and practical nature are known. The historical problems which are also real often do not find a solution in the period in which they arise.

The traditional problem of monism has appeared in a number of different forms. As a historical problem its role has varied with prevailing interests, and it must be interpreted anew for different periods. As a real problem, however, it has significance apart from changing historical conditions. Those aspects of the problem which are merely historical must be distinguished from those which are real, and the latter must be considered in relation to the structure of knowledge and the nature of reality. It is essential to make clear the programmatic character of the goal of the unity of knowledge, and to do justice to the relative independence of the facts of experience.

It is because of its ulterior significance that the concept of monism has played so conspicuous a role in the history of thought, despite its ambiguity. This significance has changed at different periods, the ideal of unity being radical or conservative, depending upon the leading interests of the time. To see this clearly, however, it is necessary to indicate the type of monism—materialism or spiritualism, for example. Although ontological dualism has conspicuously served conservative interests historically, that was not the case for the philosophy of Descartes, where it was useful in securing autonomy for scientific thought. This entailed emancipation from the authoritarian tradition in the intellectual and moral realm—of primary importance at the time. The English, with less need to compromise, and in early response to the new motives of commerce and industry, made a more thoroughgoing break with the feudal-ecclesiastical tradition in the form of a materialistic monism. Thus we see two conflicting programs in response to the same kind of motivation. This indicates the value and at the same time an essential limitation of historical method in philosophy. By means of such examples we can advance a reasonable explanation of what would otherwise be a strange succession of intellectual efforts. It will suffice to explain and to dissolve questions of merely passing significance; and it provides a bond of relatedness to the field of philosophy which is essential for a complete theory of philosophy. But the historical method is not adequate to solve problems which have a systematic meaning besides serving historical interests.

The interest in establishing monism is deeply rooted in the philosophical quest. Spinoza's elaborate argument for a monism of substance (ontological monism) is the classical prototype of all arguments for the unity of reality in modern philosophy. Spinoza has shown with consistency what follows from the concept of complete being when considered along with the concept of absolute infinity. The basic concept of Spinoza's system is substance, which is defined as "that which is in itself, and is conceived through itself"; and this turns out to be equivalent to God, defined as "a being absolutely infinite—i.e., a substance consisting in infinite attributes, of which each expresses eternal and infinite essentiality." This absolute being is all at once; it involves no negation. The difficulty of maintaining the thesis of complete being results from the need to eliminate or circumvent time, for a temporal world is never absolutely complete. *Sub specie aeterni* (assuming the perspective of eternity), all temporal changes or relationships are regarded as relative, resulting from a limited point of view. Hence the unreality of time follows from Spinoza's premises. The argument fails if one refuses to grant the possibility of transcending all temporal relations, and considers such a process to be as illicit a procedure as would be the closing of the series of natural numbers with a greatest number. A general theory of unity should not sacrifice anything of the concrete reality of the world of experience, whose horizons present us with an open world. The world of experience is a finality for all purposes, ontological as well as scientific and practical; and no theoretical construction may violate its nature.

B. Royce's Argument for Monism

The immediate background of the present interest in the problem of unity was furnished by such philosophers as Lotze, Bradley, and Royce, who advanced idealistic arguments in defense of the thesis of monism. The historical outcome of idealism is the doctrine of the universality of spirit. The idealistic arguments for the unity of reality brought on a strong reaction in the interest of actual existence. James's pluralism registered a protest against a monism that "derealized the only life we are at home in,"[1] while calling attention to the nature of facts and experience. James clamored for a world in which adventure and risk have a place. This was in keeping with the facts of our experience—and of the world of competitive enterprise.

It will be sufficient for present purposes to select Royce's argument in *The World and the Individual*[2] as an example of the efforts of idealists to establish monism. Royce reasons that if completely independent beings were supposed, they could not be related in any way, and that no two of them could be in the same space, for space would be a link between them. This is a questionable point, for space can be so conceived that allowance can be made for such hypothetical entities. There is a difference between effective and merely metrical or geographical "links." Royce argues further that no two such independent beings could be in the same time, or in any physical connection, and no two could be parts of any really same whole. Furthermore, the mutual independence which has been supposed cannot later be changed to any form of mutual dependence. This is the first part of Royce's argument. What his procedure really amounts to is the attempt to show that complete independence would imply complete unrelatedness, including also the absence of spatial and temporal relations. It is hardly a genuine argument, and turns rather upon an analysis of an assumed meaning. It is assumed that space

[1] Cf. William James, *A Pluralistic Universe* (New York: Longmans, Green, and Co., 1909), p. 49.
[2] Josiah Royce, *The World and the Individual* (New York: The Macmillan Co., 1900), Vol. I, pp. 121 ff.

and time necessarily provide effective relations between entities. The definition of "different real beings" involves mutual independence. Two real beings are regarded as different if no change in one of them need correspond to any change in the other; whereas if any less mutual independence than this existed, the two beings would be parts of one complete Being. It would not be difficult to reduce such a notion to an absurdity and to instate the desired alternative of monism if the analysis were carried no further. But one must allow for relevance, or for the idea of a quantitative minimum of proximity when determining relations. That is required by the essential individuality of things, which is different in different fields.

Royce's second thesis,[3] the disputed second part of his argument, has been submitted for reconsideration by Professor W. E. Hocking. When objects have a character in common, it is said that the same quality is present in both of them. For example, the same redness can appear in two cherries. But, it is argued by Royce, two independent beings cannot have any real quality in common, beyond the mere fact that each exists. If one supposes that they have, then by hypothesis he can imagine one to be destroyed without the other being affected. Hence they are not the same. This reasoning is intended to hold for a part, or for a part of a part, etc., that is the same. Independent beings would therefore be devoid of all relations. This is advanced as a *reductio ad absurdum* of such a notion. Royce concludes that if real independent beings have no common features and true relations, they are absolutely separated and can never come to get either ties or community of nature. A critical examination of the ideas "common character" and "the same as" would have prevented Royce from making out his case as he did. There are strictly speaking no common characters; no two things or constituents of them are absolutely the same. A more careful, nonassumptive use of the concept of a relation, with due regard for the great variation of types of relations, would have compelled him to alter his position in important respects. The same patterns of relations can be illustrated in events of the same type. No two events are identical. A great many events may, however, have similar features which are described as the same on the conceptual level. Sameness is in short the product of thought. The difference between relational events, which are real, and relational objects, which

[3] *Op. cit.*, pp. 129 ff.

are conceptual, must be recognized. Among relational events it can be seen that some are constitutive of entities, and others are extrinsic; and, as already noted, there are relevant and irrelevant, effective and noneffective relations. In the cognitive realm there are relations that are proper to a given system, and others that are strange to it. These distinctions have an important bearing upon the problems grouped together under the title of monism. Awareness of them is necessary in order to avoid a forced construction to answer an oversimplified problem.

The theory of a unified Being which Royce defends is based upon the principle that thought is prior to existence. He asserts that in the world as he defines it there can exist no fact except as a known fact, as a fact present to some consciousness.[4] The only conception of Being that can be expressed without absolute self-contradiction is held to be the doctrine that what is, is present to the insight of a single Self-conscious Knower, whose life includes all that he knows. Royce's world possesses Ontological Unity, insofar as all its types of Being, concrete and abstract, appear as various aspects of one type of Being, and he maintains that the whole of this world stands or falls together. But experience tells us precisely that there are events which are not known, to state it paradoxically—in other words, there is sufficient evidence of the occurrence of independent events. Royce's positive program is no more successful than his critique of the thesis of independent events, and his view is by no means the only alternative to the assumption of a manifold of unrelated events.

C. *The Diversity of Systems and Domains*

The idea of a domain has been seen to be of basic importance in the analysis of judgment. The various sciences of reality, the physical, biological, and social sciences, make use of universes of discourse which are selections from the domain of real existence, or reality. There is theoretical as well as practical justification for treating them separately, as distinct systems. Reality admits of such analysis and treatment; its facts behave in such a way and are so organized, that we may distinguish various levels or systems of existence. They are not entirely distinct, for the more complex levels presuppose the less complex, and certain logical and ontological principles hold for all levels. The transition from one

[4] *Ibid.*, pp. 397 ff.

level to another is accomplished by the addition, or, as may be, the modification or omission of special principles, in keeping with the kind of organization found. The fact that logical and mathematical principles are found to hold for reality does not alter the situation, for they hold in the sense of possibilities, or possible patterns of relations. An undifferentiated monistic theory of events would have little to say about particular events. The differences between the activity of living things and inert matter must appear in their description.

The formal sciences of logic and mathematics add greatly to the diversity of systems of knowledge. They operate with the idea of possibility, which must be taken as fundamental in philosophy if all knowledge is to be included in its scope. If we may speak of distinct domains in the special sciences, this holds all the more so in logic and mathematics, where it is seen that each system involves a domain.[5] An infinite number of domains is formally possible with the treatment of all possible classes of objects.

It would be futile to attempt to define the idea of a largest conceivable domain, for, even if that could be done, it would not allow for the individual differences of objects, which may only be regarded as inclusive at a given time. This point of view effectively rules out the claim of any dogmatic monism, which presumes to deduce all knowledge from an absolute principle or set of principles, and which in its various forms oversimplifies the problem. There is no closed universe with which to operate. Our propositions must express facts which are found in the world of experience, or which hold for that world. The universe as the domain of possible occurrences is an open one in all directions and respects, so far as we know. On the descriptive side, therefore, we must regard the collective system of knowledge as limited and tentative in some respects. On the other hand, explanatory principles must be employed, or pure sciences of relations developed and applied to given sets of facts. The great diversity of relations and relational properties shows that that cannot be done, if the goal is to determine one principle of unity. Even the thinnest relational invariants are plural in character as well as in number. Some philosophers may think that they find unity of possible characters, such as "Every event is possibly relatable to

---

[5] Cf. M. Farber, "The Method of Deduction and its Limitations," *The Journal of Philosophy*, XXVII, 1930.

a thinking being." But such relations are merely extrinsic, and do not aid in the determination of unity.

The existence of the various systems of knowledge may appear at first to imply ontological pluralism. The term pluralism as here used includes dualism as a special case. A distinction should be drawn between ontological and logical pluralism, the latter meaning that there are distinct and irreducible systems of knowledge. Four possible combinations may result: (1) ontological and logical monism, (2) ontological and logical pluralism, (3) ontological pluralism and logical monism, and (4) ontological monism and logical pluralism. The main objection to the first possible view, combining ontological and logical monism, is that it sacrifices the diversity of things in the interest of unity, and that such unity would not be practically desirable in any case. The second possibility must face the objection that it is obvious—all too obvious—that all events have a place in physical reality, a point of view which is justified by scientific analysis, although this is ignored or circumvented by many traditional philosophers. The third combination of standpoints, ontological pluralism and logical monism, is an impossible one in fact, since the nature of a pluralistic world would preclude a monistic formulation of it. There remains the fourth possibility, that of ontological monism and logical pluralism, which appears best adapted to the ideals of philosophy and the existing state of knowledge. A theory of ontological monism may go along with a diversity of types of organization and even with relatively autonomous and independent regions of reality. It may in fact allow for dualism, or the distinction between ideas and objects.

The statement that there are separate and distinct systems of knowledge may appear ambiguous at first. So far as existence in the world is concerned, the basic object-units are not different in the various systems. It is the type of organization or activity of the object-units that differs in the various fields of knowledge, and these differences are indicated by special postulates or principles. Let us consider the classification of the various fields of knowledge in four groups, consisting of the formal, physical, biological, and social sciences. The specific differences between them may be illustrated by some of their typical ideas or principles—the formal sciences by class, system, propositions, inference, probability, consistency, infinity, number, order, and function; the physical sciences by time, space, events, causality, the conservation of energy, and principles describing chemical change; the biological sciences by life, variation, inheritance, and the conditions for survival; the social sciences by conscious purpose and social institutions. Each of these sciences may be conceived as constructed in such a way that the fundamental ideas or units of its subject matter are distinguished from its fundamental principles or postulates. In the analysis of the object-units we are interested in the "what," whereas in the description of their organization and activity we are primarily interested in the "how," or in the behavior of things. The physical interpretation of reality may be said to hold for all groups and levels of real existence. The problem of comprehending both the sciences of real existence and the formal sciences within one unified frame will be considered in further detail in later sections of this chapter. The principle of parsimony in thought forbids the supposition that anything other than physical reality enters into the objects of other levels. Monism in this sense should be conceived as a program, not claimed as a finished solution. The basic object-units are held to be the same throughout all fields of existence, despite the greater complexity of organization discernible on the biological and social levels. The explanation of all chemical phenomena as numerical and spatial relationships, as Planck has expressed it,[6] could in a sense be entertained for other fields of knowledge, but it would not exhaust their nature.

A description of a given situation is always accomplished in relational terms. Modern relational logic makes it possible for logic to comprise all knowledge and adapt it to the changing structure of scientific knowledge and to the needs of experience. Freed from the limitations of the older logic, it can apply to all possible relations. Objects, which may be determined descriptively or by definition, fulfill variables; and this is also true of relations, which fulfill relational functions or forms. When we speak of relations, we usually mean relational forms. We find that numerous and varied situations may fulfill the same set of variables, or be formally similar while materially different. The relational logic thus gives a far more fruitful clue than did the logic which Kant used for the determination of the categories, or the basic concepts of knowledge. It makes possible a postulational approach to the ontological problem of unity. This includes the postulational de-

[6] Cf. M. Planck, *The Universe in the Light of Modern Physics* (London: George Allen & Unwin, 1937), p. 17.

termination of infinite domains. There are more properties of relations than reflexiveness, symmetry, and transitiveness, and all the more when more complex relations than the dyadic are considered, or when one takes further terms into account. In dyadic relations, to take a simple example, a relation may be applied to any number of terms, and may hold or fail for each pair. There may be an infinite number of different relational combinations, and each one has an indefinite or possibly infinite number of interpretations. The range of variation of a given pattern is determined by the domain for which it is significant, as in the case of factual reality. The relational properties indicated are merely selected from the total complex of properties which define events, so that unity can only be exemplified in limited aspects, i.e., to the extent to which the variables are satisfied by a given situation. The monistic view that is becoming more and more complete because of the progress of science should not be extended to become a theory of logical or relational monism; for it is a mistaken ideal to attempt to reduce all activity patterns to one basic set of patterns, or to attempt to reduce all concepts to one basic set of categories. The structure of the various logical systems in formal science alone, in which special postulates characterize individual systems, shows this to be impossible, unless it be at the cost of specific knowledge. It does not follow that rival mathematical systems are all equally true, for the truth of a formal system consists in its application to the real world. Validity should not be confused with truth. The point is, then, that the description of the real world in all of its aspects is not accomplished by one set of principles except at the sacrifice of its concreteness and complexity. The mystical pantheists have illustrated the residuum which remains after the subtraction of specific knowledge, to cite the most extreme case. The natural number system and people in lineal descent fulfill the same relational variables for serial order. But that is not a fruitful fact, nor is the people-in-lineal-descent situation exhausted by this observation. A great many other situations do not illustrate that kind of serial order. Such considerations help us to dispel a false ideal of unity. They show us that patterns of unity are always selective, and that the situations exemplifying them must be determined inductively.

This view may and should go along with relational pluralism, which will require a closer discussion of the nature of relations.

D. The Reality of Internal and External Relations

Relations are real, but do not exist independently of objects. The object-units exist, as objects which are in various and varying relations. There can be no objects without relations, and no relations without objects. It is not necessary to assign being to relations, in contradistinction to the changing world of existence. The relations may be regarded as ways of existence and change. The concepts of relations that we form do not have to refer to relations that subsist. It is not necessary to hypostatize them. The concepts of relations are patterns exemplified in experience and physical reality. Philosophers should take care not to confuse a necessity of thought with a necessity of existence.

The interpretation of relations is of pivotal importance in ontology, as shown by the controversy over the status of internal and external relations. That issue must be decided for the definition of events or objects. The alternative answers are, broadly, that all relations are internal and define the essence of an object, a view which leads to the unification of all things in a spiritualistic philosophy; or that relations are extrinsic and are real apart from the objects. The question which is then raised is whether a thing can be related to something outside itself, and still not be affected. It would be difficult to distinguish the inside from the outside in some instances; and the inside is always a related inside. Every real thing has spatiotemporal relations and exhibits unity in at least that respect. The absolutists regard relationships as founded on an absolute principle, which is purely hypothetical in character. On the other hand, the idea of an external relation that is real is grotesque and, like its rival, incurs the fallacy of hypostatization.

The alternative theories of relations that have been presented do not exhaust the possibilities. It is necessary to take the nature of objects into account more explicitly, since every object or event is embedded in relationships. Accordingly, three versions of objects and relations may be defined. Either (1) an object may be defined by itself as an absolutely independent entity possessing uniqueness; or (2) a thing may be regarded as constituted by every relationship into which it enters, the "what" of a thing thus being defined operationally; or (3) the mediating view may be maintained, that there is a certain minimal set of relationships, such as those of space and time, which holds for all events. Strictly speaking, there are no relations in the sense of universals, any more than there can be redness apart from particular red patches, although we find it convenient as well as necessary to refer to types of relations conceptually. Adopting the language without the ontological thesis of Whitehead, it may be said that there are relational events, but not relational objects. All claims that there are relational objects in the sense of universals have thus far remained unfounded, and may well be incapable on principle of adequate foundation. The second view, which holds that things are constituted by all the relations into which they enter, implies that everything is what it is because of its activity. This is in direct opposition to the standpoint of essence, as set forth by Aristotle and by those who derive from the Aristotelian tradition. It abandons all attempts to define things independently, regarding their identity as an open problem of speculative philosophy. What can be meant by the identity of a given entity? It must have identity for knowledge, for that is the way of knowledge, which envisages things as unities. The synthesis of identification illustrated in all regions of experience has already been noted. However, that does not imply identity in reality. The presupposition of permanence must be eliminated, and the idea of identity held in question. According to the constitutive theory of relations, an event is always defined by its relations. The mediating view, holding that not all relations are constitutive of an event, regards a given event as being a "what" plus a "how." It might be suggested that it would be better to hold the complete constitutive theory for events, and the mediating view for things or objects with endurance in experience. But it would be difficult to separate the passing relations from the relatively stable ones. If such separation is a practical matter, then no compromise is necessary—stability of relations could be adequately determined by frequency of occurrence. Accordingly, an individual event may be defined in terms of the activity with which it pervades its spatiotemporal region, and classes of events may be treated inductively in terms of the relational patterns which they exemplify. In this way we are committed firmly to what we have as a matter of fact.

Some of Hocking's illustrations of internal relations, which may be referred to as effective relations, afford instructive evidence of the modifying influence distinct terms may have upon one another.[7] People who enter into friendship influence one another. Marriage is an example of a lasting type of mutual influence. This is also seen in the context of physical nature. It is desirable that automobile tires and highways affect each other as little as possible; ideally they would be independent, but actually they are not. Such cases indicate the relational character of independence. The distinction between ideal independence and actual independence is pertinent and calls attention to the need for keeping apart abstractions and concrete realities. But is it possible to conceive a world of completely independent entities, even in the ideal? It would not be possible to conceive an independent human being, for a human being is essentially bound up with society and a long tradition. Even the most abstract or grotesque of constructions must be conceived as determined relationally.

Are both internal and external relations illustrated in the world, and are both types irreducible? Both unity and diversity are illustrated in experience and reality. There are facts or events which have nothing to do in any direct, effective sense with most of the universe, although the irrelevant portion of the universe is nevertheless related in another sense, as conditioning the events in question. Let a definite event be labelled e_1, the relevant circumstances Ce_1, and the rest of the universe U_r. The history of any single event e_o in U_r may not affect e_1; but the fate of e_1 is certainly bound up with that of U_r in general. Thus, a great cosmic catastrophe affecting U_r would act upon e_1, whereas minor catastrophes sufficiently remote would have no effect upon the event. A principle applies here which may be called the principle of sufficient relevance, or of quantitative effective relevance. Monists may argue that the moving of one's hand makes a difference to the entire physical universe; or that the existence of every individual person makes a difference to society in general. But it is a simple fact of experience that one event, the death of one individual, for example, may have no effective influence upon another event, say the course of a war. The sufficiency in question is therefore twofold: it refers to sufficient nearness in space and time, and also to the necessary minimum of weight in a causal situation. If the loss of one individual is not sufficient to turn the course of a war, the loss of a larger number may do so.

On the other hand, despite all diversity and complete relevant

[7] References to Hocking's views are based upon one of his metaphysics lectures, and upon subsequent discussion with him.

independence, it is meaningful to talk of all existence as a unitary domain. All that is required to make such statements meaningful is the possibility of selecting general features which apply universally to events, such as relations of space and time. In this way, it is seen that existence as the correlate of our knowledge can be regarded as unified, regardless of the relative autonomy of its parts.

E. Basic and Formal Unity

The original object of experience is regarded as unitary in the sense that it is labelled the natural world. The practical aim to control the world makes monism appear most desirable. Moreover, all sciences cooperate, despite their peculiar characteristics; and the most general sciences, the physical sciences, comprise the less general biological and social sciences. There is abundant motivation for the achievement of unity. The question "Why unity?" is readily answered.

We understand a subject matter best when we conceive it as a unity, or as a matrix of laws which are interrelated. The systematic search for invariants and the progressive tendency to reduce various theories or systems to one basis are ways of understanding. Thus, one important kind of understanding consists of the inclusion of propositions, or of whole systems of propositions, within one fundamental system. The determination of all facts and laws by means of one set of laws, ideally by one formula, would be the logical limit of such understanding. The concepts of unity and inclusion are related but are not identical, as shown by the fact that understanding also requires the recognition of diversity and conflict.

It is necessary to distinguish the various meanings of unity in order to determine the real problem. There are, first of all, the substantive and the causal meanings. Thus, two things may be held to be unified if they are analyzable into the same kind of components, or made of the same kind of substance. Furthermore, they belong to the same domain if they are causally related to one another. The unity may also refer to logical or cognitive relationships, or merely to relatedness. These meanings will be classified to begin with in three groups, applying to reality, knowledge, and experience.

(1) The unity of reality has the traditional meaning of being composed of one kind of substance, either in the sense of onto-

logical monism (monism of substance), or of causal monism if the element of causal relatedness is taken as essential. This monism of kind is compatible with a doctrine of unique and hence plural events, so long as the events allow the possibility of causal relatedness or of reduction to one kind of substance. We may also be interested in the aspect of reality as a causally determined system. Such a monistic system would be expressed by means of a unified system of knowledge in which the principle of the excluded middle holds universally, i.e., every proposition would be true or false. The question of the possibility of reconciling the universal application of the law of causality with the relative autonomy of various causal systems must also be considered. This raises the issue of ontological pluralism, according to which there are entities or entire regions which are causally unrelated to one another. The analysis of the possible relations of ontological and logical positions (in Section C of this chapter) has shown that ontological pluralism involves logical pluralism, for the various autonomous regions would have to be expressed by means of independent and irreducible systems of knowledge. The converse does not hold, however, for logical pluralism may be taken to refer to the independence of formal systems, as well as to the partial independence of systems dealing with selected aspects of the real world. In this sense logical pluralism is compatible with ontological monism.

(2) It is possible to treat all features of reality by means of systems of knowledge, whereas a purely ontological inquiry would not in turn do justice to systems of possible knowledge. That this advantage may lead to a one-sided program is illustrated in contemporary philosophy, in which there is a tendency to consider the unity of knowledge in isolation from its historical conditions, and without doing justice to the full nature of experience. The concept of unity is construed in terms of definableness and deductibility ("definable in terms of," or "deducible from"). The version of unity as definableness has led to the ideal of conceptual unity, or the ideal that all concepts are reducible to, or definable in terms of, one fundamental concept. Historically, such an attempt has been made in terms of the concepts of matter, mind, and sensation. If the great variety of ordered systems of knowledge is included, more than one fundamental concept must be admitted as the ultimate basis of all knowledge. The ideal of basic unity means that all basic concepts of the various fields of knowledge, such as

physics, biology, and the social sciences, are reducible to one fundamental basis.

The question of basic alternatives has been raised by Carnap:[8] can one proceed from mind or from a physical basis with equal right in the treatment of cognitive structures? In his view, physical objects are reducible to psychical objects, and conversely. This means that statements about physical objects can be transformed into statements about perceptions, and hence about psychical objects. The statement that a particular body is red is transformed into a complicated statement, such as that under certain circumstances a particular visual sensation of red will appear. Statements about physical objects which do not concern sense qualities immediately are also regarded as being reducible to them, the point being that they would otherwise have no discernible characters and so be without significance for science. On the other hand, to every psychical occurrence there corresponds a parallel occurrence in the brain, and hence a physical occurrence. Thus, to every property of the psychical event there corresponds uniquely a definite, even if entirely different, property of an event in the central nervous system. Therefore every statement about a psychical object is held to be translatable into a statement about physical objects, despite our present inability to provide the general rule of the translation.

Carnap uses the terms reducibility, transformation, translation, and coordination in his exposition. These terms are not equivalents, neither can they mean reducibility in the sense of scientific analysis. The dangers and obstacles which beset his view arise from several circumstances. The possible tacit use of some form of the subject-object limitation of reality is suggested by the idea of intertranslatability. There is also a difficulty arising from the use of scientific method. No matter how far scientific knowledge and perceptual experience may reach, there is always a region of physical reality beyond the actual limits of perceptual reality, hence the necessity for the explanatory phase of science. This does not present a difficulty in principle, for a coordination between knowledge and reality is ideally possible. But it is important to recognize this coordination for what it is. Furthermore, the difference be-

[8] Reference is here made to Carnap's early publication, *Der logische Aufbau der Welt* (Berlin-Schlachtensee: Weltkreis Verlag, 1928), pp. 77f. Cf. also his *Unity of Science* (London: Routledge & Kegan Paul, Ltd., 1934), "Testability and Meaning," *Philosophy of Science*, III, 1936, and "Logical Foundations of the Unity of Science," *International Encyclopedia of Unified Science* (Chicago: The University of Chicago Press, 1938), Vol. I.

tween the actual experience of individuals and the objective qualities which are perceptual in a never to be perceived manner must be drawn clearly. Finally, there is the danger of confusing correlated series of properties with a real reduction or even a genuine translation. As a matter of formal technique it is possible to coordinate psychical and physical events without raising the question of prior reality. The idealistic principle that being is essentally related to a knower would have to be invoked in order to make possible a real reduction of the physical to the psychical.

Logically distinguishable from the concept of basic unity is that of postulational or formal unity, with the postulates determining the ways in which the basic concepts are or may be related. Attempts have been made to deduce all postulates from a simple ultimate principle. Riehl[9] regarded the principle of identity as ultimate in logic; and Brentano thought the principle of noncontradiction was fundamental.[10] Much more prominent has been the view that it is a set of principles from which the postulates of all systems can be deduced. Logical principles alone would not be sufficient for the deduction of sciences of the real world. Physical principles must be added, and also principles appropriate to the various levels or regions of fact to be considered. It is the idea of formal possibility that separates the formal from the real, and which prevents their reduction to a common basis.

The limiting case of postulational unity would consist of determination by one principle. But postulational unity refers to entire systems of knowledge, no one of which has ever been defined by means of a single principle; and it means that the postulates of one system becomes theorems in another. In the event that basic conceptual unity in terms of one fundamental concept could be achieved, the great multitude of different types of organization of the units in question would nevertheless have their individuality described by means of relational propositions expressing their be-

---

[9] Cf. A. Riehl, "Logik und Erkenntnistheorie," in *Die Kultur der Gegenwart*, ed. P. Hinneberg (Berlin and Leipzig: B. G. Teubner, 1907), Vol. VI, p. 88, where he states that logic does not require the theory of knowledge for its foundation. As J. Cohn points out in his *Voraussetzungen und Ziele des Erkennens* (Leipzig: W. Englemann, 1908), p. 507, Riehl is able to make this separation because he deduces all logic from the principle of identity. Riehl maintains (*op. cit.*, p. 76) that the only principle of logic is the principle of identity, or expressed negatively, the principle of contradiction.

[10] In his *Wahrheit und Evidenz*, Brentano was inclined to reduce all axiomatic insights to the principle of contradiction (or, more exactly, noncontradiction). Cf. *Wahrheit und Evidenz*, ed. O. Kraus (Leipzig: F. Meiner, 1930), p. 155. But he vacillated on this, as seen in his *Versuch über die Erkenntnis* (Leipzig: F. Meiner, 1925).

havior; and the diverse descriptions would be reflected in postulate sets of distinct systems.

(3) There remains the conception of unity applied to the process of knowledge, as distinguished from the structure of knowledge considered in the preceding type. Both unity and dualism can be illustrated in the process of experience. Cognitive dualism (or pluralism) is true as a matter of fact, i.e., the distinction between experience and object, or between content and object, must be granted. This is entirely compatible with the unified explanation of cognition in terms of physical events which are subject to causal laws. Individual differences among knowers, as well as the variability of experience in general, give rise to the ideal of harmonious experience and of agreement over objective reality.

The relationships between the foregoing types of unity have been indicated. The first and second types, real unity and knowledge unity, do not mutually imply one another, for knowledge is not restricted to the domain of reality. Knowledge comprises hypothetical systems and involves the use of fictions. But the unified system of real knowledge would imply ontological monism. Cognitive dualism is compatible either with monism or with pluralism. The possibility of separating the content and the object of experience not only provides for error, but also for the use of fictions of any kind.

F. Kinds of Pluralism

The different meanings of pluralism follow readily from the analysis of monism. The opposite of unity is here taken to be plurality. Other possible opposites, such as chaos or partial unity, will be considered separately.

(1) Applied to reality, ontological pluralism is the doctrine that there is more than one kind of substance. Mind, matter, and God were viewed as different kinds of substance in Descartes' philosophy. As has been pointed out, pluralism may also be used to mean the existence of more than one causal system, unrelated to one another causally. If the concept of relation is used without restriction, and if, for example, "different from" and "unrelated to" are admitted as relations, then this meaning is untenable. There are furthermore different kinds of relations in a practical sense, as well as in respect to essence and form. The distinction between relevant and irrelevant, and between effective and ineffective rela-

tions, has already been noted. As for essence, we recognize relations that belong intrinsically to things, and also those extrinsic relations into which things enter and which they may leave without being modified essentially. It is also possible to conceive reality as consisting of partially independent causal systems, with both universal and restricted causal laws. According to this view the various causal systems preserve their identity and mutual independence in some respects, while being conditioned in others.

The limiting case of pluralism is that of complete independence, with no relational stability. That might be so if the cosmos were a chaos of unique events. It is a possibility, although quite an empty one, that the entire cosmos of the present, with as great a finite span as one wishes to have it comprise, is one unique event which is a part of a chaos of infinite becoming. Again, it is possible in the same empty sense that this chaos is twofold and also includes a chaotic distribution of unique and independent events throughout infinite space, a condition which seems ordered to us because of our finite perspectives. The term chaos is used to name the extreme case of pluralism even though grounds may be given for rejecting such an empty possibility. Thus, it may be argued that the thesis of chaos is not sustained by the facts, in view of our success in establishing unity; that the empty possibility of chaos is of no interest in view of the actually discerned order, and our practical success in the smaller sphere relevant to our experience. Indeed, it may be argued that chaos is a name for another kind of order than we are able to grasp within the present limits of our horizon. Dropping the troublesome term chaos, one can find it meaningful at least to speak of a complex of unique events with minimal stability. Strictly speaking, all events are unique. We never experience absolute sameness, and we probably never have subjective states exactly similar to those of our neighbors, or at two different times. The events of nature and experience approximate to the ideal forms and conditions by which we describe them; but it is improbable that the events coincide with the ideal forms, just as it is improbable that they coincide with one another. Even if they did, there would be only partial identity, never complete. The elements of time and continual change preclude complete identity.

(2) In knowledge, the analogues of the first two meanings of pluralism applied to reality given above—i.e., more than one kind of substance, or more than one independent causal system—are included under the caption of conceptual pluralism or diversity.

If there are irreducible concepts or indefinable terms on various levels of knowledge, then clearly no basic unity is possible. If, furthermore, the postulates of various systems are irreducible in the sense of not being deducible from a common set of postulates, then we have postulational or logical pluralism. Specific principles hold for specific subject matters; and no factual knowledge is deducible from logical principles. The same also holds for the physical principles, which are necessary but not sufficient for the description of the behavior of events on other levels. Special principles must be added for the various systems. For a universal system of logical physicalism, it is necessary to subtract postulates or defining characteristics for special systems, so that they may not be used beyond their limits of proper significance.

(3) The separation between content and object is essential to experience; and individual knowers are unique, in that no two have exactly the same experience. As has been noted, the meaning of unity in this context is the attainment of objective knowledge, both in the sense of the correspondence of an individual knower's experience to reality and as the agreement among all knowers about the facts of reality. Agnosticism, skepticism, and pragmatic relativism have been pluralistic forms of denial of this view of truth.

In addition to the cognitive dualism already mentioned, dualism may be designated as quantitative or as qualitative. The contrast between the finite and the infinite illustrates what is here called a quantitative dualism. The place of the mind and experience in the existing world makes such an opposition inescapable. Taken generally it presents an insoluble problem in the literal sense of the problem of induction. The mathematical theory of infinity is a device to bridge the gap; but, as already seen, it in turn raises new questions. The formulation of paradoxes has been possible because of the use of insufficiently clarified concepts. It should always be possible to remedy such defects satisfactorily, if it is true that all rational questions about the world are answerable in principle.

Qualitiative dualism has proved to be of only historical and passing interest. The analytical progress of science has made clear the relationship of the organic to the inorganic, and the application of scientific method to the field of human conduct, including thought, has finally dismissed qualitative dualism. The assimilation of man and all his thought processes to nature, which was proclaimed by the broad evolutionary movement, has been accomplished by the progress of the sciences. The situation has appeared to be complicated by the ideality of meanings. Observing strictly the distinction between the ideal and the real, it is seen that the only way in which the ontological status of meanings can be conceived is by an analysis of judgment-meanings in terms of meaning-events. That is to say, if a meaning is to have a place in reality, it must be reinterpreted as a meaning-event. Ideal meanings cannot be rendered literally in existential terms because they are essentially nonreal.

The question then arises whether an unclosed plurality of thought-productions can be embraced to physical nature.[11] That such a plurality is unclosed is due to our contributing activities in the process of thought and experience. Our ability to act upon the basis of formal systems which are not known to be true or wholly true shows that we are able to provide new causal conditions in experience, and strongly justifies the use of a reflective method in philosophy. There is little danger of oversimplification in conceiving physical reduction, if one bears in mind the elements of meaning and history, for which a place must also be provided in physical reality.

The distinctions incidental to experience are merely complicating factors, bearing upon real unity and knowledge unity. In other words, the difference between the content and the object of experience, made clearest in the case of error, and quantitative dualism, due to our limitations as knowers, are simply matters of fact. Unity of knowledge must therefore include reference to the unity of reality and of experience.

G. *Application to the Problem of Monism*

It will be helpful to sum up the various theses required to clarify the concept of unity. The real problem of monism is the title of three groups of problems which must be distinguished despite their mutual relevance. The reduction to the same kind of

---

[11] Hocking has questioned the "conclusion that human behavior can prospectively be plotted on the physical plane," giving the reason that "human behavior sprouts out of the untamed multitude of systems of possibility, and is the primary engenderer of such systems." In his view, because the human mind engenders the unclosed plurality of systems of possible knowledge, and since human behavior is shaped by the system, taken to be real or realizable at a given time, there is little likelihood that physical relations will contain the conditions of behavior. This argument turns upon the meaning of the concept of engendering and of the realization of a system of knowledge.

substance—for example, the reduction of the organic to the inorganic—is one meaning of unity which belongs to the program of science, and not to philosophy. The basic units of the physical level are unique, and there is good reason to hold that they are related causally. The temporary inability of scientists to determine subatomic relations presents an additional problem rather than a refutation of the principle of causal law. The complexes of physical units, such as organisms, do not manifest the same kind of behavior as the units themselves, and this is accounted for by postulational pluralism. There is no such thing as absolute independence of any events if that is taken to mean having no spatial relations, although there are relations which exercise no practical influence. Hence there can only be relative autonomy and independence. Furthermore, it is possible to achieve basic unity, but not postulational unity, in the systems of formal thought. Real systems can have basic unity in an analytical sense (referring to more elementary units), but not in the sense of complexes making up the subject matter of the autonomous real sciences. This fact is recognized in the conception of postulational or logical pluralism. The unity of all knowledge, including formal and real knowledge, is only possible on a physical basis, if at all. Finally, the demonstration of the possibility of objective knowledge underlies all other doctrines. The challenge of such views as formal relativism, according to which all truth is relative to assumptions, and the analysis of experience as involving reference to a transcendent reality, must be met as the first condition in establishing a satisfactory theory of objective reality and knowledge.

The importance of treating knowledge and reality separately is due, for one thing, to the element of formal possibility that characterizes systems of knowledge in general. Formal possibility is conditioned by noncontradiction as applied to a given system; that general condition attaches to all systems. More specifically, systems of knowledge comprise real systems, or systems pertaining to reality and limited by the evidence that has been established, and formal systems, limited only by formal possibility. There are accordingly several types of unity which may be achieved. The real systems may be regarded as unified basically (conceptually) or postulationally (by derivation), and the same holds for the formal systems. There then remains the further problem of determining how these two types of system are related, both conceptually and postulationally. A clue to the treatment of this problem will be given later in this chapter.

The question of the objective significance of the progressive achievement of cognitive unity illustrates the need for separating the provinces of experience and knowledge. Experience is subjective in one of its poles of reference, whereas knowledge is objective. The systems of real knowledge could not be unified, either basically or postulationally, unless there were an objective ground in the domain of reality. Whether there is also such a relationship between formal systems and reality is not immediately evident. It must be proved in each case, and many formal systems will never be applied to reality. The reduction of fictions and facts to a common basis would have to be accomplished to begin with, by means of a general theory of meanings and objects.

Freed from all elements of dogmatic assumption, the subjective approach is valuable and in fact, as a method of discovery, indispensable to the objective determination of the conditions of reality. The contention that the category of unity has no meaning apart from experience (or knowledge), any more than the world as such has, may be met by pointing out that the term meaning renders the statement tautologous. There is an intended reference to actual or possible knowledge in it. Hence no ontological consequences may be inferred from this statement.

The problem of monism is also illustrated in the field of social philosophy. External bonds of compulsion may serve to obscure real, underlying antagonisms between social classes. If it is true that real distinctions are sometimes ignored, it is also true that nonexistent issues are on occasion advanced as real questions. This holds for the rather artificially constructed textbook issue between individualism and collectivism. There are no partisans of either extreme position in reality. The logical analysis of extreme alternatives gives no clue to the actual alignment of social forces. The rational solution of the problem of social justice shows that each side has its region of justification. But it is not implied that such a rational solution will precede in time the actual historical resolution of the conflict. Nor is it asserted that a solution of real problems can be brought about by introducing a synthesis before the combatants have had an adequate opportunity to test the mettle of their opponents. In any case, rival claims must be adjudicated, and the solution of a conflict results in a new unity. Thus it can be seen how a dualism both implies and leads to a unity.

H. Real Unity and the Diversity of Systems

It is necessary to split up the problem of monism, as has been seen. Many questions are packed into it. One must first make clear what is under consideration—the universe of discourse must be determined. One may be interested in the world of actual experience; or, again, in the world of all physical existence, which is not experienced completely because of quantitative limitations (but not because of any inaccessibility in principle); or, finally, in the realm of thought, which includes the realm of physical existence as one of its worlds, and which includes possible and even impossible worlds besides. There can only be unity in certain respects, never complete unity in all respects. The uniqueness of events and of objects of thought prevents complete unity in the sense of sameness, definableness, or reducibility.

The analysis of the concept of unity calls attention to the existence of regions of physical reality, as well as to distinct systems of knowledge, some of which are meaningful in one area of existence and meaningless in another. Specifically biological questions should not be applied to the physical realm, and, similarly, there are questions that are peculiar to human conduct. In the field of abstract thought there are systems of knowledge entertaining fictions which could not find any possible realization in experience or in physical reality, but are nevertheless valuable for purposes of thought. Such systems are at least partly hypothetical in character, and deal with domains of conceptual objects. They must necessarily conform to logical principles if they are to have the structure of systems. Although they are reducible conceptually to the basis of logic and thus have basic unity, they are not deducible without residuum from the principles of logic. The general thesis holds that basic unity does not necessarily imply postulational unity, although the converse does hold true. It might appear at first that violence is exercised in reducing all abstract concepts to one basis. That is not so, however, for the abstractions refer to general conditions, and the properties that are involved in their respective systems of knowledge permit of replacement by abstractions that are framed somewhat differently. Even though there may be no internal reference, in a hypothetical system of knowledge, to real systems of knowledge, the system as a whole may be considered in relation to reality. The fact that formal systems are constructed in response to our interests, cognitive and practical, determines a bond which connects all systems of knowledge. This shows how it is always possible to find relatedness and hence unity in one respect or another.

The words relatedness and unity have been used interchangeably here, for unity is understood in its broadest sense. Inasmuch as there are relations of exclusion and incompatibility as well as of inclusion and compatibility, it is important that these concepts be defined carefully. The term unity should be interpreted as co-membership in a system or domain, in any universe of discourse. Proposition p excludes not-p and it is incompatible with many propositions included under not-p; but both p and not-p are members of the system of propositions.

The discussion of unity has resulted in the recognition of a diversity of types of relatedness. When one looks for constancy and identity, diversity is sure to turn up. The recognition of the fact that the examination of diversity leads to unity is sufficient to warrant a redefinition of the traditional problem of monism. As Hocking has expressed it, the problem of defining a chaos of unique events becomes a part of the problem of whether the examination of (defined) diversity leads to the recognition of an implied unity. The defined diversity exhibits patterns of relatedness, even though such patterns may vary from time-point to time-point. Thus, although it is true that a defined diversity is at the same time a defined field in which distinctions can exist, the field itself may be causal and passing, and only partially unified. This field has been treated by Hocking as subjective; and, in his view, in some cases at least (as in space) it is both subjective and objective. This recalls the Kantian thesis that the conditions for the possibility of experience are at the same time conditions for the object of experience. To the extent that the subjective process involves only the means necessary for our knowledge of reality, mental constructions can be introduced freely and they enjoy a life of their own. The situation is altered, however, when truth is taken in its original meaning of correspondence to reality. It cannot then be argued that because a defined diversity can only be thought as a field, it therefore constitutes a field in the subjective sense of the term. That kind of unity remains to be defined, and it turns out to be a natural construction of thought which cannot operate other than by applying points and frames of unity to its objects. The possibility of actually determining spatial and temporal relations, as well as general causal relations, is the ground for speaking of unity amid diversity. Even the most radical thinkable uniqueness of events would have to presuppose the domain of physical reality. That is why unity must be spoken of as selective. Diversity is also selective. But they are selective in different ways, and hence they represent different aspects of the problem.

As for the Kantian thesis in this context, the conditions of experience are related to us, our status being that of finite organizations of events; and we do as a matter of fact contribute conditions to our experience. Still deeper are the conditions underlying both ourselves as knowers and the objects of experience. The fact that we as knowers illustrate the same kind of conditions found in the universe in general is not a sufficient condition for concluding that we condition the universe. Besides illustrating the same kind of conditions, we add still others, namely, conditions for ordered knowledge and meaningful experience, including the use and imposition of abstractions which enter into the construction of systems of knowledge, and which have no locus in the universe of real temporal events. The conditions for the unity of experience are entirely explicable in objective terms, and are in fact objective in character. Our individual, subjective differences as knowers are themselves objective matters of fact. Experience as a part of reality is subject to the conditions of reality. But this is not to say that reality simply contains the conditions of all knowledge, including formal, hypothetical systems.

It is different when one speaks of the logical conditions for a world. The world has its own order and structure (a world logic), which must be discovered. We endeavor to anticipate and approximate that structure or logic by means of formal constructions which define fields of possibility. The final question of unity then becomes the determination of the structures that are invariant to the epistemic (pure, architectonic) logic and the world logic. The epistemic logic contains principles that are presuppositions for rational experience and knowledge. It also provides principles for the determination of world-logical structures; and its explanatory devices, which are projected in the manner of intellectual pseudopodia, function as instruments of discovery. It is impossible to define world-logical structures in nonepistemic terms, but that does not prove that they are therefore epistemic in character. We are unable to characterize the world apart from forms cognitively supplied, except by analogies, approximations, interpretations, and extrapolations. That these methods work very well removes the need for an appeal to an ineffable, vacuous otherness, or to unknown causes.

There is an essential difference between systems of knowledge and the domain of totalities. Lewis has distinguished a system from a world by means of the principle of the excluded middle, which holds for a world and not for a system.[12] But every system is also subject to the principle of the excluded middle in a restricted form. Since there are also limitations to the propositions that hold or do not hold for a world, the nature of the limitations must be pointed out in each case. One cannot talk of a world without the use of assumptions of transcendence, spatiotemporal and causal in character. In any system of knowledge, the principles of noncontradiction, the excluded middle, and identity are necessary but by no means sufficient principles. The universal form of these principles presupposes a single, homogeneous system of everything and all knowledge. Their region of application is therefore restricted to individual systems, although they hold generally for all systems of knowledge. The formal-logical system of all propositions contains the world-logical system as a special case, and its practical value consists in its ability to aid us in determining the logical structure of the world-system. It is a case of abstract generality being necessary for the understanding of concrete particularity. That unity means different things in different contexts is clearly seen in this instance. It means relatedness in formal logic, and incompatibility is one of the permissible relations. Does this render formal logic incapable of application to the world? No, because the relations (including incompatibility) are defined generally, and the real world of events illustrates precisely these structures. The system of formal logic is illustrated by the world logic, which is a particularization of it; but the domain of all objects and relations underlying that system is united by general relatedness, and is not equivalent to ontological unity.

Lewis's distinction between a world and a system is provided for by means of the concept of logical pluralism. The construction of formal systems clearly makes that necessary. But the system of

---

[12] C. I. Lewis, "Facts, Systems, and the Unity of the World," *The Journal of Philosophy*, XX, 1923. Lewis writes (p. 145): "The law of contradiction holds of a system, but the law of the excluded middle does not. A world, however, must satisfy both of these laws; it must be such that every proposition is either definitely true or definitely false of it. In other words, a system which is not a world (a mathematical system, for example) will be indeterminate in ways in which no possible world could be."

propositions exhaustively referring to the facts of a world must be subject both to the principle of contradiction and of the excluded middle. These principles are necessary conditions for unity. In addition, the relation of implication is also required in formal systems, for example, and causal relatedness is essential to real systems. A particular formal system of knowledge is complete if all propositions which can be expressed in its terms are either valid or invalid. This represents the principle of the excluded middle in its restricted meaning, as applied to special systems. The system of knowledge that treats of formal systems cannot be complete, in view of the ever-open horizon of possible constructions of new formal systems. In other words, the collection of formal systems cannot be closed at any given time.[13] The theory of possible formal systems always remains an unfinished program for human knowledge. Can the same be said of reality? Its features of space and time must be considered separately. The dialectical insight that to know a limit means to know beyond it has been applied to the attempt to embrace everything within one whole. This would be a weighty point if the felt need of knowledge were a sufficient condition of reality. One does not have to conceive a whole in response to a demand from the imagination for limits, thus incurring an objection supplied by the imagination in its self-transcending role. Reality is a complete domain at any given time because it comprises all events in space. But it is incomplete with respect to temporal development. If time is taken to be real, the completeness of existence is restricted temporally. The domain of existence, no matter how great its temporal span may be, is big with the future and is in that sense incomplete. The determination of all future reality by means of a complete system of real knowledge presents an ideal program which can only be realized partially. But, in principle, we may speak of the set of all possible propositions about future events. The comparison between the systems of knowledge and the domain of reality thus proves to have far-reaching significance.

The question of the possible determinateness of all reality may be formulated as the question of the range of the principle of the excluded middle. According to Aristotle its range is restricted, for it does not apply to propositions about particular future oc-

[13] Cf. M. Farber, "Theses Concerning the Foundations of Logic," *The Philosophical Review*, XXXVII, 1929; "The Method of Deduction and its Limitations," *The Journal of Philosophy*, XXVII, 1930; and "Logical Systems and the Principles of Logic," *Philosophy of Science*, IV, 1942.

currences. The universal principle of the excluded middle, according to which every proposition is either true or false, implies a thoroughgoing determinism, which made it acceptable to the Stoic logicians. The point is that if every proposition about the future is true or false, then all the events referred to are either necessary or impossible. The real problem would be to find the propositions which are to be asserted about the future. In the very nature of the case it is impossible to prove the thesis of determinism completely by means of the real system of knowledge, for the horizon of the future is endless. A legitimate totality is not constituted by "all events of the future," and hence there can be no complete system of propositions about the future.

Whether there is a whole including everything is a question that must be examined critically for its legitimacy. Distinctions must be made, or else there is a danger of operating with assumptive concepts, such as the concept of a whole, which will predetermine the issue. Systems of knowledge dealing with the conceivable universe of knowledge and the real universe of existence are really collective in character; they are partial and selective within the framework of a collective system. The ideally universal system of physics may be said to be collective if it comprises subsystems which have relative autonomy. The real universe is subject to physical laws throughout, while displaying types of laws peculiar to the various phases of reality. More generally, physics, biology, the social sciences, and abstract mathematical systems are relatively independent parts of the collective system of knowledge; and they are subject throughout to logical laws which determine a theoretical bond of unity among them.

1. *The Program of Unity*

The problem of monism has been found to involve a consideration of the nature of relations, objects, things, and events. Related events are unique, and they have a history; but all events exhibit interrelatedness and types of law. Objects are also relational essentially; and even as abstractions they are involved in logical relationships. The realization that one cannot have an all-comprehensive, homogeneous system of knowledge dispels a false ideal of unity. There are systems of knowledge, and the so-called system of knowledge is collective in character. It is clearly impossible to have knowledge of all being; hence causal determinism is a hypothesis, although one that is well justified. The original practical meaning of monism is to be found in the genetic nature of knowledge. Science means organized knowledge; and the whole process of knowledge illustrates the establishment of principles of unity.

Historical circumstances will serve to explain the appearance and temporary or permanent disappearance of problems. In the case of monism the account is not then exhausted, for it represents, as a real problem, nothing less than the problem of the nature of reality, the structure of knowledge, and the integration of being and knowledge. The puzzling and apparently insoluble problem of monism is quite amenable to treatment when, with the aid of historical perspective, its traditional form is replaced by a group of specific questions distinguished according to their proper spheres of meaning. There is no basis for a one-sided, party preference along traditional lines when one recognizes the selective character of unity.

The possibility of basic conceptual unity in the collective system of formal knowledge has been established in principle by the work of such investigators as Whitehead, Russell, Sheffer, and Carnap. The definition or interpretation of points in terms of numbers, of numbers in terms of classes (and the idea of similarity), and of classes in terms of functions and variables shows how reductively homogeneous the concepts of formal science have become. The need to add special postulates in the various systems shows that we are not prepared to speak of postulational unity in the realm of formal knowledge. In fact, such unity may well be precluded by the freedom of construction of formal systems, involving the introduction of special postulates. There can be no complete formal unity in the sense of the derivation of all special postulates from one fundamental set of principles. The unity of formal science is therefore partial. The fundamental principles apply universally to all formal systems, although they are not sufficient for the derivation of all formal propositions.

The same holds for the system of real existence, for which the concepts of physics constitute the ultimate basis. Conceptual unity and postulational pluralism obtain both in the formal and real systems of knowledge. But it is impossible to define physical events reductively in terms of purely formal concepts such as class or function. Hence the only possible way to establish the conceptual unity of all knowledge is by abstracting formal concepts from real events, recognizing the physical basis as ultimate. This procedure amounts to a generalization of the method of extensive abstraction.[14] A comprehensive basic homogeneity, including the concepts of real as well as formal knowledge, can be achieved in this way. All concepts would then be located in the same domain, although the various systems of knowledge, formal and real, would still be autonomous because of their distinctive principles, which describe the behavioral attributes of real events and the peculiar features of formal objects. The propositions describing human behavior in society cannot be deduced from the propositions describing biological facts. That follows alone from the fact that the objects or concepts of various levels are peculiarly different from one another; they differ in their organization. If that is the case, then the propositions in which they occur must be peculiarly different from propositions on other levels. Although logical and physical laws necessarily hold for all regions of facts, they are not sufficient to account for all special types of fact. It also follows that propositions peculiar to a given system do not apply to the collective system of knowledge. This view accordingly forbids the assertion of judgments of value about the universe as a whole. The concept of value is proper to human beings and their relevant sphere of active existence.

It is thus seen that unity and diversity are concepts which have practical relevance. Particular regions of reality, or special organizations of events, are also autonomous in a practical sense. Depending upon the nature of the question raised, either unity or diversity can be established because they both represent actual features of reality. Absolute monism and maximal diversity are merely limiting concepts. Diversity is given in experience, and no ontological theory which disclaims it can be true. According to Hocking's statement of the ontological problem, the only question here is whether there is any sort of unity—as of source, coherence, mutual covariance, or goal—within the indubitable diversity. If unity is taken to mean causal or logical relatedness, or truly objective and systematized knowledge, then the determination of unity becomes the goal of a program of thought and action.

[14] On the method of extensive abstraction, cf. A. N. Whitehead, *An Enquiry Concerning the Principles of Natural Knowledge* (Cambridge: The University Press, 1919), *The Concept of Nature* (Cambridge: The University Press, 1920), and *Process and Reality* (New York: The Macmillan Co., 1929).

J. Summary: Frames of Unity

Unity has been found to be a regulative ideal, representing a program for cumulative, constructive work. It is not to be achieved in any fruitful sense by one philosophical coup, however ingenious. The failure of the idealistic arguments to withstand critical inspection is instructive here. The traditional concept of monism should be considered within the context of the sciences as well as in the more general domain of philosophy. The elaborate arguments for the unity of reality repose in the pantheon (or, as may be, the museum) of the history of philosophy. The Eleatic school could prove that reality is necessarily unified while apparently sacrificing the facts of experience. The tradition of pantheism culminating in Spinoza provided unity by postulation if not as an article of faith. It was unavoidable that time and change could only be regarded as real from a limited point of view. The type of pantheism advocated by Haeckel was no more than an interpretation of his ontological principle of unity, a postulated principle conforming to the demands of common sense.

The suggestion of language is ever present: the terms reality, or world, or universe name a unified whole (one recalls the argument that there can only be one universe, or that the universe must be one, for otherwise there would be a pluriverse). To say that there is one substance is to leave open alternative possibilities as to its nature, whether spiritual or material. But this also leaves open the possibility of pluralism in another sense, on the basis of a monistic principle. Thus a materialistic monism of substance may go along with a pluralistic organization of events, such that some regions of the universe are irrelevant to others in a practical sense. It may also be maintained along with epistemological dualism, which recognizes the difference between the content of the knowing mind and the object known, or between the discerned features of the object and the object as a whole. One sees that unity is compatible with diversity, and that this view must be accepted if experience is to be accredited. The watertight monism which rejects or seeks to overcome change has the unhappy fate of having to overcome experience, and consequently of being believed by no one.

The standpoint of unity must be carefully defined before everything else. The following theses represent different aspects of the question:

(a) There is one kind of substance;
(b) Reality constitutes a single system, all parts of which are interrelated;
(c) There is one system of knowledge;
(d) The content and object of experience are one.

The standpoint of diversity (or of pluralism) is similarly in need of corresponding formulations:

(a') There is more than one kind of substance (usually there are two kinds of substance);
(b') There are independent, unrelated regions of reality;
(c') There are numerous systems of knowledge which are irreducible;
(d') There is a distinction between the content and object of experience.

Depending upon how the question is formulated, either unity or diversity may be established, although in different senses as indicated by the foregoing theses. To say that there is one kind of substance is not to deny that the events which occur are uniquely different from one another. Thus, a new set of alternative theses may be formulated, which differ from traditional monism and pluralism:

(A) Reality consists of a process of unique events which have a history, but which are all such that they have a spatiotemporal locus in physical reality;
(B) There are numerous independent systems of events, for all practical purposes unrelated to one another, although theoretically capable of being related by an abstract or theoretical system;
(C) The conceptual unity of all knowledge may be established on a physical basis, whereas its diversity of organization is described by means of special principles in the various systems of knowledge, which allow for levels of organization;
(D) The distinction between content and object in experience is founded on fact, but it need be no more than a numerical distinction.

Theses B and C are concerned with the issue of the unity of science, expressed in terms of events and knowledge respectively. It is the nature of the concept of possibility used that separates the discussion of the unity of science from the general ontological issue. But both of them, the unity of science in the usual sense of the special sciences, and philosophy, must be brought together for the purposes of a general unity. This does not imply that philosophy is nonscientific. In a strict sense it must be scientific, if science is taken to mean logically organized knowledge. It is merely a matter of convenience here to separate the two types of science (for that is what it comes to), since they operate with different concepts of possibility.

It may be affirmed that there must be freedom for alternative cognitive constructions and methods, that there cannot be oneness in general in a dynamic world, and that differences are as real as sameness of structure. The regulative program of unity as expressed in one collective system of knowledge remains an ideal for investigators in all fields. Expressed in terms of systems of language, the ideal would be to have one language serve universally in all regions of knowledge. That would establish a principle of unity; but it would be a conception which goes along with diversity in other respects. In other words, all unity is selective, and the thin unity established through the use of one language must go along with innumerable differences. The analytic progress of science has shown increasingly that all real events, whether organic or cultural, have a locus in physical reality. The quest for the "what" of things leads to monism in that sense. The "how" of things, their ways of behaving, and the new and peculiar properties resulting from the different degrees of complexity of physical organization, require the recognition of distinct and irreducible regions or levels of reality—the physical, the organic, and the social. The pluralistic nature of knowledge is shown by the fact that it is organized in separate systems. That knowledge must always be incomplete is shown furthermore by the element of novelty, which must be recognized from the point of view of men in a world which is dynamic, temporal, and growing. The philosophical alternative would be a static set of facts, fixed once and for all time, and such that a human knower might hope to gain a vision of that world in its totality. The eternalistic view has always foundered on the reality of time and change.

In concluding the present discussion, five possible frameworks of unity for all knowledge, including real and formal knowledge, will be indicated. The term relatedness would be better than unity, for co-membership in a domain is what is involved.

(1) *Valuational Unity or Relatedness*. Everything is an object of interest in the field of knowledge. Cognitive as well as practical interests have status in the ethical system of interests. A pure mathematical construction with no apparent application has status in that value system, along with everything else performed by human beings. Cognitive value is also a value.

(2) *Physical Unity*. Biological or social patterns will not apply to all physical reality, but physical relationships will. The novelty arising from man's inventive activities, as in the construction of new compounds, is always within the limits of the physical system. That there must be a comprehensive system, or a whole, may be stated as follows: Every whole consists of parts; the particular things of the world are parts; and if there are parts, there must be a whole, which gives the unity.

(3) *Spatial and Temporal Unity*. All real events have a locus in space and time. Such relatedness extends over all reality, but does not comprise formal structures, except in the special sense of their being known or experienced.

(4) *Unity through the Phenomenological Reduction (Noetic and Noematic Unity)*. Everything is viewed as an item of pure experience, as a perceiving or an imagining, etc., or as the correlate of some such act. The experienced and the known as such constitute a unified realm, despite the essential differences of the various modes of experience and the structures discerned within them.

(5) *Social-Historical Unity*. Every item of knowledge can be traced out as having connections with the social organization, and as arising in a social context.

All these unities involve diversity. There is no undistinguished unity, or unity in which distinctions are obliterated. None of these ways of unity is a mystic's paradise.

The problem of monism provides an instructive illustration of the use of logical method in philosophy. The initial step of defining the problem requires a broad view of the nature of philosophical problems, both historical and real. The practical value of the program of unity may be seen in the fact that the establishment of basic unity rules out untenable dualistic theories. Its theoretical value derives from the deeper understanding of the nature of knowledge and reality which it affords. The thesis of logical pluralism, on the other hand, in calling attention to the autonomy of the various systems of knowledge, warns against an illicit transfer from one system of thought to another. The present analysis has shown why absolute monism (leading to a "block-universe," or to an absolute mind) and extreme pluralism (involving freedom and the unpredictable) are to be avoided. The oversimplified version of causal determinism, which reflects the narrowness of traditional mechanism, is superseded by a formulation which does justice to the great diversity of facts. The possibility of deducing all the laws of the various sciences from the principles of an ideally complete physical science will not be denied. Such a science would, however, still have a collective, regional character, illustrating both unity and diversity. If this science is conceived as all-inclusive in its scope, the ideal being a complete coordination between knowledge and temporal reality, the impossibility of its closure is evident. On the basis of this system there would be no talk of chance and novelty, for these concepts are meaningful in terms of actual knowledge, and not in terms of the ideally determinate system in question. That system will of course remain a regulative ideal, in keeping with the positive, programmatic meaning of the problem of monism.

CHAPTER VII

Existence and its Interpretation

A. *The Meaning of Existence*

The determination of the meaning of existence presents one of the perennial problems of philosophy. Berkeley had a definite answer in 1710:

> The table I write on I say exists, that is, I see and feel it; and if I were out of my study I should say it existed—meaning thereby that if I was in my study I might perceive it, or that some other spirit actually does perceive it. There was an odour, that is, it was smelt.... This is all I can understand by these and the like expressions. For as to what is said of the absolute existence of unthinking things without any relation to their being perceived, that seems perfectly unintelligble.[1]

This led Berkeley to formulate his view as *esse* is *percipi;* and he went so far as to deny that things could exist out of the minds which perceive them.

Berkeley's much criticized position may be compared with the view of C. S. Peirce,[2] who regarded existence as a special mode of reality, and as absolutely determinate. "Reality is a special mode of being, the characteristic of which is that things that are real are whatever they really are, independently of any assertion about them. If man is the measure of all things . . . then there is no complete reality; but being there certainly is, even then." The laws of motion, the law of gravitation, etc., are regarded by Peirce as being as real where there are no corpuscles as where there are. Even though no matter exists in many places, those laws are real there;

---
[1] George Berkeley, *The Principles of Human Knowledge* (Chicago: The Open Court Publishing Co., 1920), pp. 30 f.
[2] Charles S. Peirce, *Collected Papers*, ed. Charles Hartshorne and Paul Weiss (Cambridge: Harvard University Press, 1935), Vol. VI, pp. 237–239.

and there are many other kinds of reality distinct from existence. Peirce thus regards being, reality, and existence as distinguishable meanings. When he states that the future difference of flowers growing under different conditions is a reality already, he is talking loosely. First of all, the prediction of a difference has a probability value, however high that may be. Moreover, it is not proper usage to state that a future difference is already a reality. Even if it were a certainty, it would be objectionable usage.

The late English philosopher McTaggart shares this usage. Declaring that which is real to be existent, he states, "Now tomorrow's weather is existent, for existence is as much a predicate of the future and past as of the present."[3] He should rather say that it belongs to the field of existence, which has the dimensions of past, present, and future. But only the present actually exists. If existence is taken as a generic title for all existents, past and future as well, then actual existence is restricted to the present. McTaggart raises the question whether the term real should be used to apply to different worlds, such as the world of a Dickens novel, or of ordinary life. The concept of reality would be weakened thereby. One can speak of various universes of discourse, or of domains and systems of the most diverse kinds, and so allow for the different worlds in the field of art. Actually, however, there is one world, there is one reality, there is one realm of existence.

In recent philosophy, existence has been much discussed as a title for a group of problems. In some cases, it is being which is the goal. Existence is frequently disparaged, in contradistinction to a more permanent, higher or deeper reality. When subjectivism was so prominent a generation ago, existence as a realm beyond consciousness was problematical. Professor Hoernlé has summarized[4] the various problems connected with the term existence in the philosophical tradition. They range "from the 'existential import' of propositions, and the 'reference of thought to reality,' to the validity of the 'ontological' argument for the existence of God." There are also subsidiary problems:

... the relation of essence to existence; the distinction between "logical" and "real" possibility and the relation of each to the

[3] J. M. E. McTaggart, *The Nature of Existence* (Cambridge: The University Press, 1921), Vol. I, p. 7.
[4] R. F. A. Hoernlé, "Notes on the Treatment of 'Existence' in Recent Philosophical Literature," *Proceedings of the Aristotelian Society*, New Series (London: Williams and Norgate, 1923), 19–38.

other and of both to actuality; the distinction between "possible" and "necessary" existence; the distinction between analytic and synthetic propositions; the relation of "ideas," or, again, of "concepts," to "fact"; the relation of a class to its members; the problem of denotation; the distinction of kinds of existence, and, again, of universes of discourse; the distinction of objects of "experience" (in one or other of several senses of "experience") and of objects of "pure thought"; the questions whether existence is a "quality," and whether it is definable or indefinable; and many more.

For example, most of the scholastic refinements about *esse* have been omitted in this "rough catalogue."

Following Aristotle's procedure in principle, G. F. Stout has given two steps in the logical division of being:[5] (1) the distinction of complete being from its essential constituents, and (2) the distinction of these constituents from each other, for example, possible existence, real existence, the existence of universals, etc. The reader will no doubt find it puzzling that the possible, the real, and universals are to be regarded as essential constituents of complete being. In contrast to Aristotle, for whom a concrete individual is a complete being, Stout regards the complete being as "the universe which comprehends whatever in any sense exists, so far at least as this is capable of coming within the range of our knowledge or questioning." But, since "it cannot be properly said to comprehend itself . . . we ought not to say that it exists." The word exist originally meant "to step out or forth, to come forth, emerge." The statements that "X exists" and "There is X" (in a field of being, and in the long run the universe) are taken to be synonymous. The term intentional is used in preference to the ambiguous term subjective. "Intentional existence"[6] refers to objects or characters of objects "only inasmuch as they are present to a mind." Stout asks whether there are objects of thought with a purely intentional existence, so that they are not objective at all but owe their being entirely to "being thought of." He gives the example of Mr. Pecksniff, a character in Dickens's *Martin Chuzzlewit*, who never existed as an actual fact. There are many imaginings of Pecksniff in different minds, but there is only one Peck-

---

[5] G. F. Stout, "Are there Different Ways of Existing?" *Proceedings of the Seventh International Congress of Philosophy* (London: Oxford University Press, 1931), pp. 122 ff.
[6] Cf. M. Farber, *The Foundation of Phenomenology* (Albany: State University of New York Press, 1967) for an account of the Brentano-Husserl conception of intentional experience and its objects.

sniff we all think of. Is the existence of Pecksniff purely intentional? Does it consist merely in being thought of by Dickens and others? Stout states that to him mere being for thought is internally contradictory. His argument is not convincing here; his analogy between a book lying on a table and an object of thought as related to thought is a false analogy. The solution of his problem involves the concept of possibility—the "possibility of being real." "Objective possibility" is Stout's answer to his question. But it is really the concept of probability that is involved, and that is based upon knowledge and evidence. Pecksniff's significance as a character is due to his historical plausibility; but there is no sense at all in speaking of his existence. It is important to recognize the distinctions that must be made between real and ideal meanings. The so-called ideal order of meanings includes the concepts of pure mathematics and all sorts of fictions. All of us can make judgments about the ideality called Pecksniff as portrayed by Dickens. No two of us will be likely to have the same intentional content, although we all have the same intentional object. Stout does not draw this necessary distinction. His use of the term existence is too broad. But it is also too narrow, if we are allowed to speak of the ideal realm of existence, properly labelled.

Another revealing contemporary treatment of existence has been provided by C. J. Ducasse.[7] According to such critical realists as Santayana, Drake, and Strong, essences are images, appearances purely as such; and nothing is literally and immediately present to consciousness except an essence. But existents are objects of intent, posited by animal faith when we act, and never themselves literally and directly given to consciousness. Knowledge is thus defined in terms of the relation of any given essence to an existent. There is knowledge when the essence happens to be the appearance of an existent, as believed. The talk of animal faith to name what is the most primitive of actual facts can hardly be condoned, from any point of view.

Ducasse's own conclusions are as follows: Until the existence of something has been proved, the term existents cannot be used denotatively. One can prove the existence of some things by experience.

[7] C. J. Ducasse, "On Our Knowledge of Existents," *Proceedings of the Seventh International Congress of Philosophy* (London: Oxford University Press, 1931), pp. 163 ff. Cf. also Ducasse's recent statement of his conception of physical existence in *Modern Concepts of the Nature of Mind*, ed. J. R. Smythies (New York: The Humanities Press, 1965), p. 92.

> Existence means presence, at a place in an order-system, of a set of characters. Material existence means presence at a place in space during a time, of some set of causal properties. . . . Pure matter is empty space-time, and cannot be said to exist materially; only sets of properties having a place in it exist. The space-time of dream objects is not different from that of material objects; but the properties of dream objects are different from those of material objects. Existing and Being Real are distinct notions. Being Real is a status always relative to an interest, and consists in existence in an order-system relevant to that interest.

Ducasse defines existence broadly, including numbers as well as material existence, as follows: ". . . to say something exists, means that some set of characters specified in a definition is present at some place in an indication-system."

The broad, inclusive definition of existence incurs difficulties which must be clarified. In the context of formal thought we speak of postulation, deduction, construction, and ideality. In all these respects material existence is different. Strictly speaking, the term existence is a misnomer in formal science, if we speak of existence in its basic sense as material existence; and, in general, it may be misleading to speak of existence in the ideal realm. There is always danger that philosophers may yield to the temptation to make the ideal order the source of the material order of existence. Furthermore, we cannot limit the talk of existence to what has been proved in experience, because there is always a region for further inquiry. On the other hand, we do not want to beg the question. But one is not begging the question by speaking of a general (infinite) field of existence, of which we come to know only a very small part. The general field is indicated by the known part. It is not a mere hypothesis to speak of the larger field of existence, in which man occupies so small a space, and for so brief a time. That is a basic fact of human existence. The conception of pure matter as empty space-time is to be distinguished from the known nature of matter. In general, one should be guided by the well-founded concepts of the sciences in the use of philosophical explanatory principles. In departing from the usage of the sciences, however, in the name of freedom of speculation, one should at least use other names. Finally, it appears that the distinction between existence and being real is in need of further elucidation.

It is undesirable to separate the terms existence, reality, and being, as has been done so often in recent philosophy, especially among the existentialists. Existence requires a locus in space and time, and it must consist of physical events. To exist is to occur in nature, to be at least an event in the physical world. The term being adds nothing, if we say that existence is the being of events. The terms stuff and substance add nothing to scientific determinations; and as the "that which has such and such properties," it is merely an aid to the imagination, a deeply rooted common-sense notion. Neither does the term real add anything, although it is useful as a more general and tenuous label, which may apply to physical existence or to experience. Experiences of all kinds, including hallucinations, are real. It is necessary to make clear what it is that is said to exist. If dream objects are said to exist, that can only be as dream objects, in dream experience. They are real as intentional objects of dream experiences; but they are not elements of reality in the sense of physical existence.

The term being may be used to refer to an individual, or to a generic object. The being of an individual is simply the event itself, as a passing occurrence. There is no general being or substance which is common to all individual existents; there is nothing in which all individuals share. No metaphysical ether or cosmic reason need be snatched from beyond the clouds and declared to reside somehow in man in order to entitle him to be called a human being, in conformity with his definition. Space, time, physical and chemical determinations all exist in particular occasions. The abstractions, including the highest or widest abstraction of being, are really devoid of all determinations, and therefore they add nothing to particular existents. This is not to deny that there are general laws of events, and that such laws may be said to have being. The term being, like the term real, which may also be applied, will say no more than that the particular events occur in certain patterns and conform to (or approximate) certain principles of order.

There is also the being of a thing as known or experienced, and the being by itself, whereby no Kantian unknowable is meant. The experience of the known being is conditioned by the knower, as well as by the physical object and the physical medium. This distinction cuts across all the foregoing ones. It must be expressed carefully in order to avoid any implication of agnosticism. All things are in larger contexts; and all things we talk about are in the context of knowing. But most things do not owe their being, in any sense of the term, to the context of knowing.

There is no room for anything beyond, below, or transcendent of existence. It deceives no one to speak of a transcendent reality or being. If a transcendent being does not exist, it cannot be effective; and if it does exist, it cannot be beyond existence.

It is a fallacy of long standing to suppose that where there is a word, there is a thing. It has long been the practice of philosophers to invent new terms, or to twist old terms into new forms, with the assumption that they are really talking about something. The large literature devoted to metaphysical subjects will certainly prompt the reader to reflect upon the themes which occupy so many philosophers. It is understandable why philosophers talk to so large an extent about the errors of other philosophers, their extravagances, or their use of language. Many of them appear to be forever traversing the same ground, without much encouragement from results.

B. *Existence and Possibility*

Existence has the three temporal dimensions of past, present, and future. The present is always a passing present. The plane of existence of the passing, present moment is called a duration by Whitehead.[6] It names a "cut" through nature, simultaneous with a present happening, a "concrete slab of nature." It is not possible to conceive of time apart from existence, or of existence without time; or, to put it more exactly and to avoid the misleading metaphor suggested by the noun time, it is not possible to remove temporality, or "passingness," from existence. That all existence recedes, that change is universal, are other ways of saying the same thing. The field of existence comprises the totality of all happenings, past, present, and future.

With regard to the past and present, one can only speak of actuality, or actual existence. There is no "ontological possibility." There is no referent for that term in the past or present, so that it is a redundant expression for actuality. Could one say that every actuality is a possibility, but not every possibility is an actuality? One can speak of possibility with respect to the future, but only with respect to the order of knowledge. Hence it is an

---

[6] Cf. A. N. Whitehead, *The Concept of Nature* (Cambridge: The University Press, 1920), Chap. III.

error of language to state that an actuality is a possibility. In an extended sense, the same may be said of the future, for what will be, will be actually existent. But if we try to predict what is to be, we are operating in the realm of knowledge, and there we must speak of possibility as well as probability. In this sense, the concept of possibility also applies to what is not known in the past, or in the ever receding present. Thus, it is possible that no such person as Socrates really existed.

Possibility is a cognitive, not an ontological category. Depending upon the assumptions that may be made, one may derive paradoxes from a logic of modalities, in which possibility is included. This is shown by Lukasiewicz, who appears to be a continuator of the thought of Whitehead and Russell[9] when he derives paradoxical results from the traditional theorems of modality—e.g., "A possible proposition is true."[10] The reason is that all propositions are considered, regardless of the temporal dimension, as parts of one system of propositions. But the collection of all propositions cannot be treated as a unified totality. It has already been pointed out that the various departments of knowledge can only be organized into a collective system, in which they have relative independence and autonomy. Propositions about the future involve possibility; various alternatives appear to be capable of realization from the perspective of our present knowledge. From our time-bound, limited perspectives, we cannot predict with certainty what will be, but is not yet in existence. We could not conceive a being that would be able to predict the future with certainty, and hence avoid the category of possibility. A being superior to us could indeed be conceived—one with a less limited perspective, or one that has existed an infinite amount of time up to the present, and with unfailing memory. Because of the open horizon of the future, however, the concept of possibility could never be eliminated. The uniformity of future existence could only be assumed. The supposed superior type of being would at least have a greater region of facts to support its pre-

---

[9] Reference is here made to the paradoxical consequences of implication, such as a "false proposition implies any proposition," which result from the logical analysis of Whitehead and Russell.
[10] Cf. J. Lukasiewicz, "Philosophische Bemerkungen zu mehrwertigen Systemen des Aussagen-Kalküls," and J. Lukasiewicz and A. Tarski, "Untersuchungen über den Aussagen-Kalkül," *Comptes rendus des séances de la Société des Sciences et des Lettres de Varsovie*, Vol. XXIII, 1930, Classe III. Cf. also C. I. Lewis and C. H. Langford, *Symbolic Logic* (New York: Dover Publications, Inc., 1959), Chap. VII.

dictions of the future, and to give them an appreciable probability value, especially those for the immediate future. As for predictions involving all future existence, that advantage is reduced to the point of ineffectiveness. We, with our limited perspectives, have a comparatively limited region of facts, and our predictions of the future (in the field of nature, rather than human society) are correspondingly weaker. It is probable that our solar system will be as it is now a million years from now; the probability that it will be essentially unchanged a trillion years from now is smaller; that it will always be as it is now has a vanishing probability value. Human knowledge has no method of bridging the open, infinite horizon of the future. It appears to be powerless when confronted by an endless field of possible existence. But there is no lack of effective power when the immediate, relevant future is involved; and that is not limited to a day or a year.

The power of prediction and the more limited play of possibilities are readily illustrated in the context of human activity. A historical prediction appears to be more complex than the case of predicting an eclipse of the sun, for example. Whether it is really more complex should be carefully considered. In some respects there is greater complexity in human beings than in inanimate nature; in other respects, there is greater simplicity. The kind of question that is at issue must be clarified. The prediction of the average age at death of the class of flute players in the next year is an example of one kind of question which can be handled simply. It is quite another matter to attempt to predict the age at which Mr. X, a particular flute player, will die. Our statistical generalizations are immensely valuable in practice, and their imperfections do not disturb us greatly. But we cannot say what will happen to the class of flute players a million or a trillion years from now.

To say that the future is the field of possibility (and of probability, when we are able to quantify, and to know the relevant facts) is not to declare it to be in a region of darkness. Is certainty entirely ruled out? Is the entire quest for certainty merely a matter of wishful thinking, if not a delusion? The inevitability of death is usually regarded as a matter of certainty, although the future progress of science may make it possible to prolong life indefinitely. Our knowledge of past uniformities and the evidence that the laws of nature operate everywhere in the known universe, the unerring predictions of eclipses, the successful determination of the causes of disease and the resultant gradual disappearance of major types of disease—all such facts indicate that there is an order of existence which is being progressively discovered.

The two extreme cases of chaos and determinate order (referred to in the preceding chapter) may be contrasted here. It is possible in an empty sense that the known universe, with all its observed order, is merely a passing incident in a meaningless succession of states, each enduring trillions of years, and each one not related in any ascertainable manner with the others, so that generalization is ruled out. Thus, there may be one kind of order for a time, but chaos (the null case of order, and itself a kind of order) on the whole. Nothing speaks for this empty possibility, of course. Does anything speak against it? The only thing that can be said against it, and that may be cogent, is that it is reasonable to argue that the present fits with the past, the past with the more remote past, etc.; so that all of past existence constitutes an ordered system, even though we know only a very small segment of it. The knowledge of some order is therefore presumptive of more order. In view of the enormous success of our scientific analyses and predictions, the weight of the argument is against chaos and for order. The nature and the degree of the order must be indicated. Would it amount to total determinateness, or causal determinism, according to which everything that happens is subject to a law, and all the laws constitute a system, with unlimited application to all future occurrences? That is the ideal of the scientific understanding and control of existence. It is possible that nature is uniform in this sense; and unlike the null case of chaos, this is a real and not an empty possibility, for there is some evidence to support it.

Novel combinations of units of matter and new qualities have been held to be unpredictable. That position could never be proved, however, because we can only talk about such novel qualities after they have emerged and become known. The whole point is really nugatory. If we say that, combining such and such elements, we cannot predict what the new qualities will be, we are only speaking of our own inability to predict at this time. But we cannot prove the unpredictability. Looking backwards, after the occurrence of the novelty, we are again unable to prove its unpredictability. One must guard against a hasty circumscription of the region of possible knowledge, which is usually done for the purposes of faith.

Difficulties in the way of prediction are no objection in principle to the ideal of causal determinism. The progress of science has been too great to declare anything in particular impossible. That the general program of causal determinism may never be completely realized could only be due, then, to the open horizon of the future. Novelty occurs at least for human beings. It is often maintained that there is genuine novelty in the nature of things. That may be true. Perhaps no such being as you or I has ever existed before; and there may never have been a system of society like ours before. But perhaps, one might rejoin, nuclear weapons may have been developed by earlier cultures, even on other planets, with the resultant destruction of the peoples that developed them; and perhaps that has happened an infinite number of times. There has been time enough for it to happen, if the past field of existence is beginningless, i.e., infinite. Although there is novelty for us as finite beings, the question whether there is genuine novelty in the nature of things, in the sense of unique existence that is unrepeatable, is less easily answered. A line of reasoning similar in broad outline to the treatment of chaos and order might be helpful here in lending greater clarity to the discussion.

From the standpoint of systematic logical analysis, the concept of possibility appears to be prior to that of existence. It seems to underlie existence, in such a way that the structures which are realized in the actual world are viewed as one set of values of the variables of a possible arrangement of the world. An ontological dogmatist in the Platonic tradition reads too much into this priority, which is merely a matter of method. If, as has been set forth, possibility is viewed as an affair of knowledge, and has reference to the future or to the unknown past—in a word, if our ignorance of the future or past is a necessary condition of possibility—in what sense is there any priority at all? From the perspective of the present, innumerable possible world-patterns appear to be capable of realization; and only one may be realized. That which is realized is an actualization of a possibility, so that the possibility appears to underlie the actuality. But that is only a manner of speaking, and the term possibility no longer has an application when an actuality has been realized. Its reference being to the unknown, it may not apply to the known actuality. It is therefore prior only in a temporal, cognitive sense, which is utterly innocuous and fruitless ontologically.

How do these considerations affect the view that this is only one of an infinite number of possible worlds? Leibniz's view will be recalled: our world is the best possible world, both on *a priori* and *a posteriori* grounds. The mathematical and the theological perspectives combined to support his judgment: the world exhibits order, and God created it. Husserl's remarks about possibility will be of interest in this connection:[11] "Naturally Leibniz is right, when he says that infinitely many monads and groups of monads are conceivable, but that not all of these possibilities are therefore composible, and again, that infinitely many worlds could have been created, but not a number of them together, since they are not composible." Husserl then goes on to state, referring to his own phenomenological method, that one can first of all think of his own ego, "this apodictic-factual ego," in free variation, and thus gain the system of possibility-alterations (*Abwandlungen*) of his own self (literally: of my own self), each of which is suspended by every other one and through the ego, that I really am.

> It is a system of a priori incomposibility. Further, the fact *I am* prescribes, whether and which other monads are others for me; I can only find them, but not create what should be for me. If I think myself into a pure possibility, then it too prescribes, which monads are others for it. And proceeding further in that way, I recognize that every monad, which has validity as a concrete possibility, predelineates [*vorzeichnet*] a composible universe, a closed world of monads, and that two monad-worlds are not composible in the same way as two possibility-alterations of my ego are, and similarly of any ego that may be presupposed.

Looking backwards, and considering the world up to the present, could one say that it might have been otherwise in any respect? In other words, was it necessary that it be as it actually has been? If possibility were ruled out, retrospectively, it might appear that everything that occurred was necessary. It would have to be shown, however, how the concept of necessity adds anything to actuality. If one says, "That which has been, had to

---

[11] E. Husserl, *Cartesianische Meditationen und Pariser Vorträge* (Haag: Martinus Nijhoff, 1950), pp. 167 f.

be as it was, and could not have been otherwise," does that say any more than "That which has been, has occurred with a certain configuration, in certain relationships, as a matter of fact"? Looking forward, one could say that a certain set of facts, arranged in such and such a way (let it be the world as it later comes to be realized), need not be, or that it is not necessary. That is another way of saying that it is only possible, or only one out of any number of possibilities. Thus, it has meaning to say negatively that something does not have to be, that it is not necessary. But what does it mean to say, positively, that something is necessary? To say that its nonoccurrence, or its occurrence otherwise than is actually the case, is impossible simply raises the question of the meaning of impossibility in this context. If possibility is meaningful for the future, may its negation, impossibility, be applied to the past? Necessity means that nonoccurrence is impossible. This cannot be said of the future in every sense of the term impossible, in view of the concept of empty possibility, according to which anything may possibly happen or not happen, so that all known evidence might be invalidated for the future. Can it be said of the present, or of the past? For example, may it be said that some kind of existence, some kind of arrangement of events, is now necessary? Were one to say that the nonoccurrence of some kind of arrangement is impossible (meaning at least that it would involve a contradiction and hence be logically impossible), that would be to hold it to be necessary. But what about empty possibility? Does that allow for the case in which nothing exists; or for chaos as the supposed lower limit of order?

If the real world at any time is viewed as a special case of possible structures, or as one particular collocation out of innumerable possible collocations, it must be recognized that the possible structures or collocations are elaborated in relation to the real world. Knowing what the world is like now, one regards the world as not yet fully realized, and speaks of it as one possible process of realization.

The concept of possibility, like all other concepts, is generalized and constituted in human thought. One of the most interesting examples of origin-analysis in phenomenology is provided by Husserl's sketch (in his work on *Experience and Judgment*[12]) of the origin of the concept of possibility in prepredicative experience.

[12] *Erfahrung und Urteil* (Prag: Academia Verlagsbuchhandlung, 1939).

Not only is the concept of possibility derived from the rudimentary elements of direct experience; it also has a history, and its significance varies throughout intellectual history. This is clearly true for real possibility, and for all other types except those that are formally defined.

The genetic derivation of philosophical possibility from the subject matter of the special sciences must also be considered. The real world, in its physical and social-historical aspects, is the primary and effective basis of all knowledge. This genetic truth has been recognized not only by empiricists but also by such transcendentalists as Kant. One should never lose sight of it, whether in formal thought or in phenomenology, where forms are treated as disengaged from their natural setting for the purposes of analysis. The genetic point of departure for all knowledge is actual experience, which is thus antecedent to the elaboration of a general relational logic. The basic facts emphasized in the present work: that experience always occurs in a social context, that it is conditioned by a vast and complex tradition, and that it has a place in the natural world—these are facts which are often forgotten or ignored by writers on philosophy. This is not to say that the theories of man and the world at a given time are to be taken as absolutely valid. The pronouncements of scientists are not necessarily the voice of nature, or of human existence.

Several different types of possibility have been distinguished,[13] notably, logical, formal, real, technical,[14] and empty. Although all of them are derived from human thought, they are generalized to different degrees and they have different functions. From the point of view of logical possibility, meanings which are abstracted from experience can be ideally treated as a set of variables, one set of the possible values of which is the real world itself. Such a complete relational logic does not exist and it may well be out of the question for us to formulate it, if only because the future is not predetermined with respect to our actual knowledge. Thus one does not operate with an *a priori* theory of pure forms which are in all ways independent of the real world, or antecedent to

---

[13] Cf. Chap. IV, Section D.
[14] Cf. H. Reichenbach, *Experience and Prediction* (Chicago: The University of Chicago Press, 1938), pp. 38 f.: ". . . technical possibility . . . concerns facts the realization of which lies within the power of individuals or of groups of men . . . it is surely technically impossible to build a bridge over the Atlantic." But the latter is physically possible, meaning that "the fact in question is conformable to physical laws." The perpetual motion machine and a visit to the sun are both cited as physically impossible.

it in a real sense, when he uses the formal concept of possibility. The basic criterion of logical possibility is freedom from contradiction. In other words, anything is possible which does not involve contradiction. If a contradiction can be shown to occur, that is evidence of a defect in the construction of the system. To say that a contradiction is not possibble (logically, that is) in a correctly constructed system is to assert a tautology; for by a correctly constructed system is meant (among other things) a system which is free from contradiction. With that restricting condition, there may be great freedom of construction. Special concepts of formal possibility are defined for each system of knowledge. Thus, the system of arithmetic not only conforms to the broad requirement of noncontradiction, which holds for all systems, but also to the special requirements which govern arithmetic. The concept of empty possibility imposes no restrictions whatsoever, and allows complete freedom of construction.

Real possibility is another matter. It has a more restricted range, in accordance with the known structure of reality. Caution must be observed lest one introduce absolute principles which have played a prominent role in formal thought to legislate for the order of facts. Can it be said that noncontradiction is a negative condition of possible reality, as Husserl stated it? Does a principle which is necessary for ordered discourse also apply to reality? All that can be said is that it is analytically meaningless or absurd to speak of a contradictory reality (since by definition the contradictory is the absurd). There is no analytical assurance, however, that reality will necessarily have any characters whatever, whether contradictory or noncontradictory. That a contradiction may in fact occur, and indeed, that contradiction is a universal feature of reality, is maintained by dialectical philosophers. Are they talking about the same thing? If by a contradiction in reality is meant a conflict, a state of affairs which is unstable due to inner tension, then this differs from the formal-logical sense of the term. The profound dialectical insight into the contradictory nature of reality may easily be vitiated by the failure to observe this distinction. When Plekhanov (in his *Fundamental Problems of Marxism*) states that the traditional law of noncontradiction ("not yes and no") is superseded by the dialectical formulation ("yes and no"), he is clearly protesting against a static conception of logic and reality. The traditional, inadequate formulation of the logical laws in question (noncontradiction and excluded middle) must give way to a more adequate formulation. Their abrogation is not involved, however. A logic of change need not be a changing logic, at least not in the same sense. The conflicts that occur in the world are expressed by the content of the propositions; and a proposition expressing a conflict, if it is true, rules out its falsity, or the proposition that there is no conflict.

C. *Problems of Existence*

If one asks "What is existence?" he must be prepared to assign this question to a system of knowledge. Where does it belong; and is the question meaningful in terms of the assigned system? Instead of asking whether there is a general problem of existence it is better first to examine the very question for its legitimacy.

Although the term existence is used in the context of mathematics, the usage is unfortunate. One may also ask what existence means for the events or characters in a given domain, as in history, biology, etc. The question about existence in general belongs to ontology, in which the meaning of existence is raised in its most universal form. One may question existence for its meaning in experience, as one does in phenomenology, the answer being provided by descriptive analysis. The account is limited to the structures of experience, however; the distinction between real existence and illusion, etc., is determined descriptively in terms of experience, but without undertaking to provide a criterion for the determination of existence in a given case. The question about existence in the context of experience does not coincide with the objective ontological question about existence.

The basic facts and principles which have been seen to apply in the discussion of experience and the problems of philosophy must be borne in mind in this context. They tend to be ignored to so great an extent that it is well to emphasize them repeatedly, when examining the various fundamental problems of philosophy. That existence is historical; that it has an infinite past, and an infinite future; and that the development of man is a recent event in the historical process of existence, are facts of far-reaching significance for philosophy. If there was a time when there were no human beings, and if there may be an infinite period in which there will again be no human beings, it follows that the talk of the dependence of existence on the human experience of it is a naïve error. No epistemological analysis which violates these basic truths of existence can have the least plausibility.

The term existence should not be construed in philosophy in a sense radically different from its use in the sciences and in ordinary experience. It should not be taken to mean human existence; nor should it be used in the sense of the human effort at self-understanding, or self-interpretation. Either complete descriptive expressions should be employed, or new terms coined. Only confusion can result from such misleading uses of the term existence.

Another guiding precept always to be borne in mind by the philosopher is that he should be careful never to violate the testimony of general experience and the sciences. The philosopher does not have unlimited freedom of construction. Neither is he completely free in projecting interpretations, any more than is the case for the special scientist. There are logical criteria to be observed, and plausibility in the light of the given and related systems of knowledge. If an epistemological analysis and argument lead to the conclusion that existence is not independent of cognition, then either the argument is fallacious, or the philosopher has not drawn the proper consequences from his analysis, or, as may be, he has simply misinterpreted his findings. His definitions may be assumptive, or his premises unwarranted. The philosophical literature for centuries abounds in illustrations of such unhappy errors. Why do they persist? The best answer, apart from detailed explanations in given, particular cases, is the historical explanation. There has been a market for spiritualism, for example; and numerous philosophers have provided the desired point of view. The assumptions made use of in their reasoning enabled them to arrive at their preconceived position. Sometimes their ingenuity was sufficient for them to contrive new arguments. But the result was always essentially the same.

In order to know existence, it is not necessary to be identical with it. Existence is known partially and selectively. The knower, who is one item of existence, perceives another existent, for example, that tree. Since it is a basic truth that the knower is extrinsic to existence (except, of course, in the case of subjective or intentional activities, where thought may be creative), the knower does not make a difference to the tree by knowing it. There is no constitutive relationship so far as the physical tree is concerned. The knower makes a difference in another respect, however, for he selects a certain content in each successive phase of perception, and all the contents are fused into a single perceptual object. Thus, one may experience what is not there—in this case, an apparently unchanging object. There is a difference between the experienced content and the physical object, which is never completely perceived. There can be no talk of the identity of the knower and the known.

Is there a general problem of human existence? An individual has his problems of health, maintaining himself economically, developing culturally, and rearing a family. Society has the many tasks involved in securing its existence, including planning for the future. There are problems of social existence as well as of individual existence. But is it desirable to speak of them as problems of existence? Not all of them condition existence in the same way, or to the same extent. Are there then degrees of existence? When Aristotle separated value from being, it was recognized that there may be degrees of value (more or less value), but hardly degrees of being or existence. One may speak with greater truth of levels of existence, in the organization of matter, but also of degrees of the realization of potentialities. A human being may exist on the animal level, or on a minimal economic level, meaning by that the indispensable minimum needed to maintain himself and his dependents. The majority of the people in a modern industrial society belong to that class. Do such individuals enjoy a complete existence? If one can speak of completeness in this context, that implies degrees of the development or fulfillment of existence, and not degrees of existence. Every existent is complete in itself, as such. How could it be otherwise? It is also incomplete in the sense that it is capable of further development; there is always the potentiality of more or of different existence. Even if there is physical decline, and impending death, there is still some degree of potentiality left. The complete realization of a potentiality is an ideal which perhaps never occurs. Strictly speaking, the adjective complete should not be applied to existence. Either it is redundant, or it is an elliptical expression referring to the potentiality of the things in question. Thus, if there are not degrees of existence (more or less of it), there are stages or levels of development, involving potentiality.

There are, moreover, degrees of value which human beings may realize, even without considering the factor of potentiality. If their potentiality is disregarded, their actual interests may be fulfilled to a greater or lesser extent; a greater or lesser number of interests may be fulfilled, and there may be degrees of fulfillment of a particular interest, say the need for food.

D. The Dimensions of Existence

In the language of common sense, every existing thing, or real event, is said to have a locus in space and time. To say that something is in space, or in time, is to use a metaphor, which is often misleading. It helps to make plausible an interpretation of space as a three-dimensional receptacle, which is real in itself. Similarly, time is frequently regarded as a one-dimensional form, with its own reality. But there is no independent reality of space or of time in which things can find a place. The events which we experience constitute our immediate reality, our immediate field of existence. The presumably infinite universe is a vast collection of events; and events have spatial and temporal relationships, just as they have physical and chemical properties. The simultaneous coexistence of events is expressed by means of spatial relations, just as the succession of events, as well as their endurance and change, are represented by means of temporal relations.

Thinkers have reflected upon the magnitude of space and time through the centuries, and also upon the smallness of the units making up the real things of experience. Two sets of problems, which may be called macroproblems and microproblems, have resulted.

Blaise Pascal wrote (in his *Thoughts*) of space as an infinite sphere, with its center everywhere and its circumference nowhere. The horizon of time, toward the past and the future, has also been a deeply impressive fact. The reaction to the idea of infinitude has varied in different historical periods, but there are also individual differences noted in the same historical period. Generalizations must accordingly be advanced with all due caution. It is suggestive, however, that Aristotle's finitism was advanced in a relatively stable, closed slave economy, and that the dictum *"infinitum non datur"* could claim his support in the closed feudal-ecclesiastical economy of the medieval period. With the breakdown of the medieval system, and with the opening up of new trade routes, the receptivity to the idea of infinity was only natural and found ardent exponents among thinkers from Bruno to Spinoza and Leibniz. It would seem that the more recent interest in finitism is in keeping with the trend of a contracting economic system. On the other hand, one can point to convinced infinitists in Greek antiquity and at the present time. The Epicureans and the evolutionists, as well as the exponents of the mathematical theory of infinity, are sufficient warning against a hasty generalization, however suggestive and sound it may be in the facts it selects. The important thing to be noted is that such a generalization should be delimited properly, and formulated with all the restrictions noted.

In Kant's view, one may argue with equal success (or lack of success) for the finitude and the infinitude of space and time. If one argues that the world had a beginning in time, or had no beginning in time, it was, in his view, possible to discredit both positions; and similarly for space. Kant's reasoning is in part of merely historical interest, but it is also significant in that it helps to formulate problems of permanent interest. Kant thought that "reason becomes involved in darkness and contradictions, from which, no doubt, it may conclude that errors must be lurking somewhere, but without being able to discover them, because the principles which it follows transcend all the limits of experience and therefore withdraw themselves from all experimental tests." If it were true that the world must be judged to have a beginning in time, and also that it could not have a beginning in time; and if it were true that the world is limited in space, and also infinite in space; and if the other antinomies formulated by Kant were cogent —then all claims to the rationality of the universe would be shaken. But what Kant really sought to do was to discredit both conflicting positions, so that the truth about ultimate reality would seem to elude the human understanding. Space and time were regarded by Kant as forms of perception. By or in themselves, the things could not be said to be in space or in time, for space and time are our ways of looking at things. Kant's arguments, designed to show that space and time are transcendentally ideal while being empirically real, have generally not been regarded as cogent. It seemed plausible to Kant that if there is to be an infinite amount of space, it must be synthesized, and that would require an infinite amount of time. But, he thought he could show, it is not possible to maintain the position that there has been an infinite amount of time up to the present.

It is the antinomy about time which will no doubt impress the reader as most formidable. Consider the two opposing views, the thesis which states that the world had a beginning in time and the antithesis which states that the world had no beginning. To establish the thesis, one assumes the antithesis, in order to show that it is untenable; and to establish the antithesis, one assumes the thesis, which is also found to be untenable. Consider the argument for the thesis. If it is assumed that the world did not have a beginning in time, then an infinite amount of time must have elapsed up to the present. How could we have arrived at the present state of affairs, if it is true that the infinity of a series forbids its completion "by means of a successive synthesis"? Does it then follow that the world must have had a beginning? To argue next that the world had no beginning, one assumes that it did have a beginning. Was it an empty time that preceded the world, in that case? But an empty time is such that nothing could take its beginning in it; it would not be possible to distinguish its parts, so that nothing could be conceived to arise from it.

Are the two arguments equally cogent? The assumption of a beginning always prompts the question, "What was there before the beginning?" One could not say that there was a beginning to time, for that would be tantamount to saying that there was a time when there was no time. It is the world that is supposed to have a beginning. In that case, one must show how something could come from nothing, and the argument ought to be rendered in theological terms. The thesis appears therefore to lack cogency. The antithesis, on the other hand, appears to be unavoidable, although it requires further consideration. What is the starting point? The present, of course, not a beginningless past, must be the starting point. One cannot begin unless there is a fixed point at which to begin. Any fixed point in the past would be a finite distance from the present. But one could not start at the first point of the temporal process because of the assumption that there was no beginning. Looking backward, one sees that every event in time was preceded by another event, or set of events, and so on ad infinitum. The same would apply to the future, so that there are two infinite horizons, as viewed from the present. One should not think of an infinite series as limited to the form of a progression, such as $1,2,3, \ldots, n, n+1, \ldots$. Looking backward, one has a regression, such as $\ldots 0,-1,-2,-3, \ldots$. One's present position may be represented as the 0-point of the reprogression $\ldots -3,-2,-1,0,1,2,3, \ldots$. It cannot be known with evidence that there is such a double infinite; but it may be regarded as the unavoidable conclusion from the failure to prove the thesis that there was a beginning (or that there will be an end). No doubt some readers will still insist that there could not have been an infinite series of events before the present, and they will prefer either to reject both thesis and antithesis or they may be led to challenge the very legitimacy of the question, or the legitimacy of the conception of infinity which is involved. Those who hold that a question is meaningful if there is a possible, or a conceivable, method of answering it, will be inclined to reject the whole issue. The absence of such a method will not prevent most people from wondering about the remote past, and about the possibility of a beginning.

The question of the spatial extent of the world should be considered independently of Kant's notion of the nature of space. When Lucretius raised the question whether there is a limit to space, he imagined someone going to the alleged limit, and throwing a flying dart. Either it would be stopped, or it would go forward; so that if it were stopped, there must be something to stop it, which would occupy space, and if there were nothing to stop it, there must be space in which it could move. In either case, the alleged limit is not a limit. According to Einstein's conception, the universe is finite though unbounded. If space is conceived relationally, and matter is the reality which is related, it is possible to argue for a finite universe. A finite amount of matter should not be dissipated in an infinite region of space. The weighty reasons of the physical theorist will not deter the philosophical imagination from picturing an endless number of universes, so that the Einsteinian universe might be viewed as a particle in the infinite domain of existence. The imagination only stops when it is weary.

The microproblems of space, time, and matter were raised in a provoking form in ancient Greece. Some of the problems formulated by Zeno have not been solved until recent years. Zeno's purpose was to support his master Parmenides in his effort to rule out change by means of a theory of being. For Parmenides, differences of space and time are illusory, mere tricks of the senses. Nothing could become, for it is impossible to get anything into being, which is all at once. Therefore change is impossible, and there is neither past nor future. Neither could there be real divisions of being, so that spatial divisions are illusory. There can be only one plenum of being. To support this position, out of zeal for his master, Zeno pointed out a number of difficulties in the analysis of time, space, and motion.

Space does not exist, Zeno argued, because if space is, it will be in something. But that is to say that space will be in space, and so on ad infinitum. Neither may points be taken to be real. Aristotle (in his *Metaphysics*) gave the following account of Zeno's reasoning: "If the absolute unit is indivisible it would be, according to Zeno's axiom, nothing at all. For that which neither makes anything larger by its addition, nor makes anything smaller by its subtraction, is not one of the things that are, since it is clear that what *is* must be a magnitude, and if a magnitude, corporeal, for the corporeal has being in all dimensions . . . but the point and the unit do not make things larger however added." With regard to motion, Zeno observed (as reported by Diogenes Laertius) that a thing which moves can neither move in the place where it is, nor yet in the place where it is not. Since it cannot move where it is, nor yet in the place where it is not, it would follow that motion is impossible. How could such an argument be answered? The starting point must be the fact of motion; and it must be recognized that "the place where it is"—a state of rest—is not a unit of motion.

The well-known paradoxes of Zeno carry out these thoughts in further detail. They bear upon the problems that arise if one confuses conceptual units with perceptual realities, and, unwittingly, Zeno hit upon the relativity of motion and the concept of the threshold of perception. If space is made up of points, there are an infinite number of points in any given space. It is impossible to move from point A to point B, because you must first travel half the distance, and then half the remaining distance, and so on ad infinitum. By this reasoning, the reader will never be able to reach the door. But hold, says someone, there is an infinitely divisible time in which one can traverse an infinitely divisible space. The difficulty can be found in time alone, however. This hour will never end, because half the time must first elapse, then half of the remaining time, and so on ad infinitum. But it does end, someone observes, and I do reach the door. It follows that space is not really composed of nonextended points, and time not really composed of nonextended instants.

If space is conceived as made up of points, then there is an infinite number of points between any two points A and B, no matter how close together they may be. There are as many points between two close points A and B, say an inch apart, as between C and D, which are a mile apart; and even as many as there are in all (infinite) three-dimensional space. The points, as nonextended nothings, can be packed closely enough in the smallest extended distance to be placed in one-to-one correspondence with the points of larger distances or areas. In other words, the points and the entire conception of infinity are conceptual explanatory devices. Real differences cannot be constructed out of such abstractions. The only alternative is the one chosen by Whitehead, who began with real durations and proceeded, with the method of extensive abstraction, to redefine the units of time and space. In Whitehead's view, when you speak of an instant, you are really talking about the neighborhood of that instant.

According to the classical atomic theory of Leucippus and Democritus, there are ultimate indivisible units of matter, although these units are extended particles. It was inevitable that speculation should go beyond such particles, all the way to Leibniz's theory of monads, which were supposed to be absolutely simple units. Leibniz saw that it was necessary to give up extension as an attribute of the supposed units, if they are to be considered as ultimate. The monads were portrayed as infinitesimal centers of force with the property of perception, each of them self-contained and mirroring the universe.

Pascal had recognized clearly that any alleged ultimate units, if extended, are capable of further subdivision. How far could that process go? Show me an alleged simple unit, Pascal reflected, and I shall show you a complex universe—which means that it is infinitely divisible. That is true if the unit is extended, and is in keeping with the observation that there are as many points in a small line as in a larger line. At no point could we, in the process of dividing the small particles, come to a particle so small that if cut in two parts it would fall into two nothings. If that happened, one could, in the spirit of Pascal, ask whether putting the two nothings together would yield something.

Kant formulated this problem in his way, in the form of an antinomy (his "Second Antinomy"). The thesis states that every compound substance in the world consists of simple parts, and nothing exists anywhere but the simple, or what is composed of it. The antithesis asserts that no compound thing in the world consists of simple parts, and there exists nowhere in the world anything simple. This issue is just as disturbing as the issue of the first antinomy. To say that there are no absolutely simple units is to be left with an open infinity of successively smaller units. There are only compounds. But does not a compound imply consisting of parts; and if the parts are compounds, does that not imply, in the last analysis, consisting of simple parts? But why may there not be an infinite series, without a limit? One cannot rest so long as there is extension; but can one rest even with nonextended units? If the latter have properties of any kind (and, in Leibniz's hands, each monad was really a complex universe in itself, since it mirrored the whole universe), further division would seem to be thinkable. The thesis, which asserts simple parts, faces the difficulty that if the simple parts occupy space, they will themselves contain parts; and if they do not occupy space, there is the difficulty of accounting for real spatial differences in terms of nonextended units. It is therefore impossible to defend the thesis that there are absolutely simple parts. The antithesis would again seem to be an unavoidable position. Beginning with the things of our experience, which are compounds, the analysis can go further and further with no conceivable limit. Greater simplicity can always be aimed at, without ever reaching a limit. This may go on ad infinitum, which is no objection unless one can prove that there are no infinite classes.

E. *The World in Philosophy*

In ancient Greece, conceptions of the earth passed through numerous rapid transformations. It was convex and round, like a stone pillar (Anaximander); it was flat like a table top (Anaximenes); but, fortunately, it was also round. A good deal happened to the nature of the world of existence as well. It was basically made of water, or of fire, etc., or of a combination of such "elements." It was in a continuous process of change; but it was also regarded as really changeless—though by only a few, to be sure. But at least there was a world in ancient Greece, and the skeptics did not succeed in undermining its general acceptance. For atomic materialism, the true reality consisted of atoms in motion, and the world was independent of those limited collocations of atoms known as human beings. When commenting on the atomic materialism of Lucretius in the Roman period, Whitehead remarked that Lucretius was writing in the atmosphere of a farmer folk, and that for the farmer the true reality is the solid earth. Subjectivism was not an ancient doctrine.

Generally speaking, the modern mind, with all its technical and scientific superiority, has a less secure grip on the world in its philosophizing. Descartes, who doubted everything in order to know with certainty, was only able to reinstate the external world with God's help. He preferred the conception of an independent world so far as human knowing is concerned, and his acceptance of divine creation was a matter of faith, supported by specious arguments. With the aim of warding off atheism and materialism, Berkeley criticized abstractions, among them matter. If it was meaningless to speak of a world of matter, on his premises, it was enough to have a divine mind with its ideas. The world therewith becomes an incident in the contents of a divine mind. Having dispensed with the equipment of a mind, and without the support of a divine being, Hume was left with a stream of perceptions as his starting point. Since the causes of impressions were held to be unknown, the question of an independently existing world was transformed into the question of the way in which we come to believe that there is such a world.

It is noteworthy that it is the natural world which is in question, rather than the social world. It has always been easy for a philosopher to dislocate, reinterpret, or even annihilate the world, but it does not seem to occur to him that his social reality is at all affected thereby. The social relations, class distinctions, vested interests, and special privileges all remain what they were before the philosophical transformation of the world.

Leibniz's world consisted of extensionless spiritual points of force. There was a plenum of spiritual reality, conscious and unconscious; and the hierarchical features of the existing world were preserved.

Kant's anticipation of Laplace in the formulation of the nebular hypothesis is well known. There is such a thing as development in the natural world. But his theory that form is contributed to the world by the mind, and his view of time and space as forms of perception, leave unanswered (and also unanswerable) the question as to what the world is like by itself, apart from human experience.

Hegel's world of nature is the self-alienation of spirit. The earth is a dialectical synthesis of the sun and the moon. From the point of view of the absolute, everything is spread out all at once, although from the point of view of man and experience, things follow one another in time.

The world of the evolutionists is an illimitable universe, without beginning or end in time, and infinitely extended in space. To offset the limitation of Einstein's finite though boundless universe, Eddington's expanding universe may be selected by those who find any suggested limits confining. If temperament will not adjust to theory, theory may be chosen to suit temperament.

The feudal world was finitistic in its conception. The authority of Aristotle could be invoked in support of the denial of an actual infinite. Not all the Greeks were deficient in this respect, of course. The concept of infinitude could be traced back to Anaximander. Aristotle's distinction between the actual and the potential, and his rejection of the infinitude of the world, provided a welcome support to the finitism of the Church. If reality is finite, there may be an uppermost limit, or a first cause.

The modern period was heralded by the cult of infinitude. It was in accordance with a spirit of endless expansion, and an open horizon for social and scientific progress. Infinitism was the prevailing view until quite recently, when finitism became a mode of response to the periodical change from an expanding to a contracting economic system.[15]

In general, a contracting social system motivates finitism. An expanding system is capable of further growth on its own basis. It ceases to be expanding if it is undermined and hemmed in by its own inner conflicts. This is illustrated by industrial and commercial history in the modern period. Because of the development of industries in hitherto backward countries, the leading industrial powers were confronted by new competitors in a dwindling world market. The expanding system began to contract (at least periodically), and the horizons changed from infinitism to finitism. That is not to say that finitism or infinitism ever disappeared wholly. It is a question of the relative prominence of the one idea or the other, as responses to dominant motives.

Other changes in ideas can be noted in the transition from a contracting to an expanding system, or vice versa. The confidence in scientific laws, and in the possibility of establishing rigorous

---

[15] The words expanding and contracting are used rather than open and closed, because it is a question of degree rather than a finished condition. One cannot say the present state of capitalism is one of closure, for there are occasions of expansion which reverse the curve of contraction for a time.

causal connections everywhere, was characteristic of the modern period until its contracting phase began. Anti-intellectualism as a general trend anticipated many changes. The revolt against the scientific method was manifested in a number of ways. The frontal attack on the intellect by Bergson won the acclaim of William James, but did not penetrate much further among reputable and trained scientific scholars. But the old concepts of cause, determinism, substance, matter, time and space, etc., were re-examined and supplanted by more adequate ideas. As though prompted by a feeling of social insecurity, changes in scientific concepts came to be understood as a breakdown in an old, outmoded scientific method, and it was inferred by many writers that there are limits to science. A strictly methodological problem was misconstrued as an impasse to the possible use of scientific method. This pleased not only traditional philosophers; even scientists of high repute could be seen in the ranks of those proclaiming limits to possible knowledge. Such phenomena require a social-historical explanation, which includes both science and philosophy within its scope. The dominant interests of a social system motivate, encourage, and seemingly unite the efforts of those who prefer to preserve it, with all its inequalities and vested privileges. The demonstration and clarification of such connections in concrete cases present a vast and rewarding program for inquiry.

F. *The Destruction of the World in Phenomenology*

Perhaps the strangest adventure experienced by the world occurred in the realm of phenomenology. One of the sections in Husserl's *Ideas* is entitled "The Destruction [*Vernichtung*] of the World." This amazing incident was not caused by nuclear explosions. It was due entirely to the flexible use of language, and a certain amount of pardonable enthusiasm on the part of Husserl. The context in which the destruction occurs consists of an elaborate analysis of the phenomenological method, which requires a reduction to pure conscious experiences. The reduction involves the suspension of all judgments of existence and validity. It follows that the existence of the world must be placed in question, and that it be bracketed. That is not real destruction. The judgment that there is an existent world is suspended. The world is then a meant objectivity, for the purposes of the method. The entire progress of Husserl's thought, and his general exposition, make this clear, even though he may at times be tempted to overstate his case and proceed to an ontology. Strictly speaking, he is committed to a procedure of descriptive analysis, and he should not allow himself to advance arguments designed to instate an idealistic metaphysics. The text of his *Ideas* betrays this weakness often enough to prove that Husserl never freed himself from all antecedent, philosophical commitments, despite his claims of neutrality and evidence. Be that as it may, the world was never really destroyed in phenomenology. But the world became a problem nevertheless, a problem of constitutive phenomenology. Incautious readers of Husserl who are prone to repeat a confusion of which the master was guilty even in his first book *(Philosophie der Arithmetik)* may fail to distinguish the constitution of meanings from the constitution of real objects. In phenomenology, it is a central aim to show how more complex meanings are built up out of simpler meanings. The world, as a complex meaning, is to be accounted for on the basis of direct experience, within the framework of a purely reflective procedure. It is important to make it clear that the "world-problem" of phenomenology is a problem of the organization of pure experience, treated as detached from its natural setting in existence. It is a problem of the constitution of meaning. To mistake it for the construction of the real world would be as grotesque as to suppose that the mightiest of giants, the phenomenologist, actually destroys the real world. How this misunderstanding affected Max Scheler will be seen in the next chapter.

CHAPTER VIII

Human Existence and its Interpretation

A. *Man in the Tradition of Philosophy*

Like the world, man has been portrayed in a variety of forms. Does the conception of man conform to the conception of the world, or is the reverse the case? A correlation between them cannot be established in so obvious a way. The point is, however, that there is some degree of correlation between ideas of man and ideas of the world. Man changes himself more rapidly than the world of nature could possibly do it. Changes in ideas are most rapid of all, and they go along with social changes, both as causal factors and as effects.

It is understandable that the depreciation of man was institutionalized in the finitistic medieval world, where the scourging of the flesh was a natural consequence of the doctrine of the decrepitude of the body. The rehabilitation of the flesh was one of the avowed objectives of philosophers heralding the great French Revolution. The consciousness of the endless perfectibility of man is characteristic of the eighteenth-century French philosophers, and also of the modern period in its expanding stages. The depreciation of man becomes a more conspicuous theme and trend in a contracting era, with greater emphasis on his irrational aspects, and a rapidly growing awareness of psychological and psychiatric problems.

Oversimplification must be avoided. The ways in which ideas are related to cultural changes may not be simple and direct. The causal situation is complicated by a great many circumstances. In the transition from one social system to another, there is not a complete change, socially or culturally. Many past intellectual and religious ideas tend to survive, or to be gradually adapted to the new conditions. Some of the established interests of the old regime continue to find a place for themselves. A feudally descended privileged group of a given country may retain a place in the modern commercial structure, and continue to defend its past ideology. Religious history provides a prime illustration of the survival of institutions in modern commercial society, with the greatest possible preservation of ideas and traditions. But even they are compelled to change in response to new conditions; and the emergence of new religious forms in the modern world can be traced directly to social-historical changes. Although the official views on man may not change, it becomes necessary to take account of the new types of men who have emerged. Thus, the right of the worker to live in at least modest comfort has been recognized, while consigning the poor to the generous care of the rich. But man remains a lowly creature, and to err is considered quite human, with the good offices of an organized religious institution required for his salvation. If the body is corrupt, death cannot be an evil. Some later forms of development show a greater degree of influence of scientific thought, all the way to religious humanism, which places the greatest emphasis on human values and happiness. The coexistence of many different forms of religious tradition in the same social system calls for special explanation, and can only be satisfactorily accounted for when psychological factors have been considered along with social motivation and the interest of the various traditions in preserving themselves.

Hobbes, writing in the seventeenth century, saw man as impelled by a continuous lust for power which ceases only in death. One rode armed, lest he be attacked; doors and chests were locked, to avoid theft; etc. Sovereignty was, however, "from below," conferred by the people on a sovereign; and man, as one body among other bodies, was the maker and material of the great Leviathan.

In terms that were to become familiar to all Americans, Locke spoke of the inalienable rights of all individual men to life, liberty, and the pursuit of happiness. The interest in the rights of the individual is characteristic of the beginning of the modern period, and of every new bourgeois society. It is in direct contrast to the authoritarianism of the feudal-ecclesiastical tradition, in which the very status of the individual is a philosophical problem. In the modern period, the justification of sovereignty is a problem—an initial problem, that is to say. The new man, capable of carrying through the industrial revolution, is first seen in England, and it is in England that his philosophical justification and the explanation of his psychological nature are attempted. The nature of man is sketched repeatedly, all the way to Bentham and Mill. The self-seeking man of Hobbes is finally subordinated to the principle of the greatest good of the greatest number, following Bentham's introduction of his calculus of pleasures. But even the subsequent invention of adding machines and modern experimental devices for measuring human reactions would have done little to support his theory.[1]

The evolutionary movement of the nineteenth century undertook to reduce man to nature, with man depicted as the highest development of the animal kingdom. Despite the strong opposition encountered, the evolutionary philosophy steadily gained ground and made a place for itself as a support for the competitive social system, national and international. The "risen animal," the man of evolution, was in competition with his fellows in the struggle for existence; and what has held true of individuals was applied on a larger scale to conflicts among countries. The "less fit" went down in the struggle (or, rather, they were "less fit" because they went down in the struggle), and it was said to be better that they should disappear. Mankind should not become soft and decline. This type of philosophy, called pseudoevolutionism by the present writer and also known as Social Darwinism, had its vogue in the closing decades of the nineteenth century and early in the twentieth century. The fact that it persisted somewhat after World War I, which sounded the notice of the end of a long period of expansion, is simply evidence of cultural lag. Carver's *Essays in Social Justice* (1915) is an illustration of the pseudoevolutionary literature contributed to by many writers. The ruthlessly competitive man of pseudoevolutionism was one of the last products of the expansionist era. This was just as much a reflection of social realities as William James's pluralism was a metaphysical response to the need for a view of the world which would provide a place for risk and adventure.

The influence of the various religious traditions throughout the modern period, and their close relationship to many philosophers, accounts for views of man in opposition to the scientific and evolutionary writers. The reduction of man to nature has been hotly disputed, by philosophers as well as by theologians. Reductionism has practically become a name for a fallacy. But the real,

[1] Cf. the following chapter for a discussion of hedonism.

historical meaning of the evolutionary reduction of man to nature (or the assimilation of man to nature) need not be rendered fallaciously or crudely. If there can be no reality outside space and time, and if everything in space and time is in nature, it follows that the idea of a "supernature" must be dismissed as baseless. The reduction to physical nature is in question, and the doctrine of levels is a warning against oversimplification. Since there are materialistic anti-reductionists, representing the strongest form of materialism, we cannot conclude that the opposition to an oversimplified reductionism was solely the historical achievement of scholars deriving from the idealistic tradition.

The theory of emergent evolution, with its ascending levels of development, provides for the future emergence of a deity. In other words, God is not yet an existing being, so that there is no divine responsibility for the evils of existence. Man apparently has a great future for emergent evolution, in the direction of the higher level to come, so that this view belongs to the expanding period. It appears to be a more moderate development of evolutionism, which bridges the gap between science and religion. Despite the occurrence of two world wars and what may justifiably be called the age of perpetual war, emergent evolution has nothing more to say of further higher development, other than to repeat its general, speculative prediction that something higher is to emerge—a vacuous prediction so far as any present evidence is concerned.

Philosophers have always expressed themselves in terms of the means at hand, and with an eye to cultural and political realities. Thus Spinoza, himself a liberal in all departments of practical thinking, subordinated everything to the concept of God, in a pantheistic scheme. Man is a limited part of an infinite substance, and he is enjoined to achieve a vision of the whole, with all things viewed under the aspect of eternity. Spinoza's man does all that he can do in the seventeenth century. Above all, he loves and he cannot hate God. He belongs to no party, and is not aligned with any social forces. In short, he is a detached Hollander of the seventeenth century, with no prospects; and if he is not particularly interested in the poor and suffering, neither does he have colonial ambitions. Unfortunately for the total representation of Spinoza's man, it must be observed that woman was not his equal (cf. the closing portion of his *Tractatus*). This will be disappointing to the admirers of "Blessed Spinoza" who have not troubled to read his text. Like so many before and after him, Spinoza was a son of his time, and woman was still far from being accorded equality, even potentially.

Kant also chose what would seem to us today a devious route for the declaration of the dignity of man. The moral man was for Kant the ultimate purpose of nature. In this sense, man is in God through all eternity; man is an innate son and not a created thing. It will be recalled that Kant was suppressed by the Prussian censorship. His doctrine of human worth, which forbade making man a mere means to an end, was in accord with the most advanced social thought at the close of the eighteenth century.

The general theme of the nature of man was thus given expression in widely different ways. If there was no general agreement, neither was there a simple structure of society. The ways in which ideas are causally conditioned must be traced above all to the nature of the social reality.

One further expansionist view of man remains to be considered. It is the view of Marx and Engels and their followers, and will be called the Marxian conception of man. Marx was specifically interested in the working class, and in man as a worker under any conditions. The progressive man in Marx's view was the man who endeavored to inaugurate a classless society, which meant, essentially, a society of productive workers. Avowedly a materialist, and closely linked with the positive findings of the evolutionists, man is viewed by him as the product of a long process of biological and social development. Darwin's work excited Marx's interest and admiration.[2] The work of Lewis H. Morgan in the field of ethnology was also welcomed warmly, and Engels integrated it with the Marxian view in his *Origin of the Family, Private Property, and the State*. In view of the fact that the leading evolutionary philosophers Spencer and Huxley accepted a society with class distinctions, just as Comte had done before them, the Marxists constituted a completely separate movement. It is a curious fact that evolutionism, with its conception of gradual development, should have become a support for ruthless competition.

The Marxian view of man is a thoroughly naturalistic conception, in opposition to supernaturalism. Man is depicted as bound to nature by his process of work, which in Marx's view (as set forth in his *Capital*) is the everlasting nature-imposed condition of

[2] Cf. W. Liebknecht, *Karl Marx, Biographical Memoirs* (Chicago: Charles H. Kerr and Co., 1901).

human existence, with the earth man's original tool house. The importance of tools is emphasized in the self-transforming process in which man is engaged throughout all history.[3] It is fundamental to the Marxian view that, before all else, man must secure a livelihood, so that economic relations determine man in important respects. Social relations and cultural traditions are held to be conditioned by the basic economic structure of society. The economic structure, in turn, is to some extent affected by cultural factors, so that a one-way economic determinism is ruled out, at least by Marx and Engels themselves. These are among the general theses of man involved in the Marxian conception. There is unquesonably a Marxian theory of man, even though Marx's greatest interest was in historical types of men. Once the goal of a classless society is achieved, in his view, all efforts should be directed toward the more secure mastery over nature and the enhancement of human happiness. As a revolutionary doctrine, it is expansionistic; but it remains expansionistic in its more ultimate intentions. There are no ontological, psychological, or social-political reasons why it should cease to be applicable at any time. This point is of some importance, in view of the frequently expressed interest in what can follow the achievement of a classless society.

Modern society in its contracting stages presents an especially complex problem for analysis, so far as the philosophy of man is concerned. In recent years, the growing prominence of philosophical anthropology and existentialism has indicated a shift in emphasis, with a tendency toward withdrawal or renunciation of the world. In a complex society, there are bound to be diverse and conflicting modes of participation. There is also a variety of modes of renunciation, some of them not easily recognized as such. For example, if the Occident is doomed, for fundamental organic and historical reasons, then there is nothing to be done about it. If the status of man is depreciated, renunciation of the world is the only outcome. A forlorn man with a primitive experience of anguish, a being thrown into this world, is hardly motivated to participate in changing the world. Far from being interested in human progress, he can only look to a mysterious transcendence for his ultimate needs—a theme now prominent in the literature of existentialism.

The social sciences, on the other hand, exhibit their own pecu-

---

[3] Cf. F. Engels, *Dialectics of Nature* (New York: International Publishers, 1940).

liar modes of adaptation to the tendency toward contraction. To fail to see the forest because of the trees has been a familiar pattern for many writers on social science. This is suggested by the local area studies which have been favored by cultural anthropologists, whereas broad generalizations about human development have been viewed with suspicion. A social worker may be interested in particular needy individuals, but not in the broad problems of distribution of wealth and the socioeconomic structure of society. Positivism in social science may become a means of avoiding causal analysis, and of missing the crucial social problems.

In philosophy this tendency has been carried to the extreme by logical positivists, who as a matter of methodological principle did not talk about reality, and whose self-imposed restriction to logical forms and procedures removed the philosopher from active participation in the affairs of society. Nonparticipation is in effect renunciation.

It is now pertinent to review the place of man in the cosmos from the evolutionary perspective, in juxtaposition to the effort to elevate man by way of a kind of ontological emancipation from the natural world, as attempted in recent philosophical anthropology.

B. *The Place of Man in the Cosmos*

We are accustomed to thinking of the process of organic evolution as a long one, involving hundreds of millions of years. Man is a result of development within the animal kingdom, rather than a being who has been thrown or has fallen into this world. The evolution of the earth is a long process when compared with the recency of human existence. But it is in turn a brief episode when compared with the evolution of our galaxy. How far back can one go in his reflection? Suppose we think of the more remote past, say a trillion times the age of our galaxy. That is a very long time for us. For the cosmos it is merely a passing state, preceded by a beginningless, infinite process, just as it is to be succeeded by an endless, infinite process. There may be no earth in the remote future, but there will be other organizations and distributions of matter.

The great evolutionary movement of the nineteenth century regarded man as a part of nature, while recognizing the importance of cultural development. There were no special prerogatives of man, no faculties or metaphysical principles which raised him above the subject matters of the various special sciences. Naturalism displaced supernaturalism in the theory of human existence. Although philosophical criticism had long before anticipated this result, it was the large array of scientific evidence offered by Darwin which delivered the most distressing blow to the supernaturalists. Despite Darwin's own cautious attitude, the full impact of his work was felt quickly, and was largely made effective through the writings of the evolutionary philosophers Spencer, Huxley, Fiske, and Haeckel. The evolutionary concept was applied to human development by Morgan, whose significance for ethnology parallels that of Darwin and Spencer for biology. Morgan, who lived in Rochester, New York, made extensive studies of the American Indians, and attempted a systematic evolutionary formulation of human development in his famous book on *Ancient Society*. Although some of his assumptions have been subject to criticism, his perspective on the emergence and disappearance of private property has been welcomed by Marxists. For present purposes, however, it is sufficient to indicate the place of man in the cosmos as seen by Haeckel.

In his *Riddle of the Universe* (1899), Haeckel criticized the fallacy of anthropism—"that powerful and worldwide group of erroneous opinions which opposes the human organism to the whole of the rest of nature, and represents it to be the preordained end of the organic creation, an entity essentially distinct from it, a godlike being." Three different dogmas are involved: (1) The anthropocentric dogma culminates in the idea that man is the preordained center and aim of all life, or of the universe, which is in line with the Mosaic, Christian, and Mohammedan theologies. (2) The anthropomorphic dogma, which is also connected with the creation myth, regards the creation and control of the world as similar to the artificial creation of an engineer or mechanic, or the administration of a wise ruler. God is conceived to have made man to His own image and likeness. The older, naïve mythology is pure "homotheism"; the gods have flesh and blood. That is more intelligible, in Haeckel's opinion, than the modern mystic theosophy "that adores a personal God as an invisible—properly speaking, gaseous—being, yet makes him think, speak, and act in human fashion; it gives us the paradoxical picture of a 'gaseous vertebrate.'" (3) The anthropolatric dogma (anthropolatry meaning "a divine worship of human nature") results from the comparison of the activity of God and man, and ends in the apotheosis of the human organism. A further result is the belief in the personal immortality of the soul, and a dualistic dogma of the nature of man.

This anthropistic view was opposed by the monistic view of Haeckel, who believed that the cosmological perspective of his monistic system would sweep such errors away. Haeckel enumerated a number of cosmological theorems which expressed very well the evolutionary perspective of the late nineteenth century: (1) The universe, or the cosmos, is eternal, infinite, and illimitable. (2) Its substance, with its two attributes (matter and energy), fills infinite space, and is in eternal motion. (3) This motion runs on through infinite time as an unbroken development, with a periodic change from life to death, from evolution to devolution. (4) The innumerable bodies which are scattered about the "space-filling ether" all obey the same "law of substance"; while the rotating masses slowly move toward their destruction and dissolution in one part of space, others are springing into new life and development in other quarters of the universe. (5) Our sun is one of these unnumbered perishable bodies, and our earth is one of the countless transitory planets that encircle them. (6) Our earth has gone through a long process of cooling before water, in liquid form (the first condition of organic life), could settle thereon. (7) The ensuing biogenetic process, the slow development and transformation of countless organic forms, must have taken many millions of years—considerably over a hundred. (8) The vertebrates outstripped all other competitors in the evolutionary race, in the later stages of the biogenetic process. (9) The most important branch of vertebrates, the mammals, developed later (during the Triassic period) from the lower amphibia and the reptilia. (10) The most perfect and highly developed branch of the class mammalia is the order of primates, first appearing by development from the lowest prochordiata at the beginning of the Tertiary period—at least three million years ago. (11) The youngest and most perfect twig of the branch primates is man, who sprang from a branch of manlike apes toward the end of the Tertiary period. (12) Consequently, the so-called world history —i.e., the brief period of a few thousand years which measures the duration of civilization—is an evanescently short episode in the long course of organic evolution, just as this, in turn, is merely a small portion of the history of our planetary system; and as our mother earth is a mere speck in the sunbeam in the illimitable universe, so man himself is but a tiny grain of protoplasm in the perishable framework of organic nature.

This summary was intended by Haeckel to give man's true place in nature, and to dissipate the illusion of man's supreme importance. His book was not well received by fideists of any kind, including professional philosophers. Professor Friedrich Paulsen said that he read it "with burning shame," and expressed indignation that the book was so widely read by a people having a Kant, a Goethe, and a Schopenhauer. Professor Adickes, a well-known expert on the philosophy of Kant, declared Haeckel to be a philosophical nonentity. He had to contend with "venomous attacks on his person and work" and "storms of painful obloquy" (in the words of Joseph McCabe).[4] It has been a rather common professional sport to single out the scientific weaknesses in Haeckel's book. His monism of substance and numerous scientific statements must admittedly be dated. The critics of Haeckel have, however, largely failed to do justice to the living and historically important aspects of his work. He was able to draw significant consequences from the concept of evolution while professional philosophers were still debating the extent to which the mind conditions reality, and even whether there is a reality apart from the mind.

C. Human Existence and Philosophical Anthropolgy

Attempts of various kinds were made to stem the rising tide of evolutionary naturalism, and scientific philosophy in general. This was a primary motive of philosophical idealists at the close of the nineteenth century and in the first part of the twentieth. Members of diverse tendencies and schools, who were normally at war with one another or otherwise engaged in internecine doctrinal strife, were in unison in opposing the naturalistic conception of man and his works. Prominent among the German philosophers were Rickert, Eucken, Dilthey, Simmel, Weber, and Husserl; and similar reactions against naturalism were to be seen in other countries. In the United States Howison and Hocking may be cited as examples.

Husserl's collaborator and follower, Max Scheler, was pre-eminent among the anti-naturalists. Scheler's philosophical anthropol-

---

[4] Cf. W. Bölsche, *Haeckel, His Life and Work* (Philadelphia: George W. Jacobs & Co., 1906), pp. 320 f.

ogy was designed to provide an alternative to the theory of man of the special sciences which would be acceptable to fideists. He was a most determined critic of the evolutionary theory; and he extended the arena of his critical activities to include Marx and Freud. The sociology of knowledge which he did so much to popularize is an example of the adaptation of Marxian thought which has found a place in academic circles. For years an ardent spokesman of Catholic thought (Scheler had a Catholic period), he was also in some respects an ideological precursor of the Nazis.[5] Fortunately for himself, however, he died before the accession to power of the Nazis.

In his book on *The Place of Man in the Cosmos*,[6] Scheler presents a summary of the main points of his philosophical anthropology. The questions "What is man?" and "What is his place in being?" are central for Scheler. He points out that the problems of a philosophical anthropology had become of central importance in Germany in wide circles, including that of philosophical scientists. In his opinion, the existing degree to which man had become a problem for himself had reached a maximum in all known history. He states that the "mighty treasures" of the special sciences must be utilized to develop a new form of self-consciousness and self-intuition. That Scheler was not the person to attempt to use those "treasures" is amply shown by his text, here as well as elsewhere.

Scheler reflects: If one asks an educated European what he understands by the word man, three sets of incompatible ideas occur to him, deriving from the Jewish-Christian tradition, from ancient Greece (reason, the logos, etc.), and from modern natural science and genetic psychology. Thus there is a theological, a philosophical, and a natural-scientific anthropology, but, Scheler declares, we do not have a unified idea of man. This is a strange conclusion. The scientific view supersedes the others, as a matter of fact, and it is really unified, unless one injects a special requirement of unity into the discussion which cannot be fulfilled scientifically. Scheler betrays his misgivings. In his opinion, the ever growing number of special sciences which are concerned with man conceal the essence of man more than they illuminate it. He seems to be playing an assumptive game with the term essence. Is

---
[5] Cf. V. J. McGill, "Scheler's Theory of Sympathy and Love," *Philosophy and Phenomenological Research*, II (March, 1942).
[6] *Die Stellung des Menschen im Kosmos* (Darmstadt: Otto Reichl Verlag, 1928).

the essence of man predetermined as something different from the findings of the sciences? Presumably it must be something which no microscope or chemical tests can reach, and which no descriptive observations can ascertain. Scheler states that all three views of man cited above are greatly shaken, and that the Darwinian solution of the problem of the origin of man has been completely discredited.[7] This is hopeful thinking on his part. Scheler's interest is in the essence of man in relation to animals and plants, and in a special metaphysical place for man.

The problem of determining man's special place requires that the meaning of man be defined appropriately. For Scheler, the term man must not be used to name the special characteristics possessed by men as a subgroup of vertebrates and mammals. It seems clear that the concept of man is treated assumptively from the outset, so that man is irreducible to nature. According to the traditional conception, the concept of man as the image of God presupposes the idea of God as a central point of reference. This concept of man, which is designated the essential view of man, is declared by Scheler to have a totally different meaning from the natural-scientific conception. Whether this essential concept of man—which assigns a special place to man as such in contradistinction to all other living species—has any right at all, is the theme of Scheler's discourse. His opposition to the view of man which is determined by the special sciences indicates his motivation clearly.

For Scheler, there is a new principle which makes man to be man, a principle which is opposed to life in general and which cannot be reduced to the natural evolution of life. The term spirit names this principle. It is supposed to comprise the concept of reason, the intuition of essences, goodness, and love. The act-center in which spirit appears within finite spheres of being is called a person, in contrast to all functional life centers, which are called mental centers, viewed from within. In Scheler's view, man alone, insofar as he is a person, is able to rise above himself as a living being, and from a center as it were beyond the space-time world, to make everything, including himself, the object of his knowledge. But this center cannot be a part of this world, Scheler maintains, and hence it cannot have a definite locus in space and

---

[7] Scheler's anti-evolution is set forth in some detail in his book, *Der Formalismus in der Ethik und die materiale Wertethik* (Halle: Verlag Niemeyer, 1913-1916). Cf. M. Farber, *Naturalism and Subjectivism* (Springfield, Ill. Charles C. Thomas, 1959), Chap. VIII.

time. It can only be situated in "the highest ground of being." Thus, man is portrayed as an essence supervening upon himself and the world. But Scheler does not in the least justify his contention that man's center of activity is not a part of the world. The reader must reconcile himself as best he can to the thought of a real being without a locus in space and time. If he is accustomed to using words without bothering to inspect their meanings, he will perhaps go along with such expressions as "beyond space and time," just as he will think he is making a significant statement when he speaks of the highest ground of being.

Like his predecessors in the idealistic tradition—Schelling, for example—Scheler regards spirit as the only being that is itself not capable of being an object. It is construed as pure actuality, and as having its being only in the performance of its acts. The center of spirit, the person, is therefore neither being as an object nor as a thing, but only an essentially determined, ordered structure of acts. Other persons are also not capable of being objects. We must "post-perform" and "co-perform" their free acts, and identify ourselves with the willing, the love, etc., of a person. This line of thought leads readily to the "one supersingular spirit" which, Scheler thinks, we have to assume on the basis of the unbreakable connection of "Idea" and "Act." The assumption of an order of "Ideas" independent of human consciousness is taken to require such a spiritual being. The "Ideas" are not "before the things," but are *with* the things, and are held to be generated in the eternal spirit in acts of continuous world-realization. When we think "Ideas," we do not merely find a being or essence already independent of us, but it is rather a "co-bringing-forth," a "co-generating" of the "Ideas" and of the values coordinated with eternal love, out of the "origin of the things themselves." It is a curious fact that Scheler should use expressions such as "origin" and "the things themselves" without explanation. How anything could originate from his supposed metaphysical source may properly remain a mystery. The use of the expression "the things themselves" is perhaps merely an interesting case of perseveration. It is a long way from Husserl's famous slogan, even though the same words were used. Scheler is far away from the facts of experience here, with his talk of eternal love, spirit, and generation.

In order to make more clear the peculiarity of spirit, Scheler considers the act of "ideation" as a specifically spiritual act. It is supposed by him to be an act completely different from all technical intelligence. What Scheler means by a problem of intelligence will be elucidated by an example which he gives: I now have a pain in my arm; how did it arise, and how can I get rid of it? That is a problem of positive science. But, Scheler goes on in his chosen philosophical direction, I can grasp the same pain as an example of the very strange essential condition, that this world has pain, evil, and suffering at all. Then I shall ask differently: What is pain itself, apart from the fact that I now have it here, and how must the ground of things be constituted for something such as "pain in general" to be possible? The reader will be tempted to ask whether this is an "in general" kind of question. The importance of nerves for pain would indicate that the answer is always "in particular," at least for the natural world and actual experience. To be sure, a better example could have been chosen, and the performance could have been more skillfully executed.

"Ideation" is taken to be independent of the number of observations which we make, and of inductive inferences. The "essential forms of construction" of the world are grasped in one example of the region of essence which is in question. The knowledge that we thus gain is regarded as holding in infinite generality for all possible things which are of this essence. Such insights are taken to be valid "beyond the limit of our sensuous experience" and to be *a priori*. Scheler sees such "essential knowledge" as fulfilling two different functions: (1) It is said to provide the highest axioms for all the positive sciences, which first of all show us the direction of a fruitful observation, induction, and deduction through intelligence and discursive thinking. Scheler does not justify this bold, empty contention. That concepts are used in hypotheses will be agreed to by all, but no scientific methodologist would think of calling them *a priori* in Scheler's sense. Investigators in the positive sciences do not look to the alleged highest axioms for the direction of their observation. (2) There is the function for metaphysics, whose final goal is described as knowledge of absolute being. They are described in Hegel's words, as "windows to the absolute." Denying that essences can be reduced to empirical causes of a finite kind, Scheler argues that they can only be ascribed to the "one supersingular spirit." He is quite sure of that, but gives no evidence for his view; his procedure is simply to speak, or to write, depending upon the circumstances.

Scheler speaks of Plato's vision of "Ideas" as turning the soul away from the sensuous content of things and into itself, in order to find the "origins" of things. This he takes to be the meaning of Husserl's procedure when he connects the knowledge of "Ideas" to a phenomenological reduction. Scheler refers here to the procedure of "crossing out" or "bracketing" the accidental coefficient of existence of world-things, in order to gain their "essentia." While not in complete agreement with Husserl's theory of the reduction, Scheler asserts that in it the act is meant which really defines the human spirit. Scheler's conception of the phenomenological reduction appears to be crude and incorrect. He seems not to have grasped its real methodological nature, and to be viewing it in accordance with his own standpoint and needs. A rather objectionable mystical product results from his exegesis, which comes close to the misunderstanding that the reduction involves the discarding of reality. Thus, Scheler asks what it means to speak of "derealizing" (or "deactualizing") or "ideating" the world. He disagrees with Husserl's view, that it means withholding judgments of existence; and he takes it to mean that the reality-factor itself is suspended by way of experiment, that it is annihilated, and that the "fear of the mundane" is set aside therewith. It is evident from his text that Scheler sees something that is correct, and that he even catches a glimpse of the play of a method; but also that his antecedently accepted articles of faith and the firm drift of his philosophical persuasion lead him to talk of annihilation and emancipation from the "fear of the mundane." He presents a quaint figure in his endeavor to wreck and remove worlds without an instrument. Scheler talks of the ascetic act of "derealization," and states that, if existence is resistance, it can only consist in the suspension of that life-drive, in relation to which the world above all appears as resistance, and which at the same time is the condition of all sense perception of the accidental here-now-thus. But, in his view, this act can only be performed by that being called spirit. Only spirit in its form as pure will can effect the inactualizing of the "feeling-drive-center" that Scheler regards as the mode of access to the "being real" of the real. Man thus turns out to be the living being that can be ascetic toward its life. Although Husserl's methodological terms "putting out of play," "suspension," "accidental here-now-thus," etc., are used, there is little evidence of descriptive analysis. The admonition of the founder of modern phenomenology, to begin with the suspension of all beliefs in the interest of a radical philosophy of knowledge and experience, is certainly not illustrated by Scheler. He has shown how easy it is to adapt the general phenomenological pattern to theological uses. Such practices—annihilating the world, asceticism toward life, the assumptive use of the term spirit and its transformation into "pure will" when needed, and the like—could best be obviated by a proper appraisal of the truth of naturalism or materialism, which means, on the basis of a science-oriented philosophy.

Life and spirit are conceived by Scheler as essentially different, and yet related. Spirit is said to "ideate" life, whereas life alone enables spirit to get into activity and to realize works. Scheler criticizes the naturalistic theories, both mechanistic and vitalistic, for mistaking the relationship of spirit and life. They are accused of overlooking the essence of life in its peculiar nature and the peculiar structure of its laws, and of completely missing the "originalness" and independence of the spirit.

Marx is mentioned under the heading of the "naturalistic-vitalistic" types, and Scheler refers to his critique of Marx's historical materialism in his "Sociology of Knowledge."[8] His brief rendering of Marx's thesis is as inadequate as his rendering of Husserl proved to be, and just as misleading. Marx is quoted as talking about "Ideas that have no interest and passion back of them"—and that means, states Scheler, powers which come from the "vital-and-drive sphere of man."

As for himself, Scheler is optimistic with regard to history. In his view, history in the large shows an increase in the role of reason, by way of an increasing acquisition of "Ideas" and values. He looks to philosophical anthropology to provide the basis for a philosophy of history and of culture. It is assigned the task of showing how, out of the basic structure of man, all specific contributions and works of man go forth—language, tools, ideas of right and wrong, the state, myths, religion, science, etc. The basic structure of man is obviously to be treated apart from its naturalistic and cultural conditions, since all naturalistic theories have been renounced. And yet, everything that is known by way of the special sciences and the much despised naturalistic theories must be packed away, in an appropriately frozen essential state, in order to make possible the "going forth" of the "works of man." Only a well-stocked hat ever allowed a rabbit to "go forth" from it. It

[8] M. Scheler, "Soziologie des Wissens," in *Die Wissensformen und die Gesellschaft* (Leipzig: Der Neue Geist Verlag, 1926).

is simply dishonest to renounce naturalistic procedures and then to make use of them covertly.

The question about man's place in the cosmos leads Scheler to ask finally: "Why is there a world at all, and how am 'I' at all?" The reader will reflect that not every string of words constitutes a real question. Presumably Scheler would not refer his question "How am 'I' at all?" to an obstetrician. His line of thought and his theological interests lead him in quite a different direction. He states that one should apprehend the essential necessity of the connection between the consciousness of the world, the self, and the consciousness of God, whereby God is apprehended here as a "being through itself" with the predicate "holy." This sphere of absolute being, whether it is accessible or not to experience or knowing, is regarded as belonging to the essence of man just as constitutively as his self-consciousness and world-consciousness. World-consciousness, self-consciousness, and God-consciousness are held to form an indissoluble unity of structure. Scheler regards the "world-ground" as being in man, as immediately apprehended and realized in man.

What has Scheler contributed toward determining man's place in the cosmos? To some extent he has contributed novelty: in degree and kind of obfuscation, in manner of crudeness in misrepresenting phenomenology, naturalistic theories, and Marxism. But also, curiously, there is novelty in the way in which he seems able to recognize significant ideas which might be made fruitful if treated subject to the canons of logic and on the basis of the sciences. As matters stand, Scheler presents a sorry, confused, and eminently unworthy picture in his attack on scientific philosophy, as well as in his dogmatic defense of selected articles of faith.

D. *The Philosophy of Existence*

The name existential philosophy, or philosophy of existence, does not refer to existence in the generally understood, naturalistic sense. There is a special terminology for existentialism, which quickly betrays its metaphysical leanings. Thus, in one of its varieties, being is distinguished from existence, which involves consciousness. An individual is in a world to begin with. That is very good, of course, but everything depends upon the way in which the world is defined. The existentialist attempts to get back to that which is most primitive. The critical reader will be interested in ascertaining what such an attempt could possibly gain, just as he will be interested in establishing its motivation. It seems to have much promise in the existentialist philosophy. There is an air of radicalism about it, of probing to depths hitherto missed, supposedly screened from us by the concepts of contemporary science and philosophy.

What kind of world is it in which one makes his appearance as a philosopher? The answer is the same world as for the scientist, the politician, or the coal miner: a world in which there are conflicts, obstacles to be overcome, and problems to be solved. There are no inaccessible depths to be probed.

As already shown, the existent world should not be contrasted with a world of being. Existence means having a locus in physical reality, and that includes physical, organic, and social or cultural events. All of them exist in this sense. Of course, more is to be discerned in organic and cultural events than is allowed for on the physical level, in the selective sense in which the term is now used. This is important in accounting for differences of viewpoint arising from cultural causes.

Human beings have different attitudes and points of view. It is misleading to make them the core of the concept of the "existential." That is to play fast and loose with idealism, without resorting to the usual supporting arguments. The differences of attitude and point of view are to be accounted for causally, without neglecting relevant factors on any of the levels of organization—physical, organic, or cultural.

Existentialism, which takes attitudes toward existence as structural finalities, avoids causal explanations, and gives the impression of scorning them. A truly descriptive view of attitudes and of interpretations of existence is not opposed to causal analysis. It is misleading to have what purports to be a descriptive view function as something superior to causal analysis. The methods for determining causes are themselves descriptive. Hence it is simply pretentious to speak of rising above or digging beneath the methods of causal analysis and of scientific description. The most important features of natural reality are apt to be lost thereby, which is precisely what has happened in much of the literature on existentialism.

Man partakes of all the known levels of existence. May one

abstract from the physical and the biological levels when considering human existence? That is impossible because of the dependence of human needs and interests upon them; and also because of the physically and biologically conditioned needs themselves. Man is the meeting place of existential problems of all kinds. The special sciences are concerned with existential problems on each of the levels. Are there any peculiarly philosophical existential problems? The inspection of human attitudes toward existence, including human existence and its place in the world, may be undertaken by a cultural anthropologist, or by a psychologist. What has philosophy to say?

There are subjectivistic and objectivistic answers to this question. The purely reflective procedure of phenomenology is designed to view all things in detachment from our beliefs and explanations. Its descriptive analysis is carried through in a framework distinct from that of the special sciences, which operate with the natural view of the world. If the phenomenologist neglects or improperly weights the importance of such natural factors as the material conditions of life, he is doomed to a sterile and pointless performance. The existential approaches of Heidegger and Jaspers may be viewed as understandable developments of subjectivism. A comparison with the objectivistic procedures of scientists and naturalistic philosophers, when they treat of man's place in nature and in history, and of the interaction between ideas and social-historical conditions, brings out the basic differences. Since a procedure is always devised in relation to a problem, or a group of problems, it is essential to bear in mind the motivating problems for each type.

The conditions that influence ideas, the way in which man changes himself as he changes the world, the explanation of the patterns of ideas of a class or of an individual—these are leading problems for objectivistic inquiry. Philosophers should undertake to make their contribution in cooperation with special scientists. A reflective procedure is needed, which sees the reflecting scholar himself as socially and historically conditioned. It is a naturalistic type of reflection, and it is based upon the findings and the principles of the special sciences. The logical or methodological problems, as well as the problems of synthesis, clarification of basic ideas, and the instatement of values, all fall to philosophy.

The procedure of naturalistic reflection is regarded as naïve by subjectivists, in the sense that there are unexamined assumptions. While radical in his way, Husserl was himself naïve with respect to human society and history. He knew very little about the positive findings of social scientists and objectivistic philosophers, and he was really not very much interested in socioeconomic problems. He was interested in a nontemporal ("supertemporal") order which he extolled as being above the lowly mundane order of problems. Even his treatment of intellectual history in one of his most mature writings[9] was detached from the realities of history. Philosophical positions and issues which were merely so much routine material for his lectures and discussions for a half century finally assumed the role of decisive historical forces in the modern period. Apart from that, the concept of essence, to which the pure reflective procedure of phenomenological subjectivism is restricted, serves to remove the subjective realm from the existing world.

The subjectivistic limitations of phenomenology brought on efforts to correct them within the fold of the idealistic and fideistic traditions. Existence had to be dealt with, or at least the word existence had to be brought to the forefront of interest. The extravagant claim has been made that the problems of existence and of being were at least lost sight of until recent existentialists called attention to them. Heidegger has been given credit for deepening the understanding of these problems, despite the unusual amount of plodding necessary to extract meanings from a frequently opaque text. The results are largely disappointing and unsatisfactory. Banal platitudes are dressed up to serve as profundities; sweeping generalizations (such as care as a fundamental feature of existence, and the role of the idea of death) are foisted upon the reader as absolute verities, with no attempt at critical justification; and linguistic turns, whether subtle or outrageous, are trumpeted as philosophical advances. The persistent fog and the awkward difficulty of the text seem to have the function of protecting the small amount of thought and magnifying its importance. There are presumably hidden depths which are not to be plumbed by the nonexistentialist eye. In its long history, human existence has had its trials and tribulations, not the least of them being such interpretations of existence.

[9] Cf. E. Husserl, *Die Krisis der europäischen Wissenschaften und die transzendentale Phänomenologie*, ed. W. Biemel (The Hague: Martinus Nijhoff, 1954).

E. Existence and Value

The predicates that are proper to existence in general do not include value. As Professor R. B. Perry stated it,[10] nature is devoid of value without the bias of life. It must be pointed out that value in the human sense is meant here. If the term is used more broadly and is given ontological significance, as is done by Whitehead and Alexander,[11] for example, that must be carefully pointed out. At best, however, the usage is unfortunate and misleading. It would be much better to invent or use different terms for the purposes of a general ontology. If one speaks of value in a cosmic sense, and supposes that value is being realized in nature, he is talking about something quite different than human happiness or unhappiness.

It may seem too drastic to hold that existence is devoid of value; to some that may be to deprive it of its very essence. It is necessary first of all to make clear the meaning of value. Like so many other philosophical terms, this term is notorious for its ambiguity. There are objective characteristics and subjective factors to be noted. Value is only meaningful in its reference to living beings; and it is of greatest interest to us in its reference to human beings. To speak of the bias of life is to name a fundamental truth that does not apply to inanimate nature. If one thinks of the earth before the emergence of life, there can be no talk of the fulfillment of interests, of the satisfaction of the need for food, and of the preservation and enhancement of life. Where there is no life, there can be none of the values of life. Is it possible to look back at that remote period, including the period preceding the origin of the earth, and to assert that nature must be good if it eventuated in living things? Such judgments must be declared to fall outside the system of proper ethical judgments. If living is acknowledged to be a good, then it would seem that nature as a whole must be good since it results in life. But it would also appear to be evil if life disappears, perhaps in some billions of years, and if that is followed by an endless period of lifeless nature. Such total judgments about the nature of things turn out to be pointless, and to

---

[10] Cf. *The Moral Economy* (New York: Charles Scribner's Sons, 1909).
[11] Cf. A. N. Whitehead, *Adventures of Ideas* (New York: The Macmillan Co., 1933); and S. Alexander, *Beauty and Other Forms of Value* (London: Macmillan and Co., Ltd., 1933).

neutralize one another. Optimism and pessimism are restricted in their area of significance to the context of human affairs. They are properly significant with respect to the life-plans of individuals, and the values realized by social-historical groups. Human existence in general should not be judged in that way; the span is too large for the concepts involved.

In a typical value situation, there are certain objective, structural features, and there is an experiencing organism. In aesthetic enjoyment, there is the beauty of the sunset, or of the mountains; and there are the feelings of the persons enjoying them. Value in this sense is not realized unless there are human beings. That there are objective features which existed before there were any human beings is certainly true. There is no contradiction here, not even a paradox. The old question as to whether there is a sound if a tree falls in a forest in the absence of human beings to hear it is easily disposed of by pointing out its ambiguity. There is a physical sound, but not an experienced sound, as indicated by the question itself. Similarly, if the term value were taken to name the objective conditions involved, there would be value apart from human beings. But if—and this is the usual meaning, which is preferred here—relatedness to human experience and organisms is essential, there obviously cannot be human value without human beings. That does not restrict our conception of existence in any way. The patterns and qualities which inspire us with pleasure, awe, or fear, occur far more often by themselves than in relation to human beings. They are contained in nature as parts of the physical world-order; hence to deny that value inheres in nature is not to deny their reality. But they should not be called good, or even beautiful, if such concepts involve human interest or enjoyment. Different terms should be used in order to avoid confusion. If the ontological realist who applies value terms to all existence means to embrace human concepts as well, he may be charged with overextending the range of his concepts.

On the other hand, a subjective theory of value restricts unduly the range of the concept of value. Value does not consist in a feeling of satisfaction, or of enjoyment. Both the experiencing subject and the object must be present in a typical value-situation. The object need not be material. It may be ideal, as when a mathematician derives aesthetic enjoyment from the contemplation of a formal system, or the proof of a theorem. The very investigation of the mathematician, say in the theory of numbers, has moral significance as well as possible theoretical value for thought. It is morally significant in the sense that every human interest is a condition of value, as a part of a life-plan or of a cultural system, or in itself as a comparatively isolated interest. Finally, one may be interested in the analysis of subjective states; in that case, there is still a subject-object relationship. The report of that relationship (whether the object be music or a subjective state, for example) is objective if it is a correct report of the facts. It may then be general in its significance, with due allowance made for subjectivity in the account of existence.

CHAPTER IX

Approaches to a Philosophy of Values

If man's place in the cosmos and the nature of human existence are in fundamental dispute, it is understandable that there is so large a number of theories of human values. Nowhere in philosophy has there been more evidence of conflicting views, or disagreements which affect the very first definitions. Some of the difficulties encountered by philosophers in the attempt to achieve a satisfactory philosophy of values have a historical explanation. The impact of social interests and institutions is most directly felt in the field of ethical thought. Religion plays a large part in the influences; and so does one's social position.

The history of ethical philosophy nevertheless records lines of progress, even when extreme views are defended and found wanting, as in the case of hedonism. Something is gained in the process of formulating a one-sided view as a general principle of value, and in having its inadequacy pointed out in the general controversy which follows. But that there should still be survivals of such a traditional view as intuitionism, despite scientific progress, is striking. Unlike metaphysics, the philosophy of values is restricted to the finite field of human interests, so that answers to its questions should be not only possible but conveniently at hand. The situation is different in the case of authoritarian moralists who are members of a religious tradition. The authoritarian spirit was perhaps never better illustrated than by Pope John XXII, who commanded two bishops to read a book by William of Occam and condemn it.[1] The appeal to authority is an appeal to a vested power. There can be no logical defense of authoritarianism in ethics. As indicated earlier, every authority may be challenged for

---

[1] Cf. W. J. Townsend, *The Great Schoolmen of the Middle Ages* (London: Hodder and Stoughton, 1881), p. 272.

its justification, and if it must be defended it surrenders any claim to absoluteness. The grounds which support it—the superior wisdom, or power, of the alleged authority—may then be examined, and the argument turns upon questions of fact: is there such an authority in existence; and are the claims of wisdom and power really supported by facts?

On the other hand, it must be made clear that definitions of values are not arbitrary. There must be a descriptive basis for the philosophy of values, and that requires an understanding of human individuals in relation to their social system. The choice must then be made, whether human judgments of value are to be investigated, or whether values are to be considered in terms of human interests and needs, i.e., objectively. Both lines of inquiry are legitimate, but they involve different disciplines. The investigation of the judgments of value which people happen to make is a department of social science, and, while it is of great significance for philosophy, it is not a part of philosophy. The objective consideration of values in terms of human interests and needs is the way to a normative science of conduct.

A. Hedonism and the Principle of Quantity

A hedonistic theory could arise under any system of society, so long as human beings are constituted as they now are. Hedonism may be the expression of an upper-class desire to find a justification for a life devoted primarily to pleasure, as illustrated by Aristippus of Cyrene. In the hands of Bentham and Mill it becomes a larger theory, with some social implications.

The acceptance of pleasure as value does not place one in any definite position with regard to social problems. It need not be associated with a conservative view, although that has been the case historically. It has also been an element of the Epicurean philosophy, which advocated abstention from political life. The acceptance of hedonism can be combined with materialism, naturalism, socialism, or the defense of capitalism. Only those who depreciate the body, for religious or other reasons, could not allow the recognition of pleasure as a basic condition of value. In social doctrines, the concept of pleasure has served opposing forces at various times. On the eve of the French Revolution, it was used in opposition to the feudal-ecclesiastical philosophy of renunciation; and at another time, for the Epicureans, it was an element in a different kind of renunciation. For shrinking the area of desirable actions to personal pleasures (or the avoidance of unpleasantness) meant in effect abandoning the happiness of mankind.

But when one considers the nature of the frustration of people who are in want, it is clear that the trouble is not primarily an insufficient amount of pleasure, but, rather, the nonfulfillment of needs. Pleasure enters in naturally enough as a concomitant of successful functioning; it is a condition normally present in the satisfaction of needs. People who lack adequate food, shelter, etc., are interested in better living conditions. This is not to deny that pleasure is ever an actual motive of conduct. Some of the time, it is an actual motive; and the degree to which it is a motive varies for different persons, classes, and social systems.

To make pleasure the aim of a political movement could be merely a diversion. It could very well go along with the perpetuation of the institutions responsible for unfulfilled wants and frustrations. An increase of pleasure on the part of those in want could occur without disturbing basic inequalities of opportunity.

The ideal of pleasure involves quantity. If a unit of pleasure is good, then an increase in the amount of pleasure is necessary for an increase in the realization of value. In order to elaborate a hedonistic philosophy it is necessary to set up a calculus of pleasures and pains, or a balance sheet. Pleasures which are followed by greater quantities of unpleasantness, measured in terms of intensity and extensity, have negative value. It is quite unlikely that anyone could realize a preponderance of pleasure if he lived in want, or if his chief desires were unfulfilled. The desires represent the central point of interest in ethics, not pleasure.

It is unnecessary to repeat what the ancients knew about the difficulties in the way of a life of pleasure. That it would be self-defeating was a familiar theme.

Although hedonism was wrong in its psychological premise, in maintaining that the pleasure motive is universal, and although it failed to be effective for the purposes of a social philosophy, the criterion of quantity was a significant idea. This criterion could only be applied if pleasures were all on the same plane, i.e., if no one pleasure were regarded as inherently superior to any other pleasure. Once qualitative differences, in the sense of inherent superiority or inferiority, are introduced, it is difficult if not impossible to set up a hedonistic calculus. If it is argued that certain pleasures are more important than others—for example, the enjoyment of a musical composition, as contrasted with the enjoyment of food—that can only have meaning in terms of consequences, or in terms of the place of such a pleasure in the total system of pleasures of one's lifetime. For some persons, a musical composition would occupy a lower level than food, or perhaps a wrestling match on the basis of the system of pleasures involved.

The principle of quantity must be detached from utilitarianism, which is the generalized form of hedonism. It has an indispensable place in ethical reasoning, even though there are difficulties in the way of its application. The principle must be studied in its application to the lives of real individuals in an actual social system. For the analysis of an individual's values, the units must be needs and interests. The total organization of values for an individual, as expressed by means of his life-plan, becomes the unit for the purposes of a social value theory.

Quantity is a useful criterion for many cases: two fulfillments of the need for food are better than one, better meaning that there is more goodness. A thousand units of such fulfillment would be still better; and so on. As applied to a social system, if the fulfillment of one life-plan is good, the fulfillment of two is better, and of a thousand still better. This is all very well in the abstract. But actual cases must be considered, and it will then be possible to amplify the criterion of quantity in its abstract, general formulation. A number of questions which will arise and require further analysis will now be considered.

Take the case of a person who has an intense desire for a certain type of article which he collects. Nonfulfillment might seem to be only a small item in his total system of interests. But he may brood over his failure, and so adversely affect his future realization of value. In fact, he may be led to commit a crime in the effort to satisfy his desire, and so bring about his total undoing. Such a case may turn out to be of psychiatric interest. To suggest that such a person should not attach so much importance to one thing, may be to introduce the criterion of quantity in an objective sense. In terms of his well-being and his potential realization of value over a long period of time, it is judged that he is wrong in attaching so much importance to a particular desire.

Where there is a preponderance of quantity for or against a given line of action, a decision can usually be easily reached. But where the quantity is approximately equal, or where there is a ratio of 3:2, or even of 4:2, one is less sure. Furthermore, the estimate of quantity may not be accurate. What seems to be 3:2 today may turn out to be just the opposite when the ultimate effects and significance of an action have become known. As with the Aristotelian mean, there is no doubt of there being a quantitative determination, but it is difficult to ascertain. There is just the right amount of eating, drinking, and exercise for a given person, even if it is difficult to determine that amount. The same applies to all other aspects of human conduct. Any deviation from the right amount is a move in the wrong direction, toward the sacrifice of value. It should be noted, of course, that the deviation must be sufficient to make a real difference.

In many cases even a probability estimate may be merely a rough guess. Should a child learn two foreign languages, or give a greater emphasis to music? Such questions cannot be answered without a study of each child concerned, and also of the opportunities and practices of the social system. One is not likely to emerge from such a study with a definite probability value in favor of any one course of action.

If the quantitative index of individual interests is difficult to determine, it is to be expected that the problem becomes more complex when social problems are considered. On the social level, individuals are treated as units, with the assumption that their life-plans are well-defined systems with an assignable index of quantity.

For utilitarianism, each person is to count as one, and no person for more than one. It then seems simple enough to determine a system. The hedonist must presuppose that he already has his method of calculating pleasures for an individual, and that he can now operate on a social scale. Some of the difficulties in the way of determining a hedonistic balance sheet for an individual have already been indicated. Everything that has been said about the problems in the way of determining quantity for an individual applies also to the hedonistic view, in addition to the special difficulties incidental to the pleasure-pain theory.

B. The Principle of Equality and the Criterion of Quantity

Although human beings are not equal in capacities and aptitudes, they are declared to be equal in rights by a basic principle of ethics. A social system could not be constructed at all unless the units were equal in some way, or unless assumed inequalities were rendered determinate. The majority of the people will never be satisfied very long by an assumed hierarchy of rights, whether the result of socioeconomic relations or of conquest. To speak of equality in rights is not to imply equality in individual capacities. Individual differences must be recognized as a matter of fact. If the basic equality of rights is denied, a satisfactory reason must be given for that denial. Usually, factual inequalities—physical, intellectual, or cultural—are cited in support of the proposition that men are unequal. But the question is rather, should they be unequal in rights, and specifically the right to fulfillment of needs and interests? Unless one has the support of a rigid caste or class system, he is unable to justify inequality, even speciously. And yet there is a sense in which inequality is morally called for, even though equality is a basic principle. Granting the basic principle that "each counts for one, and no more," as meaning equality of right to fulfillment, it turns out that choices must be made in the light of social needs, as well as individual aptitudes. The principle of equality alone could not justify such choices. The general principle of quantity, added to the principle of equality, can be used to support the selection of some individuals for a given occupation and the disappointment of many others who may desire the same thing. The good of the whole, or the maximum good, is defined as the maximum satisfaction of the greatest possible number of life-plans of individuals. This requires that a selection be made, and it is only by considerations of quantity that a means of making a decision can be achieved. The "equality of right" goes along with inequality in fact for many persons. Some are better fitted than others for education, physics, or medicine. It even turns out that a selection must be made from among those really fitted for a certain profession, if the number of candidates is greater than social need justifies.

The present discussion is being carried on in the abstract. In present-day society, economic opportunity plays a big part in the selection of a vocation. Engineering provides an example of a vocation which is at times overcrowded, with a resultant decrease in the student bodies of engineering schools, and at other times a growing field. There is rarely a dearth of candidates. Many students are financially unable to train for expensive, specialized vocations, so that there is an economic factor of selection in our society. In addition to that, however, there is an attempt to apply standards of aptitude and general fitness, even though such procedures are admittedly still rudimentary in character.

It is conceivable that society may so develop technologically that work as it is now known may become largely unnecessary, with the result that there could then be a far greater degree of freedom of choice of a life-plan. Such a remote fantasy need not detain us here. The fact remains that in societies as we know them it is necessary to have a widespread differentiation of functions, which means that a selection must be made for the sake of social values. Here it is helpful to deal with society in the abstract, and then make application to an existing social system. Every selection of a vocation, which is the dominant factor in the formation of a life-plan, is to be made for the greatest social good. That may mean the sacrifice of some persons, as in the case of the scientific investigator who loses his life or is injured, and the disappointment of others. Disappointment may be illustrated by the artist who must do something else, because there is less need for him as an artist. In the abstract, one sees how such things cannot be avoided, while recognizing that as technological progress continues, the number of neglected interests may decrease progressively.

To point out the unavoidable occurrence of selection and frustration in the abstract is not, however, to condone existing conditions and practices, or to imply that the existing modes of frustration are morally justifiable in terms of the principles of the abstract system-form. Despite great technological progress the degree of frustration may actually increase because of the problem of unemployment. It would be of far-reaching significance to examine in detail the facts of fulfillment and nonfulfillment within the various occupations, including the tasks of unskilled workers in our industrial system.

The principle of quantity provides a broad criterion if the quantitative difference is sufficiently great to preclude doubt.

Thus, individuals who threaten the welfare of society must be suppressed. Where there is a conflict of interests between two individuals who may wish the same job, or who may be business competitors, or where there is a conflict between one individual and two others, the test of quantity is not so obvious. One may be able to show that one of the conflicting parties is right, in that his cause is aligned with the interests of the majority in society. If cases of simple conflict between equals in quantity should arise, as a matter of fact, no decision could be made with this criterion. But even where differences are obvious, the practical difficulties are very great. Could the principle of quantity be invoked in the conflict between capitalists and laborers, or between two rival countries? Of course, this is a gross oversimplification. The economic and historical relations between capitalists and laborers must be considered. In actual practice their issues are settled by a series of compromises, following pressures and counterpressures, and at times physical force.[2] The appeal to the principle of quantity would have no effect, except among certain moralists. The basic principle of equality is violated whenever there is a privileged class; and the principle of quantity cannot apply without equality.

In the illustration of armed conflict between two countries, say Latin-American country A, with a population of twenty million people, and Latin-American country B with a population of ten million people, should the decision go to the former because it has more people? Those who anxiously added up and compared population figures of the Axis powers and their opponents in World War II were not looking for a quantitative moral decision. They were interested in manpower reserves, and in the prospects of victory. No informed person would make the mistake of treating the countries as units. The countries have their internal class antagonisms, and there are also conflicting interests in the commercial class.

These considerations call attention to a set of problems and dangers, as follows: (a) the difference between real social issues and the abstract formulation of a problem; (b) the impossibility of deciding social issues by quantitative means alone, and the need for the principle of equality; (c) the danger of treating aggregates, such as nations, as undifferentiated unities; (d) the error of treating society as a compound composed of individuals as

[2] Galsworthy's play *Strife* is of interest in this connection.

atoms, which is a form of the atomic error; society is rather an aggregate composed of subaggregates, such as male and female, old and young, slaveholders and slaves, or bourgeoisie, farmers, and workers, a consideration which has important bearing on the application of the principle of quantity; (e) the fatuous superficiality of the mere appeal to quantity when a majority errs in its judgment, all the way from "quick justice" (a hasty verdict, or a lynching party) to "the will of the people" as expressed in an election—Hitler's majority which was based upon fraud and force, or a typical American election campaign, with its propaganda-laden atmosphere; (f) the danger of assuming that a given social system, or a given dominant group, is right—for example, ancient Athens with its slave system, and its intolerance of Anaxagoras, Socrates, and Protagoras; or America's treatment of such men as Mooney, Sacco, and Vanzetti. In this area it is especially necessary to perform an *epoché* (a methodical suspension of beliefs and judgments) and to examine all assumptions. But it is peculiarly difficult to carry through an *epoché* in moral and social-philosophical thinking, because the traditional institutions are naturally taken as unquestionable finalities. That is why it is so easy to see traces of the bias of the existing social system and its traditions so often reflected in the views of moralists—if not directly in their professional moralizing, then unmistakably when their attitudes on social relations are expressed. This was shown by various philosophers when they expressed judgments on such crucial matters as private property, the working class, and the status of women.

C. *The Individual and Society*

Strictly speaking, there is no such thing as an individual consciousness, just as there is no independent individual as a unit of society. Neither is there such a thing as society in general. There are only particular social systems, at definite times and places. In important examples of historical societies known to us, individuals are members of groups or classes within the society that may be in question. A given individual may have been a slave, and the class of slaves a part of ancient Greek society. An individual as such and society in general are explanatory abstractions.

The moral unit cannot really be an individual, and neither can the epistemological unit really be an individual consciousness. An individual is a member of a group, or a class, and is the product of a long social and natural process of development. This is true of his conscious processes as well as of his interests and needs. An individual's needs require a world of nature and a society for their fulfillment. The point has been amply emphasized that there can be no individual without a world, so that the systematically doubting philosopher begins with a cardinal falsehood when he reflects that the world may not really exist. An individual knower similarly requires other knowers, past and present, without which he could not be.

If these elementary facts are borne in mind at all times, there will be no error in dealing with society, an individual, or an individual consciousness, as abstractions. They are useful methodological devices if they are carefully controlled. Again, it may be helpful to list the errors that are to be avoided. (a) There is the metaphysical error of atomism, or of false atomism. The person who says "I am I," as the bedrock for all future thinking, finds on inspection that he is not self-sufficient. He cannot stop, in the recognition of conditions bearing upon him, before he includes the entire infinite universe, past and present. False atomism incurs a violation of causal monism as well as causal pluralism. (b) There is the psychological (or epistemological) error of positing an isolated self or knower. Perhaps Feuerbach (in his *Philosophy of the Future*[3]) showed some wisdom in recognizing a hopeless problem when he said, "The unity of I and you is God." If the "I" is taken to be an irreducible and individual entity, then it would seem best to refer the unity of I and you to a transcendent being. There can be no real "retirement to immanence" within one's own consciousness. A person carries with him his virtues and his crimes, but also many of the virtues and crimes of others—whereby one's virtues and crimes will be found to involve other human beings—and, necessarily, the long tradition of culture. (c) There is also the ethical error of false abstractionism, along with the errors of confusing ethical principles with actual ethical preferences, and of confusing the objective with the absolute.

The popular distinction between the individual and society is at issue. How artificial that distinction can be is seen in the alleged issue between individualism and collectivism. It is easy to show that both extreme views are untenable. But it would be difficult if not impossible to point to any defenders of either view.

[3] L. Feuerbach, *Die Philosophie der Zukunft* (Stuttgart: Frommann's Verlag, 1922), p. 91.

The individual and society (as such, or in general) cannot be found in the existing world. A homogeneous group would be needed to illustrate such a distinction. But the historical societies known to us are not homogeneous. Apart from the well-known class distinctions it is necessary to recognize distinctions such as old and young, or male and female, if a meaningful ethical theory is to be constructed. An individual is always a member of one or more groups in an actual historical system of society. Humanity in general, or universal mankind, are phrases which have their proper use, but that is another matter. The error in question is clearly one which involves false abstractionism.

In his categorical imperative ("Act only on that maxim that thou can'st will to be a law universal") Kant deals only with the individual and society, and there is no recognition of special groups and classes. This is an obstacle in the way of its application to present-day society. The critical points of such writers in the Marxian movement as Engels, Kautsky, and Cunow are pertinent. There is no undifferentiated society, and it is unavoidable that any significant example be taken from a particular kind of society, which means a society with class distinctions of some kind. A strikebreaker may violate the Kantian imperative; but are not the strikers also violating it?

The Marxian criticism of Kant must be seriously considered. It points out truly how Kant's ethics is itself a product of his social system; and it shows how Kant failed to consider groups between the individual and society. But this criticism has not gone far enough to pass beyond Kant to the question of normative ethical judgments as a logical problem. The Kantian attempt can be salvaged in part, however, as the concept of the categorical imperative, or of unconditional obligation, must yield to the hypothetical imperative, which takes account of conditions and consequences. The aims of normative ethics should not be overgeneralized. One need not talk of eternal or absolute values and principles. That would be to go beyond possible confirmation or achievement. It is enough to speak of societies like ours, with individuals like us. There are hypothetical and limiting conditions in ethical thinking from the outset, so that this restriction is in place. The theme of ethics is always the ethics of human beings, goodness and evil being defined in terms of the satisfaction or frustration of needs. All ethical principles must then be expressed in a hypothetical form, as follows: If goodness means the following . . . , and if the following postulates . . . are accepted, and if human society and individuals can be referred to concretely, then the following consequences can be drawn. . . .

The Marxist may now remark: That is just the weakness of the construction. Different people, groups, or classes will choose differently; some will accept your definitions and assumptions, and others will modify or reject them. When Mussolini proposed "Live dangerously" as an ideal, he rejected the principle of quantity, i.e., the more value, the better. How one could propose to convince anyone would have to be pointed out; and furthermore the way in which one's values and principles are to be realized must be shown. Could one appeal to a classless reason, in a society in which there are prominent class antagonisms? In any case, there is no way of compelling a person to be logical. Even if he is logical, he may agree to virtue in general, while refusing to make any applications in particular. Real social progress, according to Marxists, is accomplished by a part of a society which has to revolt against another part, the vested interests of the party in power. It might be argued that there is at least an implicit class ethics, expressing the point of view of the working class, which opposes the ethical conceptions of the dominant class. This point must be expressed very carefully, however, in view of the usual avoidance of an ethical appeal by Marxists. It is suggested by Engels' remark that different ethical conceptions—the feudal, bourgeois, and proletarian—may coexist and struggle for supremacy. Engels writes[4]:

> Which morals are preached to us today? There is first of all the Christian-feudal . . . which is divided essentially into Catholic and Protestant [forms]. . . . Beside them there is the modern-bourgeois and in addition to that the proletarian morals of the future, so that past, present, and future provide three large groups of moral theories at the same time. . . . Which is the true one? No one of them, in the sense of absolute finality; but surely that ethics will possess the most enduring elements, which represents in the present the transformation of the present or the future, and that is the proletarian ethics. But when we see that the three classes of modern society, the feudal aristocracy, the bourgeoisie, and the proletarian class each has its particular morals, then we can only draw the conclusion, that human beings, consciously or unconsciously, derive their moral views in the last analysis from the practical conditions in which their

[4] Friedrich Engels, *Herrn Eugen Dührings Umwälzung der Wissenschaft* (Stuttgart: Verlag Dietz, 1921), pp. 88 ff.

class is grounded—from the economic relations in which they produce and exchange.

Engels raises the question whether there may be something common to all three types. Could that be at least a part of an ethics which is valid for all time? The different types of ethics represent different stages of social development, and they admittedly do have a good deal in common. But the condemnation of stealing represents an economic order in which there is private property. If the motives for stealing were obviated, Engels holds, it would be ridiculous to proclaim, as an absolute truth, the precept "Thou shalt not steal." In his view, all previous moral theories were the result, in the last analysis, of the economic condition of society. And since until now there have been class antagonisms in society, morals were always class morals; they either justified the domination and the interests of the ruling class, or they represented, as soon as the oppressed class was strong enough, the revolt against this domination, and the future interests of the oppressed class. But can we go beyond class ethics? Engels' reply here is noteworthy: "A really human ethics which is above the class antagonisms and above the remembrance of them first becomes possible on a stage of society, which has not only overcome the antagonism of classes, but has also forgotten it for the practice of life." It is evident, then, that Engels did not deny the possibility of formulating at least parts of a really human ethics. For practical reasons he was concerned with another type of issue. The actual historical and social sources of moral judgments and moral theories were of primary interest, because he was a spokesman of one of the contending parties. The philosophical defense of absolute principles and norms within the framework of a class-society met with his strong opposition. As a matter of policy he limited his interest in ethics to the representation of social forces which would transform society into a classless structure. Only then, when all remembrance of class antagonisms had disappeared, would he consider the time ready for a really human ethics.

D. *The Problem of Objective Ethical Knowledge*

If the danger of false abstractionism is the result of ignoring historical realities, it is also true that ethical principles cannot be derived simply from the ethical preferences of people at a given time. To attempt this would be to incur the error of confusing facts with principles, whereby the range of the facts (the ethical preferences) is overextended. Only relativism can result in that way. Thus, one might speak of Ethical System I as applying to Historical System I, Ethical System II as applying to Historical System II, etc. But the matter would not be so simple. There is not likely to be a consistent set of ethical preferences in a complex social system. One might suppose that a system of bourgeois ethics would result, or of proletarian ethics. But even that would not be so, for there would not be complete consistency in the ethical preferences of any group, whether bourgeois or proletarian. The consideration of ethical preferences would not yield any ethical principles, and could only result in a set of empirical facts about the judgments of people at a certain time and under certain conditions.

Expressions of preference are certainly significant. But far more important is the determination of what is objectively good for people, in terms of their needs and interests. People must be considered within an actual social system. Although one could not expect all that is objectively good for people to be determined, many needs and interests can be pointed out. Ethics is an incomplete science, and will no doubt always be incomplete. That does not undermine its value, however, as most sciences are incomplete.

The aim of establishing objective knowledge about human values should not be understood to mean that one is aiming at absolute principles and norms. That would be another error of confusion—confusing the objective with the absolute. Absolutes are supposed to hold under all conditions. It is easy to refute such claims, for no ethical principle could be named which has not been conspicuously violated or rejected. The absolutes usually hold vacuously anyway, i.e., under abstract conditions, so that the error of false abstractionism is readily incurred.

If ethical thinking is to apply to human conduct and experience, its norms must be based upon the objectively established knowledge of human beings. The satisfaction of needs and interests constitutes goodness as known and sought for in human experience. To a certain extent, it is possible to establish a body of empirical knowledge about human beings—say, very young children, as a clear example—and to argue that a number of precepts should be observed. The knowledge of nutrition, physiology, etc., leads to the establishment of norms. These norms are not empty absolutes. They must be applied with due regard to the individual nature of a given person. How far can one go in this direction?

So long as one remains on the level of basic needs, there is not much difficulty. But one soon encounters problems involving other persons which cannot be handled so simply, if the ideal is to determine what is objectively best. An individual Male X needs a mate. Is it objectively right that he marry Female Y? Experts, including medical men and analysts, might be able to provide the necessary basis for a judgment of high probability. Certainty is admittedly out of the question in this area, as in all other empirical inquiry. If the present case is complex, what shall one say about the objective right or good involved when this individual X seeks employment, and the prospective employer Z offers a wage of g dollars? The economist can account for the amount of the wage. Can the moralist give objectively binding grounds for asserting that the wage should be h dollars? In practice, there is a long struggle over the level of wages. Even if the objectively right amount could be determined by that new emergent, the scientific moralist, there would be very little chance of its affecting the deliberations of representatives of capitalists and laborers (meaning in actual practice what passes above—and under—the table of deliberation).

There are clearly numerous obstacles in the way of an objective ethics. Nevertheless one should attempt to formulate whatever principles can be justified as normative, with their probability index, and with explicit recognition of their hypothetical and limiting elements—hypothetical with respect to basic ideas and principles, and limiting within a given historical system.

It is true that men do not come as individuals in a society, but rather as workers, capitalists, etc. There is also justification, however, for the theoretical attempt to determine what may be called the system-form of ethical theory. The system-form is the abstract form which is exemplified by the various actual historical systems. Such a form must simplify matters, and must speak of a society as made up of unspecified individuals. It can provide for the class of all subclasses of individuals, some of which are illustrated by the social and economic classes which make up our present society. This system-form does not bring any absolutes. It is limited to the human species; its basic concepts, such as needs, are treated as variables; and even such a basic principle as the criterion of quantity may be subject to modification under special conditions. Such things must be pointed out in the derived principles.

Everyone has a certain social status. He is a member of a social class, and has his own special interests. What about the objective moralist: is he devoid of individual or class interests; is he free of all one-sided standpoints? If he takes due account of all the influences bearing upon him, which might make a difference in his observation and thinking, he may be able to overcome class bias. He is committed to follow wherever the argument and evidence lead. The interests of his own class will be given their proper weight; they will not be ignored. But they will not be permitted to interfere with the quest for truth.

It is generally assumed that all questions have answers, and that all problems can be solved rationally. What if some of the practical problems turn out to be insoluble except by the use of force, whether physical or political? The use of physical force is rightly deprecated, and is to be condoned only under special conditions, when the methods of reason are not allowed to operate. Even the rule of the majority may itself be a vehicle of force and compulsion; it may be merely a front for the rule of a minority, which has sufficient resources to mold the preferences of the majority.

When Yale University asked a group of its alumni to investigate the basis of the charge that atheism, agnosticism, and collectivism were promoted at Yale, the committee reported that the charge was unfounded.[5] It is noteworthy that faculty members, while enjoying academic freedom, were expected to "exercise the proper amount of restraint," and that it would, by inference, be a serious charge against a faculty member to be found a defender of collectivism. The Yale committee of alumni included the chairman of the board of the U.S. Steel Corporation, the chairman of the board of the N.Y. Life Insurance Company, a judge, two fellows of the Yale Corporation, and two professors. Its failure to find an advocate of collectivism at Yale is a simple matter of fact. If, as may be inferred, it would disapprove of such a person if he existed, could that judgment of disapproval be regarded as objectively founded? If it came at the close of an all-sided logical inquiry into the question, that might be so, assuming that the question is capable of an answer in terms of an acceptable theory or set of basic principles. Two things must be noted, however: (a)

[5] As reported in the *Buffalo Evening News*, February 18, 1952.

the committee is undoubtedly antecedently hostile to collectivism, and is likely to have only a partial knowledge of the whole issue, or, perhaps, a rationalization of its own preference; (b) the question at issue may not be capable of a theoretical solution cogent for all concerned. There may be basic assumptions which will be disputed by one party or another. The rule of the majority must then be resorted to as the only defensible vehicle of change. The majority may of course be wrong; it is frequently wrong. But if change is always possible through future enactments of the majority, eventual progress may be expected.

A well-defined system of ethical knowledge, with its two parts —the system-form, and the application to present-day society— can become increasingly effective as a standard of evaluation and criticism of practical proposals. The erratic course of history may be improved gradually by such constant criticism. Economic and social questions become political questions, for their solution; and political questions eventually will become educational matters. Lest one fall into the habit of talking within the safe framework of a system-form which need never touch the actual world, when speaking of education, it is necessary to remind oneself of the actual limitations of the educational process in our social system. It is no accident that the dominant lines of indoctrination echo the dominant interests of our social system.

E. *The Real Meaning of Freedom*

Long ago Bentham distinguished between eulogistic and dyslogistic terms, expressing approbation or opprobrium. We come habitually to use certain words with implied praise, and others in a spirit of denunciation. Although many eulogistic terms may well deserve approval, the general habit of using them is fraught with mischief. In saving ourselves the task of thinking, we are at the same time exposed to the dangers of assumptive reasoning, for skill in insinuating meanings into presumably neutral terms may turn many minds into any desired direction.

The term freedom is one of the most prominent eulogistic epithets, just as determinism has come to be a dyslogistic term in wide circles. Such usage faces the logical objection that all assumptions must be rendered explicit, and must be tested in the light of all the available evidence. In addition to this objection, there is the further fact that the term freedom is highly ambiguous, and frequently empty or merely negative. As a general term it may be interpreted in widely different ways, depending upon the context, or the historical period. Totalitarians and exponents of equality clamor for freedom; employers of labor and workers have their meanings of freedom.

A captive who is bound hand and foot dreams of freedom, and there is a definite meaning of the term for him—freedom from his bonds. Let us suppose that this meaning of freedom as "freedom from" is generalized. How far could one go in eliminating bonds and ties of all kinds? The extreme limit would leave one with no restrictions of any kind, but also with no positive values. In order to achieve values, it is necessary to cooperate with others, and so to submit to at least some of the limiting conditions of a particular cultural system. If the limiting conditions are held to be just (another eulogistic and ambiguous term), an individual may be satisfied that he is not burdened by indefensible restrictions on his personal liberty, and he may regard it as necessary for his own welfare to submit to the principles and practices of his social system. The assumption is justice, and that involves the concept of equality. It is thus evident that the analysis of freedom requires the clarification of a number of relevant concepts and principles. It will also be evident that the abstract definition of these concepts is empty until application is made to a concrete historical situation.

In its positive sense, freedom means the power to fulfill needs or interests—in other words, to achieve values. Quite abstractly, it has been seen to be possible to define the minimum as well as the maximum of values for an individual in an unnamed social system S. That is because there is a most convenient absence of the actual conflicts, always found in real historical situations. Abstractly, one can speak of the greatest possible fulfillment of needs or interests, insofar as that can be determined for society as a whole. One does not expect more than a given level of culture can offer; there will be less on a lowly level of technological development, and more on higher levels. The abstract talk of more and less, of minimum and maximum, of an individual and of a society, may be of logical interest, and it may be pleasing to all who wish to preach virtues in general without entering into actual problems in particular. But it must inevitably come to an end and yield to concrete discussion of actual persons who belong to definite social and economic classes. The clamor for freedom is then seen to be the demand for the satisfaction of needs and interests.

In all past historical periods, progress has been achieved by repeated pressures on the part of suppressed or inhibited interests. Conflicts within a social system and struggle between rival powers—local, national, and international—have been means of change, which could by no means always be called progress in the sense of an increase in the total amount of human value realized. There has been no continuous line of moral progress, if by that is meant a steady increase in the level of general human happiness. Progress has frequently been followed by retrogression. Force has been unavoidable in the destruction of a repressive system, as America's early history readily testifies, for America was born in revolution. Will it continue to be unavoidable for social change? The answer depends upon the instrumentalities for change provided by a social system. If peaceful means for instituting improvements without limit are allowed, force disappears because it is unnecessary.

It is an accepted fact, at least in the academic world, that the philosopher *qua* philosopher does not enter into concrete social and political issues, although he may do so as a citizen. His contribution as a philosopher, if any, will be to provide renewed clarification for the analysis and gradation of values to be achieved. Instead of offering a rationalization, whether lofty or downright mendacious, to support the use of force,[6] he may be expected to assist in the effort to determine the application of forms of value to the actual historical situations. It will be recalled that the pseudoevolutionary social philosophers sought to justify war on evolutionary grounds, as facilitating the survival of the worthiest individuals and nations; and it will not be forgotten how totalitarian regimes were supported by philosophical apologists. When one speaks of the task of philosophy, or of the role of the philosopher, he is again speaking quite abstractly.

The possibility of determining what is best objectively has been denied by many; and yet it is a necessary assumption for all rational planning. Even if no greater claim than that of high probability were made for purportedly objective determinations

---

[6] One recalls the way in which many countries justified their participation in World War I on moral grounds; and the more recent totalitarian ideologies are even more relevant.

of value, that would be sufficient for practical purposes. There must always be a maximum of happiness which an individual can achieve in a given social system, although it may be difficult in fact to establish even a good approximation to it. There must also be a maximum possible realization of value for an entire social system, no matter how complex the problem of ascertaining it may be.

To speak of objective determinations is to require the use of descriptive procedures, in contrast to appeals to authority, tradition, or special faculties not subject to scientific controls. Furthermore, it means the objective judgment of what is good for an individual, rather than dependence upon his subjective preferences. If one individual (the wrong individual!) achieved all that he wished to have, perhaps no one else would have very much. Thus, the complete freedom (in this sense) of one person or group might involve the virtual enslavement of all others. Historical actualities fall short of this extreme, and yet there is a point in indicating it. True freedom, like true happiness or true value, must be determined objectively if reason is to prevail instead of conflict and force.

A pediatrician can decide with considerable evidence what is good for a child. Experts—present or future—will be able to provide data about everyone, to be used as a guide in defining life-plans. In every case, the goal will be the maximum value that could be realized; and value is defined basically in terms of the satisfaction of needs. Since an individual cannot be considered in isolation from his social system, his life-plan must be subject to the greatest good of the system itself. In other words, the individual and the social system are correlatively determined. Subordination of the individual and some degree of sacrifice are unavoidable for the greatest good of the group. Freedom cannot be defined without this dual frame of reference. What holds for a national group holds in principle for the future international group, the world brotherhood of man.

This is the ideal goal. It may seem unnecessary to indicate how far the actualities are removed from the goal, but it is well to do so in order to make sure that we are amply aware of the difficulties confronting us. Our competitive socioeconomic system illustrates keen and often fierce conflicts—strikes and trade wars, for example. There is usually a large reserve supply of labor, but even under conditions of scarcity of labor, workers are to some extent in competition with one another. There are conflicts within and between economic classes; and this is true of nations, and of groups of nations, culminating in world wars. One country may be well liked in many ways in numerous parts of the civilized world. But other countries are not prepared to acquiesce gladly in the face of competitive production, which might adversely affect their own industries and a host of other activities. Might there not be a situation parallel to the hypothetical individual who satisfied all of his desires, on a national and world scale, with one country dominating the industrial activities of the world? The parallel is in part faulty, to be sure, because the hypothetical one country would not be a unit, and would have conflicts within itself.

Would it be possible, in principle, to determine objectively what is best for all mankind, regardless of distinctions between classes and rivalry among nations? Only general and abstract criteria could be indicated, but they are always important in reminding us of the ultimate ideal. The quantitative criterion, the test that what is best is determined by the good of the greatest possible number of people, requires the principle of equality. It is not honest to profess the democratic principle of decision by the majority unless one really recognizes the basic and inherent equality of right to fulfillment on the part of each and every individual, and, still more important, unless one tries to do something toward instituting such equality. There must, then, be no discrimination because of color or creed; no fiction of race or nation. The approach to this ideal still lies in the future, although there is evidence of ever-growing numbers of people who accept it. Social equality is not enough, however. There must be effective equality in the economic sphere, which in turn requires planning in the light of human values. Such planning would finally remove man from a vast and protracted historical jungle, with its record of struggle and its sacrifice of value. It is not enough to preach brotherly love or neighborly love: all too often such love means, in practice, fondness of a secure place on the backs of hapless "backward" peoples, who—so the rationalization goes—are uplifted by the contact with a culturally superior people. Like tumors, cases of the imperialistic or paternalistic domination of technologically weaker peoples may be classified as benign and malignant, with the observation that no one wants even a benign tumor. The last echo of a weakening defense of such domination is seen in the bleat that "freedom is certainly desirable, but this is not the time for it." Count Witte of Czarist Russia favored the emancipation of the Jews, but at a later date, when they and conditions were to be ready for it. For that matter, there is the story of the proverbial gallant gentleman who favored virtue—"but not yet."

Grandiloquent maxims such as Kant's categorical imperative, especially his insistence that fellow human beings should be viewed as ends in themselves, and never as mere means, must be connected more explicitly with the economic realities. There can be no talk of effective equality if wealth is largely concentrated in a few hands, and if some persons profit at the expense of others, no matter what legal sanctions there may be. "Equality before the law" is no guarantee of economic, or moral, equality. "Equality before the law," or political equality, will, however, afford the means for progress toward equality in all senses, through the enactment of appropriate laws. In this way political democracy makes endless progress possible. There is no part of human society which could not be changed by peaceful, legal means in a country—or a world—committed to democratic means of change and progress. It must be ascertained, however, whether the democratic powers function effectively, or whether particular social forces have learned how to manipulate them to their own advantage.

Mention has been made of the philosophical procedure of suspending all beliefs in order to undertake a thoroughgoing critique of knowledge. Unexamined beliefs, no matter how commonplace they may be, perhaps conceal dogmas. In any case, they must be re-examined for their evidence. Even though the philosopher is presumably a man of reason, he is expected to begin radically, with a "clean slate." It is still more important for him to practice such radical reflection in the sphere of practical affairs, where preconceived or antecedent beliefs are frequently the expression of class privileges or personal interests. In so doing, he views all human problems under the aspect of humanity as a whole, and he aims persistently at the greatest possible realization of values for all people. Freedom has only a partial meaning, or at best is merely negative in reference, apart from these considerations. There will be no illusion about the prompt, widespread adoption of this point of view. Most people, including scholars, follow immediate aims; they fail to see themselves in their one-sidedness, and do not completely understand the conditions which restrict them.

In reacting against such restrictions, they strive for freedom. The real meaning of freedom as maximum happiness for all humanity —defined in terms of the satisfaction of needs and interests in a society planned to yield the most for all on the basis of equality of right—must be clearly grasped and held up in all its implications by scholars, teachers, writers, workers, and all members of society for whom reason plays a role. In time, it will make itself generally felt, and will act as an ever greater directive force. Real freedom in this sense, like good, cannot be a static condition. It is an activity, a process of continuous adjustment and realization, a process which can never rest in the nature of things.

F. Summary: The Nature and Scope of a Theory of Value

Human values must be founded on life and experience. To be scientific, ethics must be constructed "from below," not derived "from above." Method is of paramount importance in ethics, as in all other fields. The general precept of method, which requires that every statement be referred back to the method by which it was derived or instated, also applies to ethics. It is even more important here than in other fields, because human conduct is involved. The ideal goal of ethics as a science is an objectively justified set of principles which are fundamental enough to hold for all particular situations. Actually, however, no finality may be expected, any more than complete prevision of future human beings and their problems could be expected.

The methods of knowledge that may be used in ethics are selected from those that are logically acceptable. Inductive and deductive methods are used, and there is a place for carefully controlled experimental methods. Such methods as the appeal to an absolute authority and the use of a nonrational intuition must be dismissed as illogical.

The desires or interests of sentient beings under given historical conditions are the units of the subject matter of ethics. For the clarification of this domain for inquiry, ethics is dependent upon the findings of the special sciences and the humanities.

The logical structure of ethical theory is seen most clearly when it is conceived deductively, and ethics may in its broad outlines approach that strict scientific form. The deductive system of ethical knowledge, which can be complete only in certain broad and limited aspects, is dual in its nature and may for convenience be divided into an individual system and a social system. Conforming to the pattern of a deductive system, there are basic ideas and relations, and a set of fundamental assumptions. In the individual system, the individual needs or interests are the units to be considered, and in the social system the individual agents themselves constitute the units. Moral value is not intrinsic. That is a vague term, as objectionable as intuition; and no essential insight into so-called intrinsic values can help us here. What can be said to convince a person who fails to have the desired insight, and who rejects an alleged intrinsic value?

The unit of value or goodness is best defined as the fulfillment of a need or interest,[7] and moral value as the fulfillment of an organization of interests. The term desires might be used, although a good deal of clarification would be required. The term interest may be used to include needs and desires, but not arbitrary desires. In the present account, it is sufficient to recall the basic needs without which life would be impossible. But it is also necessary to consider the cultural offerings and potentialities of the social system if the significant problems of ethical judgment are to be formulated. In both the individual and the social systems the principle of equality is the first assumption, asserting negatively that there is no inherent aristocracy of interests or agents. Provision for future interests and the criterion of quantity are further basic principles. It follows that no interest is higher than any other one, unless different quantities of interests are involved. There is thus a sense in which basic biological needs such as the need for food may be said to be prior to others, for their fulfillment is a necessary condition for the existence and satisfaction of other interests. The definition of the ethical ideal is always relational: for an individual it means self-realization, the development of his capacities, within the framework and needs of the social system; and for society it means the maximal development and satisfaction of the needs of individuals, in their relation to the values of posterity. An international organization of society is necessary for the realization of the ethical ideal. Man has attained virtual mastery over nature. His next goal is to attain mastery over human relations. There can no longer be talk of the niggard-

---

[7] Cf. R. B. Perry, *The Moral Economy* (New York: Charles Scribner's Sons, 1909), *General Theory of Value* (New York: Longmans, Green, and Co., 1926), and *Realms of Value* (Cambridge: Harvard University Press, 1954).

liness of nature, since there is now so effective a control over the food supply. If there are regimes and periods of want in an advanced country like America, the causes are to be sought in the nature of our economic relations. The time is ripe for rethinking our social and economic relations nationally and internationally, in order to prepare the ground for an international organization of society which is devoted to the ethical ideal.

The scope of the concept of value, conceived as the fulfillment of interest, is coextensive with human activities. The definition of progress is made possible at once. An increase in positive value (fulfillment) or a decrease in negative value (frustration) is evidence of progress. The concept of progress may be used in an unlimited sense, so that one can compare persons in a low economic class in a modern society with persons in a low economic class in an ancient society, and find that there is improvement. In mastery over nature, there is surely improvement. Another question can be raised, however: how far removed is the lower class from the maximum fulfillment which could be provided by modern society if it were reorganized in the light of that ideal? In other words, how does the ratio of fulfillment of modern society compare with the ratio of fulfillment of the ancient society? There are, then, different concepts of progress, depending upon the frame of reference. The importance of ethical analysis for the philosophy of history is thus indicated clearly.

G. *Moral Value and Aesthetic Judgment*

The application to aesthetic thought is also indicated. If ethics is concerned with the fulfillment of interests, the class of aesthetic interests must be included, so that aesthetics has an ethical aspect. In this respect it is like all other fields of scholarship, for no human activity is exempt from ethical significance. There should be no suggestion, however, of substituting ethical principles for the canons of art. Exponents of religious ethics, for example, are not slow to condemn works of art whose significance is felt as hostile to their authoritarian position. The same may be said of the exponents of social classes or groups who judge works of art in terms of their own values. The relevance of ethics to aesthetics is recognized only too generally. The important point is which system of ethical thought should be used in judging the moral significance of a work of art, assuming this significance is sufficiently determinate. Great harm could result from adopting one of the authoritarian traditions as a standard of judgment. The slogan "art for art's sake" indicates the need for emancipation from the inhibitory effects of moral criticism in this objectionable sense. But nothing is "for its own sake." The instrumental conception of art, like the instrumental theory of ideas generally as advanced by Dewey,[8] shows the close connection between the various types of artistic activity and the general experience of human beings. There are no irreducible distinctions between fine art and applied art.

Because of the basic relevance of ethics and aesthetics, it may seem that ethical control of artistic activities is implied. But in view of the practical danger of having the wrong kind of ethics as a standard of censorship, any kind of control would be highly undesirable. It is to be doubted whether restrictions of any kind should be imposed on creative art even in an ideal form of society. Bureaucrats typically suffer from lust for power, and most known bureaucrats tend to display a peculiar hardening of the neurones as soon as they assume office. There may be other reasons for misgivings, even under the postulated ideal conditions, but this alone would be sufficient. The people themselves must determine what is best. Even though habit and prejudice might for a time be responsible for the loss of much that is good, there is no defensible alternative.

A number of conclusions will now be outlined, in lieu of the fuller discussion which cannot be included here.

(a) The positive value of aesthetics usually is held to be beauty. The experience of the beautiful must be distinguished from the objectivity involved. Objective beauty is the correlate of some actual or possible aesthetic experience.

(b) Art is also concerned with ugliness; but it may be neutral with respect to beauty and ugliness.

(c) Art may be judged as to form and content; and it may range in its significance from greatness to triviality.

(d) The facts supporting relativism must be considered, and the full truth of relativism embraced by an objective philosophy of values. The question whether there is ever beauty apart from

[8] Cf. John Dewey, *Art as Experience* (New York: G. P. Putnam's Sons, 1934).

human beings is easily disposed of when one makes clear what he is talking about—experienced beauty, or certain objective features or forms which may be independently real.

(e) Would it be possible to state the necessary and sufficient conditions for aesthetic value? At most it could only be done incompletely, in a broad, conceptual manner, and in such a way that an unlimited number of special conditions and interpretations could be added. Limitation, significance, and enjoyment are clearly necessary for a complete aesthetic situation; and symmetry, balance, massiveness, and harmony are contributing conditions. The creative efforts of artists make extension and revision of old standards constantly necessary. The history of music shows that it is not possible to impose one set of standards upon harmony, for example.

(f) Form consists of relations and relational patterns; and the minimum of form, for aesthetics, is the minimum of significance. Significance and form may coincide in some cases. There may be logical forms with minimal significance. Interpreted forms, along with meaning for experience, are most important for us.

(g) There may be psychologically constant or indifferent factors in art, causing enjoyment in any cultural era. Thus, the enjoyment of nature is constant, although the aesthetic appreciation of mountains, for example, is comparatively recent,[9] due to the development of appropriate techniques. There are variable elements in content, depending upon social and scientific change, and the extent to which some forms of art are restricted to given groups. It is important that all members of society be given the educational and social opportunity to enjoy all possible forms of art. Ultimately, it is hoped, the aesthetic attitude of enjoyment will pervade all human activities. What is now called fine art will then rank—or its successors will—as the most significant and technically finished set of products of human activity.

(h) A philosophical theory of art undertakes first of all to make clear the significance of the human activities involved. It is always good procedure to analyze complex problems into their proper parts, and to attempt to accomplish what is possible. Objective criteria of significance and the social value of art must be determined.

(i) All art is instrumental, and should be viewed in its posi-

---

[9] Cf. C. R. Griffith, *An Introduction to Applied Psychology* (New York: The Macmillan Co., 1934).

tion in the collective system of interests which constitutes human society at work. The concepts of beauty, goodness, and truth are related in an important way. This is shown by the fact that no work of art can be called great which does not represent much goodness and truth, even though that may be accomplished by the portrayal of evil.

(j) It is possible to judge the value of past works of art in terms of man's enduring basic needs and interests, i.e., in terms of his relationships to nature and society. New needs arise, and are in fact prompted by new cultural achievements.

(k) There should be no suppression of artistic activities. Society does that at its peril. Man is fundamentally and pragmatically sound in his judgments, and only the useful or that which is free from evil can long survive. A program of censorship and restriction might lead to stagnation. Freedom is admittedly open to objection, but it is incomparably the lesser evil, and, as such, is a forced option.

(l) A just and good order of society is a prerequisite to the universal enjoyment of art in all departments of human activity. The art which, within present conditions, helps to bring about that ideal is truly valuable art. It is instrumental in the best sense of the term: instrumental to the achievement of human satisfaction and value.

CHAPTER X

Problems of the Philosophy of Religion

A. *Ludwig Feuerbach and the Problem of Belief*

How does a person come to have his beliefs? Some of our most cherished beliefs are due, as Locke pointed out in his *Essay Concerning Human Understanding*, to the authority of an old woman, or of a nurse. Tradition and authority are the chief sources of our beliefs. There are certain articles of faith which are a part of the standard equipment of an average person's mind in the various religious traditions. Beliefs that have been accepted early in life tend to be regarded as self-evident. The actual reasons why people believe are matters of fact, and they include self-interest, unconscious and conscious psychological factors, and faulty as well as good logic, in addition to the cultural traditions which act upon them.

In his book on *The Origin of the Gods*, the nineteenth-century philosopher Ludwig Feuerbach[1] expounded a provocative theory of the essence of belief. In his view, belief is nothing other than the conviction or certainty of a wish for its fulfillment. One does not wish immortality because he believes or proves it; on the contrary, one believes and proves immortality because he wishes it. Without the wish not to die, immortality would never have come into anyone's head. The animating soul of belief is the wish. A belief which is not the expression of a wish is simply dead and unworthy. The usual definition of belief, that it is "holding something to be true, or conviction on subjectively sufficient grounds" is formulated by Feuerbach in the field of religion as follows: It is in the last analysis a conviction based on sufficient wishing. The proofs of God's existence sound like mathematical demonstrations.

[1] L. Feuerbach, *Der Ursprung der Götter* (Leipzig: Verlag von Otto Wigand, 1866), pp. 48 ff., 197 ff.

But the point is, that one wishes what is thought to be more than thought.

A wish is held by Feuerbach to be the expression of a deficiency, a limitation, a "not," whether it be a not-being or a not-having or a not-able-to-do; or an expression of suffering. One wishes that these things were not. The wish is a slave of need, but a slave with the will to freedom—to overcome poverty, for example. The prominence of the wish before action is seen in the Bible, in that every creative act closes with the statement, "and God saw that it was good." But where there is no wish, there is also no good. Who can find light to be good, if he does not wish to see? Another example is cited by Feuerbach: It was not good for a man to be alone, and therefore a companion was created, as an aid. The creation of woman was thus made dependent upon a wish.

The fundamental condition of belief in God is held by Feuerbach to be the unconscious wish to be God oneself. But since this contradicts one's real essence and being, that which one wishes to be becomes merely an ideal, a thought, or believed essence. The not-man is pictured, because man realized that he is not-God. Furthermore, what man wishes, he wishes at the same time to be continuous. Man is glad to be young, and opposes being old. It is first with the loss of youth that man recognizes that he is the subject of an unyielding necessity. Youth is therefore a kind of godliness or a property of gods; but not old age, which is "hateful to the gods." Man does not attribute properties to the gods which he does not himself wish. As opposed to the good of life, all men feel that death is a harsh, hostile necessity.

Frederick Engels paid tribute to Feuerbach's earlier work, *The Essence of Christianity* of 1841, pointing out its "liberating effect" at the time. "With one blow . . . it placed materialism on the throne again. Nature exists independently of all philosophy. It is the foundation upon which we human beings, ourselves products of nature, have grown up. Nothing exists outside nature and man, and the higher beings our religious fantasies have created are only the fantastic reflection of our own essence."[2] Engels stated later, however, that Feuerbach "never quite sheds his idealism."[3] Criticism of Feuerbach was expressed in some detail in a letter to

---
[2] Frederick Engels, *Ludwig Feuerbach and the Outcome of Classical German Philosophy* (New York: International Publishers, 1941), p. 18.
[3] *Ibid.*, p. 69.

Marx in 1846.[4] The theme of this letter was Feuerbach's essay on *The Essence of Religion*, which had recently appeared. In Feuerbach's view, the orientals are related to the occidentals as rural people are to urban people, the former being dependent on nature, and the latter on man, so that "only urban people make history." Engels remarks that this is the only breath of materialism in the essay, and he finds it "ill-smelling." Feuerbach is chided with failure to see the historical conditions of the development of religious beliefs. Thus, Engels writes: "That the One God would never have arisen without the one king, that the unity of the God who controls the many phenomena of nature, is only the image of the one oriental despot who holds together conflicting individuals . . . Feuerbach thought it superfluous to state," so that "concerning the historical development of the various religions one learns nothing."

In the century which elapsed after Engels wrote these lines, an extensive literature has appeared in this field. Among liberal religious scholars it is becoming commonplace to recognize the economic and social conditions of religious beliefs since it is now taken for granted that economic history is essential for the explanation of all other historical forms. In his book *The God of the Liberal Christian*,[5] Professor D. S. Robinson distinguishes six different social orders in past history, each of which had a distinct social pattern and a special doctrine of the atonement. The close relation between the idea of God of a certain people and their general social organization was recognized by Professor E. S. Ames, whose views are quoted by Robinson:

> Thus a nomadic or a hunting social group believes in and worships animal gods, a tribe of fishermen develops fish gods, and an agricultural folk create rain and grain gods. When the life of a group becomes so complicated and diversified as to include a number of separate activities, that people is certain to develop syncretized deities, that is to say, gods which combine in themselves several specific functions previously attributed to separate deities. And when social organization advances still further to the point where great human leaders, such as sheiks, patriarchs, kings, warriors, and what not, control the destinies of the people, the gods forthwith take on the characteristics of these potentates. Moreover, that God and the social consciousness are

---

[4] *Der Briefwechsel zwischen Friedrich Engels und Karl Marx*, ed. A. Bebel and Ed. Bernstein (Stuttgart: Verlag Dietz, 1921), Vol. I, pp. 45 ff.
[5] D. S. Robinson, *The God of the Liberal Christian* (New York: D. Appleton and Co., 1926), pp. 35 ff., 125 f.

one and the same is further borne out by the fact, well known to the historian of religion, that when a race is conquered its gods become the vassals of the gods of the conquerors. Then, too, when a homogeneous group is dispersed by a more powerful rival, so that its tribal identity is lost, its god becomes a jinn, a mere ghost of its former self, or else disappears entirely and becomes a dead god.

B. *The Idea of God*

That man portrays his gods in the image of his society has been known at least since Xenophanes protested against anthropomorphism in religion. He observed that mortals fancy gods are born, wear clothes, and have voices and forms like themselves, and suggested that horses would make their gods like horses if they could paint, and oxen like oxen. Furthermore, Ethiopians make their gods black and snub-nosed, whereas Thracians give their gods blue eyes and red hair. Homer and Hesiod, he noted, have ascribed deeds to the gods that are a shame and a disgrace among men—thieving, adultery, and fraud. Xenophanes, who was a forerunner of pantheism, maintained that there is one god, supreme among gods and men, and resembling mortals neither in form nor in mind.

The heavenly order has always been a reflection of the earthly order. The conceptions of divine beings have varied historically with the changes in the structure of society. The impersonal spirit of modern religion, and the gradual rise of nondenominationalism inevitably associated with it, is a reflection of a growing international order of society. To be sure, its nonsectarian character was anticipated by ancient philosophers. Aristotle's god was pure form, the unmoved first mover, or thinking about thinking, and he supposed that there is a universal reason in which each individual participates. This god was not limited to Greece, and was easily adaptable for international purposes. The fact that Aristotle was not an equalitarian in his social thought was clearly in accord with his social position, but that is another matter. The gods of Epicurus, on the other hand, were well-equipped Epicureans. They were constituted subject to the condition that all real things consist of atoms moving in the void. They consisted of fine atoms, and dwelled in the intermundia, unmindful of earthly things. If they were not altruistic, neither were they jealous beings, and none of the evils besetting man have been ascribed to them. What has happened to the gods of Epicurus? Apparently he had provided for their gradual extinction through his version of the atomic theory. All things are forever shedding atomic films or images, so that perception is possible through contact with our organs. In time the gods disappeared, as a lasting confirmation of the Epicurean theory.

The attempt to conceive God as a person can only be carried through vacuously. Only a nonspecific person would be admissible. There can be no traits of American or Frenchman, of banker or coal miner, of male or female. No particular language is spoken by this superperson. There is no learning from experience, for there simply is no experience, only a vision of the whole of things, unimpeded by a finite perspective. If all things are already determinate for such a being, what is its function? Condemnation of the errant and approval of the faithful are definite, compresent facts for it. No wonder it does nothing; there is really nothing to do. The image of a divine person in speculative religious thought is that of an infinite blank. The love sustained by it could only be love in general, with no application to cases in particular. If it is essentially good and omnipotent, the existence of evil remains to be explained; and if the reality of evil is denied, many will be unconvinced. The growing interest in a "finite God," as represented by Professor E. S. Brightman,[6] indicates the acute awareness of this problem. Without depriving God of infinitude in all respects, it is suggested that He has limits, for something is "given" to God and constitutes a problem. Man is called upon to cooperate with God in solving the problems of his material life, for which there is no divine responsibility. Presumably this strengthens the position of the preacher who visits a hopelessly suffering member of his congregation. No doubt the unhappy person will be glad of the opportunity to help God solve the problem of his "given."

The religious traditions have favored theism, or the view that God is coordinate with the real world, and is related to the world as a part is to a part. As supernature, God is distinguished from nature. The mediating position of the Church is thus provided for. The doctrine that God is related to the world as a whole is to its parts, or that God is identical in some sense with all reality, could only be unwelcome to organized religion. It proved to be a de-

---

[6] E. S. Brightman, *The Problem of God* (New York: The Abingdon Press, 1930). According to Brightman, "God is a person supremely conscious, supremely valuable, and supremely creative, yet limited both by the free choice of other persons and by restrictions within his own nature."

cided source of embarrassment in the mystical form of pantheism. Some of the most pious men that ever lived were brought before the bar of medieval ecclesiastical justice, to learn the error of their ways. Apparently the doctrine of the mean applies to the dimensions of God. The experience of Meister Eckhart, a Dominican born in 1260, is a case in point.[7] In 1326 he was tried for heresy by Archbishop Heinrich von Virneburg. Shortly after, the friendless theologian died, before Pope John XXII had issued a bull of condemnation[8] stating: "With pain do we express ourselves, that one of our contemporaries in Germany, Eckhart by name . . . , not being contented with belief alone, wanted to know more than others, by turning his ear away from truth and toward fabulous stories. Misled by that father of lies . . . this man has planted thorns and thistles on the field of the Church in opposition to the sun-clear truth of belief . . . : he has taught much which must darken the correct belief in the hearts of the multitude; he has presented it openly to the simple folk in his sermons, and also in writing. . . ." One of the condemned propositions stated: "We become completely transformed into God and changed into him, in a manner similar to the way in which, in the sacrament, the bread is transformed into the body of Christ; so I am changed into him; he brings me forth as his own unified being, and not only as something similar." Eckhart was known as the master "from whom God concealed nothing," and it was said that no one could understand his sermons. He maintained the principle that being is God *(Esse est Deus)*. This being is in motion, but there is nothing outside it, so that only being can move it. God is therefore the only being, and God is self-moving, in an eternal flow from and back to itself. According to Eckhart's concept of "divine immanence," God is the "eternal now." The highest being has no predicates: there is no will, nor love, nor good in the godliness, which is beyond all concepts. It is worth noting that Eckhart characterized this highest being as pure nothing. Since evil has no being, it, too, is nothing, with no relationship to God.

God is regarded as the only being in which essence and existence are identical.[9] In his interpretation of the Scripture text,

---

[7] Cf. J. Bernhart, *Die Philosophische Mystik des Mittelalters* (München: Verlag Reinhardt, 1922), pp. 177 ff.
[8] For the text of the papal bull giving the twenty-eight condemned propositions, cf. *Meister Eckharts deutsche Predigten und Traktate* (Leipzig: Insel-Verlag, 1934), pp. 413 ff.
[9] Cf. M. De Wulf, *History of Mediaeval Philosophy* (London and New York: Longmans, Green, and Co., 1926), Vol. II, pp. 125 ff.

"*Ego sum qui sum,*" Eckhart finds that the repetition of the term "*sum*" indicates God's delight in reposing in Himself; that God is pure affirmation, and that all negation is repugnant to Him; that it implies the return of His being upon Himself; that there is an internal overflow of His being, which takes fire, liquefies, and boils within itself. In such a manner Eckhart shows that God has unity, goodness, justice, love for Himself, intelligibility, and simplicity.[10]

The idea of God, which was for Descartes innate in all minds at the beginning of the modern era, was the idea of "a substance infinite, independent, all-knowing, all-powerful, and by which I myself, and every other thing that exists . . . were created."[11] Spinoza, with unfailing consistency, if not with divine humor, showed that if God is defined as an absolutely infinite substance, it must be concluded that God comprises all reality. In other words, the theists were logically committed to pantheism, despite all their intolerance of pantheists. Spinoza curiously felt the need to prove the existence of God, in his sense.[12] The point was, that his definition of God must also refer to something which exists. But if God is defined as an absolutely infinite being, how can such a being be proved to exist? It is easy enough to prove that something exists; but how can one prove that an absolutely infinite being exists? What does proof mean here? Formally, a proposition is proved if it can be derived logically from a set of premises. Inductively or empirically, proof is construed as evidence. Absolute infinitude cannot be a matter of empirical evidence. Neither can actual existence be guaranteed by any set of premises, so that formal proof will not suffice.

C. *The Leading Attempts to Prove God's Existence*

(1) PASSING FROM THOUGHT TO EXISTENCE

The theist is certain that God exists; the atheist is equally certain that God does not exist; the agnostic knows that the truth is unknowable. Is it logically possible that all three positions are unwarranted? If the theist fails to achieve a rigorous demonstration, his contention must be withdrawn until he is successful. The atheist may be successful in his critique of particular traditional

---
[10] *Ibid.*
[11] René Descartes, *Meditation* III.
[12] Cf. Spinoza, *Ethics*, Bk. I, Prop. 11.

claims. Is he capable of demonstrating the nonexistence of a God in every sense of the term? As for the agnostic, what becomes of his claim if either the theist or the atheist is successful? And is he capable of proving that neither one of them could ever be successful? Logically, the presence of disproof does not follow from the absence of proof; nor may the presence of proof be inferred from the absence of disproof.

One of the best known arguments for the existence of God, the ontological argument, was advanced in the eleventh century by St. Anselm of Canterbury. Addressing himself to the Deity, he wrote:[13]

> We certainly believe that Thou art a being such that a greater cannot be conceived.... Now, such a being cannot exist merely in our understanding which conceives it. For if it were only in our minds, it could be thought of as also existing in reality, which is greater. If, therefore, that than which a greater cannot be thought is in the mind alone, the very thing than which a greater cannot be thought is that than which a greater can be thought. But certainly this cannot be. Therefore it cannot be doubted that there is something than which a greater cannot be thought, both in the mind and in reality.

St. Thomas Aquinas rejected this argument, on the ground that it passes from the subjective order to the real order. The logical weakness of the argument had already been seen by the monk Gaunilo, a contemporary of Anselm. Gaunilo pointed out that having an idea is no proof of real existence, and that the argument "proves" too much.

In his *Meditations*, Descartes devoted considerable attention to the question of God's existence. It was a delicate theme for the times, particularly for a rationalist, and Descartes expressed himself with great care. There could be no doubt about his acceptance of the existence of God, but his reasoning was hardly worthy of a great prophet of reason. In the fifth *Meditation* he reasoned:

> It is certain that I no less find the idea of a God in my consciousness, that is, the idea of a being supremely perfect, than that of any figure or number whatever: and I know with not less clearness and distinctness that an (actual and) external existence pertains to his nature than that all which is demonstrable of any figure or number really belongs to the nature of that figure or number.... But though, in truth, I cannot conceive a

[13] Cf. M. De Wulf, *op. cit.*, Vol. I, pp. 122 ff.

> God unless as existing, any more than I can a mountain without a valley, yet, just as it does not follow that there is any mountain in the world merely because I conceive a mountain with a valley, so likewise, though I conceive God as existing, it does not seem to follow on that account that God exists; for my thought imposes no necessity on things; and as I may imagine a winged horse, although there be none such, so I could perhaps attribute existence to God, though no God existed. But the cases are not analogous . . . for because I cannot conceive a mountain without a valley, it does not follow that there is any mountain or valley in existence, but simply that the mountain or valley, whether they do or do not exist, are inseparable from each other; whereas, on the other hand, because I cannot conceive God unless as existing, it follows that existence is inseparable from him, and therefore that he really exists. . . . The necessity of the existence of God determines me to think in this way: for it is not in my power to conceive a God without existence, that is, a being supremely perfect, and yet devoid of an absolute perfection, as I am free to imagine a horse with or without wings. . . .

Since existence is a perfection, Descartes believed he could infer the existence of a "first and sovereign being." God was the only being he was able to conceive, "to whose essence existence necessarily pertains"; and he saw clearly "that he must have existed from all eternity, and will exist to all eternity." Descartes was also sure "that it is impossible to conceive two or more gods of this kind." The potential implication of pantheism which was latent in his concepts was made clear by Spinoza's analysis of God as infinite substance.

When one speaks of the possibility of conceiving, or the impossibility of conceiving something, he must be prepared to furnish criteria of conceivability. Is it the psychological act of conceiving something that is meant? That is ruled out because different individuals might well disagree, and objective criteria would have to be provided. The criterion of noncontradictoriness must then be resorted to as the most general condition of logical possibility. If it would be contradictory to affirm the existence of two infinite beings, then Descartes could declare two or more gods of that kind to be "impossible to conceive."

Kant, who was called by Heine "the arch-destroyer in the realm of thought,"[14] submitted the leading proofs of God's exis-

---

[14] Heinrich Heine, *Religion and Philosophy in Germany* (London: Trübner and Co., 1882); quoted in Kant's *Prolegomena to any Future Metaphysics* (Chicago: The Open Court Publishing Co., 1912), p. 269.

tence to a searching criticism. He maintained that only three kinds of proof are possible to speculative reason:[15] the ontological (from idea to existence), the cosmological (the causal argument), and the physico-theological (the argument from design, or toward a final cause). It is interesting to note that Heine considered Kant successful with the last two, but to have failed with the ontological argument. But it was not difficult for Kant to do what had been done in principle before, to point out the error in inferring existence from an idea of a Supreme Being. He asked: Is the proposition that this or that thing *exists* an analytic or a synthetic proposition (i.e., is the predicate contained in the subject, or does it add to the subject)? If it is analytic, then nothing is added to the thought of the thing when you say it exists. If, however, a proposition involving existence is synthetic, as Kant thinks it must be, can it be said that the predicate of existence cannot be removed without contradiction? Kant considered the concept of a Supreme Being very useful, but incapable of increasing our knowledge of existence by itself, since it is merely an idea.

(2) INFERRING A FIRST CAUSE

It is evident that a Supreme Being could not be both a being comprising all reality (an *ens realissimum*) and a first cause which antedates and somehow conditions all other existence. At any rate, if proved to exist, the first cause could function as a God, although a great deal would remain to be done for religious purposes. It would have to be proved fundamentally different from all other existing things; it could not belong to the natural order. It would have to be proved infinite and necessary. But it would also have to have characteristics of mind and personality, and provide moral principles. Finally, it would have to be brought into an active relationship with present events, and be shown to have the future in its power. Hence the proof of a first cause, even if it were successful, would not achieve enough. It might merely signify a peculiar feature of the natural order of existence.

According to a representative set of theses in philosophy deriving from the medieval tradition, the existence of God as the Unproduced Cause of the universe is proved with certainty by the *"a posteriori"* method of demonstration. God is regarded as a self-sufficient and necessary being, who must be infinite in perfec-

[15] Kant, *Critique of Pure Reason*, trans. F. M. Müller (New York: The Macmillan Co., 1919), p. 476.

tion and absolutely simple. There is only one God and He is an intelligent and personal being, both physically and morally immutable. God is regarded as knowing all reality by one comprehensive concept. He is omnipotent through the exercise of His will. The Creator of the world, He conserves all His creatures in existence. Furthermore, God's concurrence is necessary for all the operations of His creatures. Thus, all creatures are under the sway of Divine Providence. Nothing less would be enough for the purposes of a traditional organized religion, if it is to retain its power and prestige. A weaker concept of a Divine Being would be a blow to confidence and faith. But everything depends upon demonstration, whether the concept of God be stronger or weaker —that is, if logic is allowed without restriction, and if there has been no earlier indoctrination to reduce its function to the ancillary role of offering reasons for something already accepted as an article of faith.

To many minds it appears plausible that there must have been a beginning of all things in the form of a first cause. If the world of the present is called p, say with a span of one day, then the world of yesterday, p', could be called its cause, and the world of the day before yesterday could be called the cause of the cause; and so on. If an infinite series were ruled out, it would be possible to conclude that there must have been an uncaused first cause. But why should an infinite series be ruled out? It would be dogmatic to hold that there could be no infinite series in reality. If infinitude has not been proved in the sense of direct evidence, neither has it been disproved. The imagination may tire in the face of ceaseless questioning, and the closure of the series of natural events be merely a fatigue symptom. Analogy plays a big role in popular thinking. All things in experience have causes, and many of them have makers. Why should not the universe as a whole have a maker who is distinct from all the finite things which are produced? This line of reasoning is assumptive, in that it treats the universe as a closed totality, despite the fact that it is forever open and incomplete, temporally speaking.

The alleged impossibility of an infinite series of moving and moved bodies was of decisive importance for St. Thomas Aquinas in his attempts to prove God's existence.[16] According to the argument from cosmic change, that which changes does so under

[16] Cf. M. De Wulf, *op. cit.*, Vol. II, and F. C. Copleston, *Aquinas* (Baltimore: Penguin Books, Inc., 1955).

the influence of something other than itself. Since an infinite series is held to be impossible, the existence of an immovable mover is inferred. There is also the inference from efficient causes to the existence of God, which is supposed to apply to a series in which the higher is the cause of the lower. An infinite chain of causes is ruled out, on the ground that it would destroy real causality and contradict the facts. In general, if there are gradations of the being, goodness, truth, or unity of limited beings, the existence of a being possessing these "perfections" in the highest degree is inferred, and it is argued that all the others are derived from it. This argument applies to real existence, and not to mere concepts.

St. Thomas maintained that the eternity of the world is not contradictory. While holding that "creation *ab aeterno*" is not absurd in philosophy, as a theologian he taught the beginning of things in time. Although he himself did not regard the world as eternal,[17] it was his view that it could not be shown by reason to be eternal or created in time. And since reason could not decide, the revelation of faith that the world was created was acceptable. It is interesting to recall that the Christian Aristotelianism of Thomas Aquinas met with opposition during his lifetime, both within and without the Dominican Order. After his death, some of his doctrines were condemned at Paris and Oxford, and for fifty years the reading of his works was forbidden in the Franciscan Order.

Let us examine the idea of a first cause more closely. If it is a real event it must be temporal, and hence it must be due to other events which preceded it. That would be so if it were like the events with which we are familiar, in ordinary experience and in our scientific knowledge. If the alleged first cause is in time, it cannot be first unless it be proved to have existed for an infinite time in the past in its identity. Then it would have to be shown how, and at what point, the infinite first cause blossomed forth in a causal series of finite existent events. Only a myth would meet that need. It would take its place among the various cosmic myths to account for the beginning of the world, and would seem to be most appropriate for the childhood of the human race. If the alleged first cause is held to be free, that could only mean "undetermined by causal law." In that case, the unenviable problem

---

[17] Cf. R. McKeon, *Selections from Medieval Philosophers* (New York: Charles Scribner's Sons, 1930), Vol. II, pp. 149 f.

of how to account for lawfulness on the basis of lawlessness would remain unsolved.

Reality undoubtedly exhibits hierarchical features. There are gradations; there are the earlier and the later, the cause and the effect, the more complete and the less complete, the better and the worse, the more beautiful and the less beautiful (or ugly), etc. There is nothing to force us to assume that there is a first, a highest, a most complete, or a most beautiful. In some contexts, there may be a point in speaking of an ideal limit. But this cannot apply to the real order of existence, which could not possibly be shown to have a first cause. On the other hand, it is incomparably more plausible to hold that reality in its indefinite or infinite past resembles the behavior of real events of the present and known past. There is something to be said for this alternative, and nothing at all for the empty possibility that there once existed an infinite cause which somehow gave an initial impulse to the order of existence as we know it. This latter view could not be actually refuted; but, then, neither could the hypothesis of successive instantaneous creation—i.e., the supposition that all reality is created anew each instant. It is sufficient to bear in mind that nothing speaks for this "irrefutable" hypothesis, which must remain a piece of idle fancy. So far as our experience and knowledge are concerned, the idea of an uncaused first cause really amounts to a contradiction in terms.

(3) REASONING FROM FITNESS TO A FINAL CAUSE

If the matter of things cannot be accounted for by a creator, may not their form be due to a supreme artificer? The design argument for the existence of God makes use of the evidence that many things are adapted to definite ends, and it calls attention to the very structure of the universe which supports life and enables human beings to further their interests.

A well-known argument from analogy may be recalled. Suppose that a watch is found on the sand by the sea. Would it not compel the assumption of an intelligent maker? Then, by analogy, the universe which contains the watch, and which exhibits structures that make purposive activities possible, will also compel the assumption of an intelligent maker. Inspected more closely, the analogy breaks down. In the first place, there were many makers of the watch, so that a plurality of universe-makers would follow.

In the second place, the watchmakers were finite beings, so that, by analogy, there would be a plurality of finite universe-makers. Furthermore, the makers of the watch did not create its matter, so that, by analogy, there would be at most a universe-architect, or a group of universe-architects. Finally, there is no reason to suppose that there is any relationship between expertness and moral character on the part of the watchmakers. By analogy, we are left with a not necessarily moral plurality of finite universe-makers, or universe-architects. The point is that if it is to be an argument from analogy, the items of resemblance and difference must be indicated carefully.

It is possible to argue that there is evidence of lawfulness on every hand. Can one also speak of fitness? Lawfulness merely means conformity to law, and nothing follows from the descriptively true statement that everything in existence occurs in conformity to laws. If the behavior of anything is not accounted for by laws already formulated, then appropriate modifications of the laws must be introduced, or new laws formulated. Certainly there is also evidence of fitness, because nothing could exist or occur unless there were sufficient conditions. There could be no organic beings as we know them without an atmosphere. It is a big step from such considerations of fitness to the thesis that there is evidence for design or purpose in the nature of things. The reader will reflect that there are large regions of the known universe where life is impossible. The physical conditions are not favorable; there is no fitness. If one argues from the fitness of the earth for life to the existence of an intelligent, purposive activity, he should also consider the absence of suitable conditions for life. There is no basis at all for the talk of a cosmic purpose, or of a transcendent being that is responsible for the apparently purposive orderliness of things. As already seen (in the discussion of monism), it is not possible to get away from order of some kind or other, and even chaos is but a name for another, unfavorable kind of order. If a case can be made out for a series of sufficient conditions leading to the present arrangement of things, we must not overlook that an enormous number of possible arrangements were ruled out at the same time. For every arrangement that is realized, a great number of other possibilities are sacrificed. Yet one argues for design, while neglecting to recognize that it is at most partial and selective. And the term design says too much. The occurrence of things can be accounted for by neutral scientific principles, so that it is unnecessary to resort to a transcendent principle of explanation.

The locus of design or purpose should be borne in mind. So far as we know only human beings are capable of conscious purpose, and of reflectively determining goals of action, although patterns of purposive action can be found in other organic beings. To carry this conception over to inorganic nature would be to incur the fallacy of an illicit metabasis (transference of a concept which is meaningful in one context to another in which it is not). The conditions for the development of purposive behavior on the human level are evident. There are organic and cultural conditions—the development of the central nervous system, and of group life. Is it necessary to invoke a transcendent explanation for the emergence of human beings, with their more complex modes of behavior than are found elsewhere; or are the naturalistic methods of the sciences adequate? It appears that the teleologists reacted to a limited set of facts, to fit an already accepted faith. With a position to be defended at all costs, the facts were simply culled in support of it.

Unlike Kant, the present writer will not express a profound appreciation of the teleological, or the physico-theological, line of reasoning. The glorification of nature, or of existence, is the only possible outcome of the argument. A supernature cannot be provided by its findings. But why should existence be glorified? It is frequently terrible, from the point of view of organic beings. The struggle and strife in the animal kingdom, the evil and suffering in the human realm: are these facts to be forgotten in a synoptic view of all existence? One does not have to go so far as Nietzsche when he said, "If there were a God, how could I stand it, not to be God?" A finite being naturally protests against his finitude. He cannot be expected to express approval of any arrangement of things—the world and the social system—in which there is a sacrifice of value and so much frustration. As an intelligent being, he feels impelled to change the world, so that he can survive and realize the greatest possible amount of value. If he should be successful, through scientific progress, it will not be forgotten that it is only man that is prospering. The cockroach is being exterminated; it has no place in the human sphere. No human being is apt to take exception to this principle of selection. But there should be no naïve or sanctimonious profession of cosmic values if the human undertaking is successful and life preserved indefinitely.

It is important above all to apply the concepts of order, fitness, and purpose to actual social conditions. When a philosopher (like Leibniz, for example) glorifies the existing world, he may do so as a social conformist, as one who accepts the inequalities and vested privileges of his social system. We must abandon the abstract conception of a Supreme Being, which may merely be an interpretation of a scientific formula or a set of equations, and consider the real meaning of God in history.

(4) OTHER ATTEMPTS AT JUSTIFICATION

Numerous other attempts have been made to justify belief in a Supreme Being. The appeal to religious experience has been convincing to some scholars, especially in the form of an experience of inner illumination judged to be a revelation of God's existence. "How can you ward off criticism that you are begging the question?" a philosopher who had only recently experienced this inner illumination was asked. "I am not begging the question," he exclaimed, "God is begging the question."

The moral argument for God's existence was made prominent by Kant. Despite his incisive criticism of the leading traditional arguments, he was profoundly religious. He undertook to destroy knowledge of God in order to make room for faith. There must be a power that makes for righteousness, in his view. The meaning of life requires belief in God and immortality. Reward must meet desert, and there must be an adjudicator. Confident that he had established the self-defeat of the human understanding on ultimate metaphysical questions, he thought he had made room for simple faith. William James carried on the spirit of Kant's approach, through his formulation of the "will to believe" on matters which could not be decided by scientific reasoning.

Each person will have to decide for himself the effectiveness of such arguments. The question remains, whether people can be educated so that they are able to retain an open mind when a decision cannot be reached by logical means; or whether wishful thinking will continue to motivate ultimate beliefs.

The fact that many who have been unbelievers through the years yield to a religious conversion when facing death is evidence of nothing except personal fear, perhaps coupled with the persistence of early influences. It proves nothing objectively. No one could predict with certainty how he would react under such circumstances. The conversion of allegedly strong minds may be balanced by the conduct of others who are unyielding and consistent.

The materialist Hobbes rejected the ready spiritual aid of the Church when he was thought to be incurably ill.[18] He was told of the power of absolution of the Church of Rome. Hobbes replied: "Father, I have debated that with myself long ago, and have no mind to discuss it now; you can entertain me better." But he permitted a bishop to pray with him, using the English prayer-book. This was not inconsistent with his considered point of view, for he allowed for a religion controlled by the State.[19] He favored the religion of Scripture and Christ, without the inventions of Church doctors and pagan influences. In his words, "It is with the mysteries of religion as with wholesome pills, which swallowed whole have the virtue to cure, but chewed are for the most part cast up again without effect."

The fact that many philosophers have been fideists has no bearing here. One might have expected Hobbes to oppose fideism, in conformity to his vision of science and its powers. Locke might have been expected to be a more thoroughgoing empiricist, more tolerant toward persons who rejected the prevailing theism. Bruno, Spinoza, and Haeckel might have dispensed with their pantheistic interpretation of reality. Albert Einstein, when accused by William Cardinal O'Connell, dean of the Roman Catholic hierarchy in America, of harboring the "sinister apparition of atheism" behind his theory of relativity, replied that his God was the God of Spinoza. He preferred to preserve the concept of God instead of placing it in methodological abeyance, pending sufficient evidence or justification. The conciliatory attitude of such outstanding thinkers is understandable in the context of their times. We have no choice but to accept their sincerity at its face value. It is also true that the intolerance of the multitude, which is so thoroughly indoctrinated, can at times attain the frenzy of a pogrom, and make conditions difficult at every step for a thinker. Progress is achieved slowly, and sometimes it occurs within the field of religion.

[18] Cf. G. C. Robertson, *Hobbes* (New York: Charles Scribner's Sons, 1886).
[19] Cf. Hobbes, *Leviathan* (New York: E. P. Dutton & Co., 1931), pp. 252, 313, 378 f.

Even a unanimous vote on the part of distinguished thinkers in favor of any article of faith would not establish its truth, just as a unanimous negative vote would not prove its falsity. Nor is anything to be gained logically by contemplating the mixed vote we actually have.

D. Consequences of Disbelief in God

In his much-discussed lecture on existentialism,[20] Sartre rejects the belief in the existence of God, and affirms his readiness to accept the consequences of disbelief. He uses Heidegger's term, forlornness, to mean that God does not exist, and that we have to face the consequences. As an existentialist (i.e., a philosopher of human existence), he "thinks it very distressing that God does not exist, because all possibility of finding values in a heaven of ideas disappears along with Him." Dostoevsky's statement, "If God did not exist, everything would be possible," is taken by Sartre to be the very starting point of existentialism. Everything is held to be permissible if God does not exist, and as a result man is described as forlorn. There is nothing to cling to, and man is on his own. In particular, Sartre finds that if God does not exist, we have no values or commands to turn to which legitimize our conduct.

In opposition to Sartre, and to his less obvious forerunner Heidegger, it may be observed that man is not "thrown into the world." He emerges after a long process of development. So far as transcendent principles are concerned (i.e., principles which are supernatural, or which have no place in the world as results of natural causes), man is indeed alone. But he need not feel forlorn if he abandons something which has never been proved to exist. Assumed explanatory entities and principles have been abandoned without forlornness, even though they were at one time well entrenched as habits, and as aids to the scientific imagination. The feeling of dependence on a transcendent being is in some cases so firm a habit that it may well destroy happiness to remove it. Different people will react differently, depending upon psychological and educational factors. In some cases there may be exhilaration at the thought of giving up a dogma and conforming to the ideal of parsimony in our thought. In others, there may be deep despair at the removal of a basis for hope. Those who are ac-

---

[20] J.-P. Sartre, *Existentialism*, trans. Bernard Frechtman (New York: Philosophical Library, 1947), pp. 25 ff.

customed to a supernatural sanction for the principles of conduct may say that everything is allowed, if God is pronounced dead. But that will hardly be concluded by anyone who knows the nature of human rules of conduct and the ways in which they are enforced in diverse societies. The divine sanction is an extraneous affair, superimposed upon rules which serve the needs of a social system, as a whole or in part. Thus a given social system tends to be preserved, with all its inequalities, by ecclesiastical means. To separate the divine sanction from the institution which controls and mediates it would simply be an abstraction. The medieval period is a good example to bear in mind, historically speaking.

If man is self-sufficient in the sense of not being dependent upon a transcendent being, he is more clearly conscious than ever before of his sole responsibility for his happiness. With the rejection of the supernatural, and its provision for an infinite afterlife, man realizes that his limited life-span offers the only opportunity for happiness. The challenge is a double one: all obstacles to happiness are to be removed as quickly and effectively as possible; and more extensive efforts should be encouraged to enlarge the span of human life. As for the "legitimizing" of our conduct, man must look to experience, to the careful study of the consequences of his actions; and he must summon all the available knowledge about individuals and the social system, to institute principles of conduct. Those principles are to be viewed in the light of scientific knowledge, as subject to modification on the basis of further experience. Man is not "condemned to be free." Unfortunately, he is far less free than is recognized by many philosophers, for historical reasons. Every approach toward the ideal of open-mindedness is to be greeted as a step toward the enlargement of the area of freedom. Intellectual freedom can only go along with social freedom; and freedom in both senses is a necessary condition for the scientific approach to the achievement of human happiness.

E. *The Meaning of Immortality*

The question of immortality usually refers to the human soul. The status of the soul is therefore of paramount importance.

Plato devoted considerable attention to the problem of the immortality of the soul. He reflected upon the apparent perpetuity of life due to the alternation of opposites in nature. Just as day follows night, so life follows death. Hence death is only an apparent break. But this reflection would hardly be reassuring to anyone interested in personal immortality. Plato's most serious argument was based upon the alleged resemblance between the soul and the ideal forms which were supposed by him to be unaffected by change. If the soul is like the ideal forms (equality, justice, goodness, etc.), then it, too, will be unaffected by change. Plato assumed that an ideal form (or Idea) is simple, and that the simple persists. He reasoned that there must be something of the order of ideal forms in us, because "like knows like" (a principle advocated by Empedocles). Hence, if there are ideal forms, there must be a soul; and since the ideal forms are held to be eternal, the soul must be immortal. This is precisely the problem, of course, because nothing could be more questionable than the eternal ideal forms. They need be no more than concepts, or idealizations. It would then follow that the soul is a concept or an idealization. In that case, what can immortality mean?

The interest in immortality in Greek philosophy was religiously motivated. Aristotle also illustrates some degree of persistence of the religious tradition in his theory of the soul. For the most part, Aristotle interpreted the soul as the function of the body; and he held that the soul perishes with the body, except for its highest level, the rational soul, which is alone immortal. There is no proof in Aristotle. It comes "from outside" and is allowed to reside in man while his perishable parts exist. To say that the soul is the form of the body is to say no more than that the potentialities of man are most fully realized while the functions exist and are active. The question of indefinitely continued activity is precisely what is at issue for most people, and that is not touched by the introduction of a metaphysical dogma.

The history of modern philosophy and psychology could only be seriously embarrassing to exponents of the immortality of the soul. Descartes retained belief in a soul, but he located it rather badly, as already noted. In the history of British empirical philosophy, the soul, the self, and, in general, spiritual substance were all challenged and dismissed as metaphysical dogmas. The concept of mental behavior superseded the belief in immaterial thought activities. The denial of the existence of consciousness by William James,[21] which had a startling effect at the time, completed the

---

[21] W. James, "Does Consciousness Exist?" in *Essays in Radical Empiricism* (New York: Longmans, Green, and Co., 1912).

destructive criticism by the empirical tradition, and helped prepare the ground for a thoroughgoing scientific psychology. The soul remains for nearly all nondenominational psychologists an unnecessary hypothesis. Professor William McDougall, however, postulated a soul for psychological purposes.[22] His process of reasoning was as familiar as it was lacking in cogency—namely, that we are compelled to postulate an existent, immaterial being in which the separate neural processes produce the elementary affections, which he calls the soul, just as scientists were compelled to postulate the ether as a necessary condition of the development of the magnetic field.

If a person really believes that the body is corrupt and unworthy, and if he firmly accepts the doctrine of the survival of an immaterial soul, death should present a welcome opportunity. Most purported fideists are inconsistent, however, and are given to intense expressions of grief. Of course, that may be merely because their bodies mourn at the loss of other bodies for which they have an irrational fondness. When Diogenes, the ancient cynic, heard a speaker portray the superior felicity of the afterlife, he is said to have called out, "Why, then, do you not die now?"

Apart from the disputed hypothetical soul, is there any meaning to the talk of immortality? Or is it an illusion?[23] How much comfort can an individual derive from Spinoza's line of reflection, which calls attention to the inexpugnable place he will have occupied in the cosmos? Nothing can efface what a person will have been, or what he will have done. Hitler and Mussolini, Newton and Einstein, Beethoven and Bartók, are all contained in the infinite sphere of being, where they have their own unique places. To express it in more dynamic terms, all people, like all real events, are etched on the infinite process of becoming. Mozart and Schubert were young men when they died. What they were is understandable in terms of the cosmos which produced them and the cultural conditions which affected them; and their death was conditioned by the relatively low level of medical science. Spinoza's perspective does not help here. A human being is no different from the Niagara gorge in having its own place in being. A finite being strives to preserve itself, as Spinoza recognized. It

[22] W. McDougall, *Physiological Psychology* (London: J. M. Dent & Sons, Ltd., 1918), pp. 168 f. His book was first published in 1905.
[23] Cf. Corliss Lamont, *The Illusion of Immortality*, 4th ed. (New York: Frederick Ungar Publishing Co., 1965).

is as natural to wish continued existence as it is to satisfy immediate needs. If a person is interested in his welfare at the age of sixty, he may also show a lively interest in the prospect of surviving to the age of one hundred and sixty. Let it not be said that further survival, for an indefinitely long period, is a tedious idea. No vacuous continuation of an "immaterial" something (which must be shown to be something really) is meant here. Physically, the human body will have completely changed a number of times in its first century of existence. With indefinite survival, the possibilities of change in each individual are most interesting. It would be difficult to speak of the same person over a period of thousands of years. If scientific progress can bring about such continued survival, it will be necessary to treat an individual person as a class of historical emergents. This is one meaning of immortality.

There are two other meanings to be mentioned. One of them is biological survival, through one's descendants. It is to be doubted, however, whether the parents of as many as thirty children would derive much added comfort from that fact. They would still be reluctant to yield up their own personal existence.

Finally, there is the means of survival through one's activities, intellectual and practical. The story is told that Brahms was once saddened by a reflection upon man's finitude. A companion hastened to assure him that his music would always be enjoyed. Brahms replied: For a time—perhaps fifty thousand years—but not always. Whether a thousand years would be a closer estimate of the survival of Brahms's music, or a million, could not be decided with great confidence. Probably the rapidity of cultural development will push even his great achievements aside; and there is no assurance that human taste will not change radically in the coming centuries. Must the same be said of the discovery of truths? If human life does not become extinct, the work of Galileo, Pasteur, and Koch, and of the creative minds in mathematics, will always remain among the important instruments of progress. There is certainly no reason for an unbridled optimism. Helen Keller's quotation of a remark by Mark Twain[24] is pertinent: "If a man is a pessimist before he is forty-eight, he knows too much. If he is an optimist after he is forty-eight, he knows too little." But there is no ground for hopeless pessimism, either. Progress through science is the chief basis of hope for the future

---

[24] Cf. A. B. Paine, *Mark Twain: A Biography* (New York: Harper & Brothers, 1912), p. 1253.

of mankind; and that means social science as well as natural science. As for the individual who wants more than is allowed by our level of scientific achievement, the only good counsel is the thought of Aristotle and the Stoics: if we are faced by conditions which cannot be changed, we can at least change our attitude. Man must be educated to master himself in the face of unalterable circumstances.

The prospect of enlarging the span of human life involves the paradox of infinitude. No matter how large the span of life may be, if it is finite it is to be followed by an infinite amount of time. If the nature of things could be reversed for human beings, to allow them first to live forever, with the ultimate prospect of enjoying their life-spans thereafter, would people then long for mortality? That would depend upon the nature of the preliminary eternal life. But enough of paradox: as a finite being, man must as a matter of fact face the ever-open horizon of temporal events, and must realize that each step forward in preserving human interests is still infinitely far from a goal that transcends every limit.

The formal treatment of infinity[25] appears paradoxical from the point of view of human experience. In reality, it is not meaningful to speak of anything following an endless process. The interest in immortality cannot be affected by explanatory theories which transcend the known order of existence. The only hope human beings can have is to extend their lives increasingly. The importance of their limited existence is inversely related to the endless period of nonexistence, which means that a finite life-span is as supremely important as it is cosmically evanescent. That is the constructive outcome of the interest in immortality.

---

[25] Cf. G. Cantor, *Gesammelte Abhandlungen Mathematischen und Philosophischen Inhalts*, ed. E. Zermelo (Berlin: Verlag von Julius Springer, 1932); and A. Fraenkel, *Abstract Set Theory* (Amsterdam: North Holland Publishing Co., 1953).

Index

ABELARD, P., 26f., 29
Adickes, E., 222
Aesthetic and moral value, 260ff.
Alexander, S., 60, 233
Ames, E., 266
Analytic knowledge, 129f.
Anaxagoras, 5, 6, 244
Anaximander, 5, 208
Anaximenes, 5, 208
Anselm, Saint, 90, 271
Anthropistic dogma, 220f.
Anthropomorphism, 220, 267
Antinomies, 203ff.
Aporetics, 110ff.
Appearance and reality, 68f.
Appraisals, 100f.
A priori knowledge, 129ff., 226
Aristippus of Cyrene, 237
Aristotle, 6, 8, 17, 25ff., 70, 72, 82, 130, 159, 175, 186, 201, 206, 210, 240, 267, 283, 286
Atomic error, 243ff.
Authoritarianism, 236f.
Autonomy of philosophy, 101ff.
Avenarius, R., 118
Ayer, A., 2, 91

BACON, F., 30
Bacon, R., 27, 29
Bakewell, C., 69
Bartók, B., 284
Beard, C., 147
Bebel, A., 266
Beethoven, L. van, 24, 136
Belief, 264ff.
Bentham, J., 215, 237, 252
Bergson, H., 24, 211
Berkeley, G., 25, 78, 89, 115, 122, 125, 184, 209
Bernal, J., 148
Bernard of Clairvaux, 1, 33
Bernhart, J., 269
Bernstein, E., 266
Biemel, W., 232
Bölsche, W., 222
Bradley, F., 132
Brahms, J., 285
Brentano, F., 32, 54, 122, 164
Brightman, E., 268
Bruno, G., 202, 280
Burnet, J., 70

CANTOR, G., 81, 286
Carnap, R., 36f., 64, 93, 163, 177
Carver, T., 215
Certainty, 127ff.
Change and permanence, 71
Cogito, 134
Cohn, J., 164
Collective system of knowledge, 176
Collingwood, R. G., 36
Common sense, 2, 4, 202
Comte, A., 217
Conceptually founded problems, 80f., 83f.
Conditions contrary to fact, 144f.
Content and object, 68f., 76f.
Cosmological theorems, 221
Cunow, H., 246
Cynics, 1

DARWIN, C., 32, 94, 215, 217, 220, 224
Deduction, 45ff.
Degrees of value, 201f.
Democritus, 6, 25, 207
Descartes, R., 6, 30, 48ff., 77, 91, 123, 127, 130, 133, 165, 209, 270ff., 283
Determinism, 175ff., 211
Dewey, J., 21, 24, 32, 39, 76, 94ff., 99, 110, 112, 261
DeWulf, M., 26f., 269, 271, 274
Dialectic method, 64f.
Dialectical materialism, 27
Dietzgen, J., 21
Dilthey, W., 222
Diogenes, 284
Diversity of systems, 153ff., 171ff.
Dostoevsky, F., 281
Dualism, 30, 150, 167f., 170
Du Bois-Reymond, E., 114
Ducasse, C., 98ff., 187f.
Dühring, E., 64, 247

ECKHART, MEISTER, 33, 269f.
Eddington, A., 210
Einstein, A., 205, 210, 280, 284
Eleatic school, 179
Emergent evolution, 216
Empedocles, 5, 283
Empiriogenic problems, 83f., 113
Engels, F., 25, 27, 32, 64, 145, 217f., 246ff., 265f.
Epicureans, 203, 237f., 267f.

Epoché, 244
Essence, 72f., 130, 134, 166, 187, 226f.
Eucken, R., 222
Euclid, 46, 75, 143
Evolutionary philosophy, 215, 219ff.
Existence, 103, 119f., 184ff.
Existence and value, 233ff.
Experience, 121f., 126

FARBER, M., 46, 52f., 83, 92, 124, 136, 148, 154, 175, 215, 224
Feuerbach, L., 25, 27, 31f., 78, 245, 264ff.
Fichte, J. G., 25, 31, 78
Finite God, 268
Finitism, 202ff., 210, 274
First cause, 274ff.
Fiske, J., 220
Formal *a priori*, 130
Fraenkel, A., 286
Frames of unity, 179ff.
Frank, P., 92f.
Frechtman, B., 281
Freedom, 252f.
Frege, G., 136

GALILEO, 285
Galsworthy, J., 243
Gaunilo, 271
God, 30, 150, 220, 266ff.
Goethe, J. W. von, 222
Gorgias, 89
Griffith, C., 262

HAECKEL, E., 179, 220ff., 280
Hartmann, N., 110ff.
Hedonism, 237f., 240
Hegel, G. W. F., 27, 31f., 64, 73, 78, 82, 111f., 141, 209, 226
Heidegger, M., 27, 231f., 281
Heine, H., 272f.
Heraclitus, 70
Herzberg, A., 33
Historical and real problems, 87f., 149, 177
Hitler, A., 244, 284
Hobbes, T., 14, 16, 30, 78, 128, 214f., 280
Hocking, W., 152, 159f., 168, 172, 178, 222
Hodgson, S., 23, 55ff.
Hoernlé, R., 185
Howison, G., 222
Human ethics, 248

Human existence, 34, 188, 201, 213ff.
Hume, D., 4, 44, 82, 90, 117, 125, 128, 209
Husserl, E., 3, 10f., 22, 24, 27, 32, 50f., 54f., 83, 99, 102, 116, 122, 124, 127, 133f., 136, 140, 195f., 198, 211f., 222, 225, 227f., 232
Huxley, T., 217, 220
Hypothesis, 44f.
Hypothetical judgments, 142ff.

IDEAL OBJECTS AND MEANINGS, 102, 168, 187, 225f.
Idealism, 58f., 100
Immortality, 282ff.
Implication, 143ff.
Individual and society, 244ff.
Induction, 43f., 73, 84f.
Infinity, 202ff., 274, 286
Intentional existence, 186f.
Intrinsic value, 259

JAMES, W., 12, 32f., 39, 54, 64, 70, 76, 116, 151, 211, 215, 279, 283
Jaspers, K., 27, 231
Judgments and objects, 138ff.

KANT, I., 14, 21f., 26, 31, 69f., 80, 82, 90, 92, 122, 124, 128ff., 138f., 156, 172f., 189, 197, 203, 205, 207, 209, 217, 222, 246, 257, 272f., 278f.
Kaufmann, F., 131
Kautsky, K., 246
Keller, H., 285
Kierkegaard, S., 32f.
Koch, R., 285
Koehler, W., 51
Kraft, V., 64
Kraus, O., 164

LAMONT, C., 284
Langford, C., 108, 191
Laplace, P. de, 209
Leibniz, G., 6, 30f., 48, 60, 78, 128, 130, 195, 202, 207, 209, 279
Lenin, V. I., 22, 27, 53, 118
Leucippus, 6, 207
Lewis, C., 99, 124, 132f., 143ff., 174, 191
Liebknecht, W., 217
Locke, J., 17, 30, 47, 71, 117f., 122, 124, 214, 280
Logical empiricism or positivism, 37f., 219

INDEX

Logical-semantical method, 64f.
Lotze, H., 12
Lucretius, 205
Lukasiewicz, J., 191

MACH, E., 92
Mannheim, K., 146
Maquet, J., 146
Marcel, G., 27
Marx, K., 14, 16f., 21, 25, 27, 32, 64, 145, 198, 217f., 220, 228f., 246f.
Marxian criticism of ethics, 246ff.
Marxian theory of man, 217f.
Material *a priori*, 130
Materialism, 27, 57, 86f., 92, 100, 104, 119, 179, 208
McCabe, J., 222
McDougall, W., 284
McGill, V. J., 92, 148, 223
McKeon, R., 275
McTaggart, J., 64, 185
Meaning-events, 168
Meinong, A., 136
Metaphysical interpretation, 57
Methodogenic questions, 64, 83, 85f., 113, 134, 143
Mill, J. S., 237
Mind, 122f.
Mind and body, 122f.
Mitin, M., 27
Monism, 78, 149ff., 180
Montague, W., 94
Mooney, T., 244
Moore, G., 53, 108
Morgan, L., 217, 220
Mozart, W., 284
Müller, M., 80
Mussolini, B., 247, 284

NATURAL ATTITUDE, 3f.
Naturalism, 57, 104
Necessity, 195f.
neo-Thomist, 17
Neutral monism, 78f.
Newton, I., 2, 92, 284
Nietzsche, F., 6, 22, 32, 34f., 71, 278
Noema, 102f., 140, 182
Noetic, 140f., 182
Northrop, F., 146

OBJECTIVE ETHICAL KNOWLEDGE, 248ff., 254ff.
Objectivism, 52f., 231, 234
O'Connell, Cardinal W., 280

Ontological position, 99f.
Ontology of man, 34

PAINE, A., 285
Pantheism, 268f.
Parmenides, 70, 205
Participation and renunciation, 19f., 114, 218f.
Pascal, B., 202, 207
Pasteur, L., 285
Paulsen, F., 222
Peirce, C., 184f.
Perceptually founded problems, 67ff., 83f.
Perennial problems, 88ff.
Perry, R., 53, 66, 79, 233, 259
Phenomenological method, 64f.
Phenomenology, 38, 50ff., 103, 111, 197, 211f., 227f., 231f.
Philo, 89
Philosophical anthropology, 222ff., 228
Philosophical neutrality, 118ff.
Philosophy, 1ff., 62ff., 109
Philosophy of existence, 229ff.
Philosophy of values, 236ff.
Planck, M., 156
Plato, 1, 6, 14, 17f., 25ff., 70, 72, 82, 85, 194, 226, 282f.
Plekhanov, G., 198
Pluralism, 155ff., 165ff., 179ff.
Pope John XXII, 236, 269
Possibility, 154, 175f., 190ff., 276
Prall, D., 123
Predicament of absolute authority, 61
Principle of equality, 241, 257
Principle of identity, 132
Principle of quantity, 238ff.
Problem of knowledge, 93ff.
Problem of the given, 124ff.
Problems and questions, 82f., 107, 112ff., 140
Proofs of God's existence, 270ff.
Pseudoevolutionism, 215
Psychological theory of philosophers, 33ff.
Purpose, 278f.
Pythagoras, 75

RADICAL ANALYSIS, 104
Radicalism in philosophy, 116ff.
Realism and idealism, 92f., 119
Reality, 142, 175ff., 179f., 184f., 188f., 276
Reductionism, 215f.

Reflexive method, 49f.
Reichenbach, H., 197
Relational events and objects, 152f., 159
Relational properties, 157
Relations, 152, 156ff., 165
Richardson, C., 86f.
Rickert, H., 222
Riehl, A., 164
Robertson, G., 280
Robinson, D., 266
Roscellinus, 29
Ross, W., 70
Royce, J., 64, 151ff.
Rule of method, 40f., 62
Russell, B., 26, 36, 50, 64, 79, 86, 92, 136, 143, 177, 191

SACCO, N., 244
Sameness and ideal meanings, 135ff.
Santayana, G., 35, 70
Sartre, J.-P., 281
Scheler, M., 145, 212, 222ff.
Schelling, F., 31, 33, 225
Schiller, F., 76
Schilpp, P., 108
Schlick, M., 23
Schopenhauer, A., 22, 32, 34, 222
Schubert, F., 284
Sellars, R., 92, 148
Sheffer, H., 177
Sheldon, W., 91
Simmel, G., 222
Skepticism, 42, 69, 128
Smythies, J., 187
Social-historical significance, 34, 37, 95f., 114f., 147ff.
Sociology of knowledge, 145ff., 223, 228
Socrates, 191, 244
Somerville, J., 21
Space and time, 202ff.
Speculation, 45
Spencer, H., 14, 32, 70, 91, 217, 220
Spengler, O., 148
Spinoza, B., 27, 30, 46, 89, 141, 150, 179, 202, 216f., 270, 272, 280, 284
Spirit, 31, 33, 78, 142, 225
Stoic logicians, 176
Stout, G., 54, 186f.
Struik, D., 148
Subjectivism, 52ff., 231, 234
Synthesis of identification, 83f.

TARSKI, A., 191
Thales, 5f.
Theism, 268
Thomas, Saint, 14, 27, 70, 90, 271, 274f.
Townsend, W., 236
Transcendence, 76ff., 81, 218
Truth, 74ff.
Twain, M., 285

UNITY, BASIC AND FORMAL, 161ff., 178
Unity of objects, 67, 182
Universals, 71ff.
Unknown and unknowable, 69f., 77, 91, 189

VANZETTI, B., 244

WALLACE, W., 64
Weber, M., 222
Weber-Fechner law, 86
Whitehead, A., 2f., 7, 24ff., 32, 36, 44, 59f., 80, 90, 99, 143, 159, 177f., 190f., 207, 233
William of Occam, 29, 115, 236
Windelband, W., 25
Witte, Count S., 257
Wittgenstein, L., 23, 64, 93
Wolfson, H., 89
World and world-logic, 173ff., 196, 208ff.

XENOPHANES, 267

ZENO, 80, 205f.
Zermelo, E., 286

Selected titles: revised December, 1967

harper ⚜ torchbooks

HUMANITIES AND SOCIAL SCIENCES

American Studies: General

LOUIS D. BRANDEIS: Other People's Money, and How the Bankers Use It ‡ TB/3081
HENRY STEELE COMMAGER, Ed.: The Struggle for Racial Equality TB/1300
CARL N. DEGLER, Ed.: Pivotal Interpretations of American History Vol. I TB/1240; Vol. II TB/1241
A. S. EISENSTADT, Ed.: The Craft of American History: Recent Essays in American Historical Writing
Vol. I TB/1255; Vol. II TB/1256
CHARLOTTE P. GILMAN: Women and Economics. ‡ Ed, by Carl N. Degler with an Introduction TB/3073
MARCUS LEE HANSEN: The Atlantic Migration: 1607-1860. TB/1052
JOHN HIGHAM, Ed.: The Reconstruction of American History△ TB/1068
ROBERT H. JACKSON: The Supreme Court in the American System of Government TB/1106
LEONARD W. LEVY, Ed.: American Constitutional Law TB/1285
LEONARD W. LEVY, Ed.: Judicial Review and the Supreme Court TB/1296
LEONARD W. LEVY: The Law of the Commonwealth and Chief Justice Shaw TB/1309
HENRY F. MAY: Protestant Churches and Industrial America TB/1334
RICHARD B. MORRIS: Fair Trial: Fourteen Who Stood Accused, from Anne Hutchinson to Alger Hiss. New Preface by the Author TB/1335
RALPH BARTON PERRY: Puritanism and Democracy TB/1138

American Studies: Colonial

BERNARD BAILYN: The New England Merchants in the Seventeenth Century TB/1149
JOSEPH CHARLES: The Origins of the American Party System TB/1049
HENRY STEELE COMMAGER & ELMO GIORDANETTI, Eds.: Was America a Mistake? An Eighteenth Century Controversy TB/1329
CHARLES GIBSON: Spain in America † TB/3077
LAWRENCE HENRY GIPSON: The Coming of the Revolution: 1763-1775. † Illus. TB/3007
PERRY MILLER & T. H. JOHNSON, Eds.: The Puritans: A Sourcebook Vol. I TB/1093; Vol. II TB/1094
EDMUND S. MORGAN, Ed.: The Diary of Michael Wigglesworth, 1653-1657 TB/1228
EDMUND S. MORGAN: The Puritan Family TB/1227
RICHARD B. MORRIS: Government and Labor in Early America TB/1244
WALLACE NOTESTEIN: The English People on the Eve of Colonization: 1603-1630. † Illus. TB/3006
JOHN P. ROCHE: Origins of American Political Thought: Selected Readings TB/1301

JOHN SMITH: Captain John Smith's America: Selections from His Writings TB/3078

American Studies: From the Revolution to 1860

MAX BELOFF: The Debate on the American Revolution: 1761-1783 TB/1225
RAY A. BILLINGTON: The Far Western Frontier: 1830-1860. † Illus. TB/3012
GEORGE DANGERFIELD: The Awakening of American Nationalism: 1815-1828. † Illus. TB/3061
WILLIAM W. FREEHLING, Ed.: The Nullification Era: A Documentary Record ‡ TB/3079
JOHN C. MILLER: Alexander Hamilton and the Growth of the New Nation TB/3057
RICHARD B. MORRIS, Ed.: The Era of the American Revolution TB/1180
R. B. NYE: The Cultural Life of the New Nation: 1776-1801. † Illus. TB/3026
A. F. TYLER: Freedom's Ferment TB/1074
LOUIS B. WRIGHT: Culture on the Moving Frontier TB/1053

American Studies: Since the Civil War

MAX BELOFF, Ed.: The Debate on the American Revolution, 1761-1783: A Sourcebook TB/1225
W. R. BROCK: An American Crisis: Congress and Reconstruction, 1865-67 ° △ TB/1283
A. RUSSELL BUCHANAN: The United States and World War II. † Illus. Vol. I TB/3044; Vol. II TB/3045
EDMUND BURKE: On the American Revolution. † Edited by Elliot Robert Barkan TB/3068
THOMAS C. COCHRAN & WILLIAM MILLER: The Age of Enterprise: A Social History of Industrial America TB/1054
WHITNEY R. CROSS: The Burned-Over District: The Social and Intellectual History of Enthusiastic Religion in Western New York, 1800-1850 TB/1242
FOSTER RHEA DULLES: America's Rise to World Power: 1898-1954. † Illus. TB/3021
W. A. DUNNING: Reconstruction, Political and Economic: 1865-1877 TB/1073
HAROLD U. FAULKNER: Politics, Reform and Expansion: 1890-1900. † Illus. TB/3020
FRANCIS GRIERSON: The Valley of Shadows TB/1246
SIDNEY HOOK: Reason, Social Myths, and Democracy TB/1237
WILLIAM E. LEUCHTENBURG: Franklin D. Roosevelt and the New Deal: 1932-1940. † Illus. TB/3025
JAMES MADISON: The Forging of American Federalism. Edited by Saul K. Padover TB/1226
ARTHUR MANN: Yankee Reformers in the Urban Age TB/1247
GEORGE E. MOWRY: The Era of Theodore Roosevelt and the Birth of Modern America: 1900-1912 † TB/3022
R. B. NYE: Midwestern Progressive Politics TB/1202
JAMES PARTON: The Presidency of Andrew Jackson, From Vol. III of the Life of Andrew Jackson ‡ TB/3080

† The New American Nation Series, edited by Henry Steele Commager and Richard B. Morris.
‡ American Perspectives series, edited by Bernard Wishy and William E. Leuchtenburg.
* The Rise of Modern Europe series, edited by William L. Langer.
** History of Europe series, edited by J. H. Plumb.
¶ Researches in the Social, Cultural and Behavioral Sciences, edited by Benjamin Nelson.
§ The Library of Religion and Culture, edited by Benjamin Nelson.
Σ Harper Modern Science Series, edited by James R. Newman.
° Not for sale in Canada.
△ Not for sale in the U. K.

1

FRANCIS S. PHILBRICK: The Rise of the West, 1754-1830. †
Illus. TB/3067
WILLIAM PRESTON, JR.: Aliens and Dissenters: *Federal Suppression of Radicals, 1903-1933* TB/1287
JACOB RIIS: The Making of an American ‡ TB/3070
PHILIP SELZNICK: TVA and the Grass Roots TB/1230
TIMOTHY L. SMITH: Revivalism and Social Reform: *American Protestantism on the Eve of the Civil War* △ TB/1229
IDA M. TARBELL: The History of the Standard Oil Company. Briefer Version. ‡ *Edited by David M. Chalmers* TB/3071
ALBION W. TOURGÉE: A Fool's Errand. ‡ *Ed. by George Fredrickson* TB/3074
GEORGE B. TINDALL, Ed.: A Populist Reader ‡ TB/3069
VERNON LANE WHARTON: The Negro in Mississippi: 1865-1890 TB/1178

Anthropology

JACQUES BARZUN: Race: *A Study in Superstition.* Revised Edition TB/1172
JOSEPH B. CASAGRANDE, Ed.: In the Company of Man: *Portraits of Anthropological Informants* TB/3047
W. E. LE GROS CLARK: The Antecedents of Man: *Intro. to Evolution of the Primates.* °△ *Illus.* TB/559
CORA DU BOIS: The People of Alor. *New Preface by the author. Illus.* Vol. I TB/1042; Vol. II TB/1043
DAVID LANDY: Tropical Childhood: *Cultural Transmission and Learning in a Puerto Rican Village* ¶ TB/1235
EDWARD BURNETT TYLOR: Religion in Primitive Culture. Part II of "Primitive Culture." § *Intro. by Paul Radin* TB/34
W. LLOYD WARNER: A Black Civilization: *A Study of an Australian Tribe.* ¶ *Illus.* TB/3056

Art and Art History

EMILE MÂLE: The Gothic Image. § △ *190 illus.* TB/44
MILLARD MEISS: Painting in Florence and Siena after the Black Death. *169 illus.* TB/1148
ERICH NEUMANN: The Archetypal World of Henry Moore. △ *107 illus.* TB/2020
DORA & ERWIN PANOFSKY: Pandora's Box: *The Changing Aspects of a Mythical Symbol* TB/2021
ERWIN PANOFSKY: Studies in Iconology: *Humanistic Themes in the Art of the Renaissance* △ TB/1077
ALEXANDRE PIANKOFF: The Shrines of Tut-Ankh-Amon. *Edited by N. Rambova. 117 illus.* TB/2011
OTTO VON SIMSON: The Gothic Cathderal △ TB/2018
HEINRICH ZIMMER: Myths and Symbols in Indian Art and Civilization. *70 illustrations* TB/2005

Business, Economics & Economic History

REINHARD BENDIX: Work and Authority in Industry TB/3035
GILBERT BURCK & EDITORS OF FORTUNE: The Computer Age: *And Its Potential for Management* TB/1179
THOMAS C. COCHRAN: The American Business System: *A Historical Perspective, 1900-1955* TB/1080
ROBERT DAHL & CHARLES E. LINDBLOM: Politics, Economics, and Welfare TB/3037
PETER F. DRUCKER: The New Society △ TB/1082
ROBERT L. HEILBRONER: The Limits of American Capitalism TB/1305
FRANK H. KNIGHT: The Economic Organization TB/1214
FRANK H. KNIGHT: Risk, Uncertainty and Profit TB/1215
ABBA P. LERNER: Everybody's Business TB/3051
HERBERT SIMON: The Shape of Automation: *For Men and Management* TB/1245

Education

JACQUES BARZUN: The House of Intellect △ TB/1051
RICHARD M. JONES, Ed.: Contemporary Educational Psychology: *Selected Readings* TB/1292
CLARK KERR: The Uses of the University TB/1264

JOHN U. NEF: Cultural Foundations of Industrial Civilization △ TB/1024

Historiography & Philosophy of History

JACOB BURCKHARDT: On History and Historians. △ *Intro. by H. R. Trevor-Roper* TB/1216
J. H. HEXTER: Reappraisals in History: *New Views on History & Society in Early Modern Europe* TB/1100
H. STUART HUGHES: History as Art and as Science: *Twin Vistas on the Past* TB/1207
ARNALDO MOMIGLIANO: Studies in Historiography °△ TB/1288
GEORGE H. NADEL, Ed.: Studies in the Philosophy of History: *Essays from History and Theory* TB/1208
KARL R. POPPER: The Open Society and Its Enemies △ Vol. I TB/1101; Vol. II TB/1102
KARL R. POPPER: The Poverty of Historicism °△ TB/1126
G. J. RENIER: History: Its Purpose and Method △ TB/1209
W. H. WALSH: Philosophy of History △ TB/1020

History: General

WOLFGANG FRANKE: China and the West TB/1326
L. CARRINGTON GOODRICH: A Short History of the Chinese People. △ *Illus.* TB/3015
DAN N. JACOBS & HANS H. BAERWALD: Chinese Communism: *Selected Documents* TB/3031
BERNARD LEWIS: The Arabs in History △ TB/1029
BERNARD LEWIS: The Middle East and the West °△ TB/1274

History: Ancient and Medieval

A. ANDREWES: The Greek Tyrants △ TB/1103
P. BOISSONNADE: Life and Work in Medieval Europe °△ TB/1141
HELEN CAM: England before Elizabeth △ TB/1026
NORMAN COHN: The Pursuit of the Millennium △ TB/1037
CHRISTOPHER DAWSON, Ed.: Mission to Asia △ TB/315
ADOLF ERMAN, Ed.: The Ancient Egyptians TB/1233
HEINRICH FICHTENAU: The Carolingian Empire: *The Age of Charlemagne* △ TB/1142
GALBERT OF BRUGES: The Murder of Charles the Good. *Trans. with Intro. by James Bruce Ross* TB/1311
F. L. GANSHOF: Feudalism △ TB/1058
DENO GEANAKOPLOS: Byzantine East and Latin West △ TB/1265
MICHAEL GRANT: Ancient History °△ TB/1190
W. O. HASSALL, Ed.: Medieval England: *As Viewed by Contemporaries* △ TB/1205
DENYS HAY: Europe: The Emergence of an Idea TB/1275
DENYS HAY: The Medieval Centuries °△ TB/1192
J. M. HUSSEY: The Byzantine World △ TB/1057
SAMUEL NOAH KRAMER: Sumerian Mythology TB/1055
ROBERT LATOUCHE: The Birth of Western Economy: *Economic Aspects of the Dark Ages* °△ TB/1290
NAPHTALI LEWIS & MEYER REINHOLD, Eds.: Roman Civilization Vol. I TB/1231; Vol. II TB/1232
FERDINAND LOT: The End of the Ancient World and the Beginnings of the Middle Ages TB/1044
ACHILLE LUCHAIRE: Social France at the Time of Philip Augustus TB/1314
MARSILIUS OF PADUA: The Defender of the Peace. *Trans. with Intro. by Alan Gewirth* TB/1310
G. MOLLAT: The Popes at Avignon: 1305-1378 △ TB/308
CHARLES PETIT-DUTAILLIS: The Feudal Monarchy in France and England °△ TB/1165
HENRI PIRENNE: Early Democracies in the Low Countries TB/1110
STEVEN RUNCIMAN: A History of the Crusades △ Vol. I TB/1143; Vol. II TB/1243; Vol. III TB/1298
J. M. WALLACE-HADRILL: The Barbarian West △ TB/1061

History: Renaissance & Reformation

JACOB BURCKHARDT: The Civilization of the Renaissance in Italy △ Vol. I TB/40; Vol. II TB/41

2

JOHN CALVIN & JACOPO SADOLETO: A Reformation Debate. Edited by John C. Olin TB/1239
G. CONSTANT: The Reformation in England △ TB/314
G. R. ELTON: Reformation Europe, 1517-1559 ** ° △ TB/1270
WALLACE K. FERGUSON et al.: The Renaissance: Six Essays. Illus. TB/1084
JOHN NEVILLE FIGGIS: Divine Right of Kings TB/1191
FRANCESCO GUICCIARDINI: Maxims and Reflections of a Renaissance Statesman (Ricordi) TB/1160
J. H. HEXTER: More's Utopia TB/1195
HAJO HOLBORN: Ulrich von Hutten and the German Reformation TB/1238
JOHAN HUIZINGA: Erasmus and the Age of Reformation.△ Illus. TB/19
JOEL HURSTFIELD: The Elizabethan Nation △ TB/1312
JOEL HURSTFIELD, Ed.; The Reformation Crisis △ TB/1267
ULRICH VON HUTTEN et al.: On the Eve of the Reformation: "Letters of Obscure Men" TB/1124
ROBERT LATOUCHE: The Birth of Western Economy. ° △ Trans. by Philip Grierson TB/1290
NICCOLÒ MACHIAVELLI: History of Florence and of the Affairs of Italy TB/1027
GARRETT MATTINGLY et al.: Renaissance Profiles. △ Edited by J. H. Plumb TB/1162
J E. NEALE: The Age of Catherine de Medici ° △ TB/1085
ERWIN PANOFSKY: Studies in Iconology △ TB/1077
J. H. PARRY: The Establishment of the European Hegemony: 1415-1715 △ TB/1045
BUONACCORSO PITTI & GREGORIO DATI: Two Memoirs of Renaissance Florence: The Diaries of Buonaccorso Pitti and Gregorio Dati TB/1333
J. H. PLUMB: The Italian Renaissance △ TB/1161
A. F. POLLARD: Henry VIII °△ TB/1249
A. F. POLLARD: Wolsey: Church and State in 16th Century England ° △ TB/1248
CECIL ROTH: The Jews in the Renaissance. Illus. TB/834
A. L. ROWSE: The Expansion of Elizabethan England. °△ Illus. TB/1220
GORDON RUPP: Luther's Progress to the Diet of Worms °△ TB/120
FERDINAND SCHEVILL: Medieval and Renaissance Florence. Illus. Vol. I TB/1090; Vol. II TB/1091
R. H. TAWNEY: The Agrarian Problem in the Sixteenth Century TB/1315
G. M. TREVELYAN: England in the Age of Wycliffe, 1368-1520 °△ TB/1112
VESPASIANO: Renaissance Princes, Popes, and Prelates: The Vespasiano Memoirs TB/1111

History: Modern European

MAX BELOFF: The Age of Absolutism, 1660-1815 △ TB/1062
EUGENE C. BLACK, Ed.: European Political History, 1815-1870: Aspects of Liberalism TB/1331
ASA BRIGGS: The Making of Modern England, 1784-1867: The Age of Improvement °△ TB/1203
CRANE BRINTON: A Decade of Revolution, 1789-1799. * Illus. TB/3018
D. W. BROGAN: The Development of Modern France. °△ Vol. I TB/1184; Vol. II TB/1185
ALAN BULLOCK: Hitler, A Study in Tyranny ° △ TB/1123
E. H. CARR: German-Soviet Relations Between the Two World Wars, 1919-1939 TB/1278
E. H. CARR: International Relations Between the Two World Wars, 1919-1939 ° △ TB/1279
E. H. CARR: The Twenty Years' Crisis, 1919-1939 °△ TB/1122
GORDON A. CRAIG: From Bismarck to Adenauer: Aspects of German Statecraft. Revised Edition TB/1171
DENIS DIDEROT: The Encyclopedia: Selections. Ed. and trans. by Stephen Gendzier TB/1299
FRANKLIN L. FORD: Robe and Sword: The Regrouping of the French Aristocracy after Louis XIV TB/1217
RENÉ FUELOEP-MILLER: The Mind and Face of Bolshevism TB/1188
ALBERT GOODWIN, Ed.: The European Nobility in the Eighteenth Century △ TB/1313
ALBERT GUÉRARD: France in the Classical Age △ TB/1183
CARLTON J. H. HAYES: A Generation of Materialism, 1871-1900. * Illus. TB/3039
STANLEY HOFFMANN et al.: In Search of France TB/1219
LIONEL KOCHAN: The Struggle for Germany: 1914-45 TB/1304
HANS KOHN: The Mind of Germany △ TB/1204
HANS KOHN, Ed.: The Mind of Modern Russia TB/1065
WALTER LAQUEUR & GEORGE L. MOSSE, Eds.: Education and Social Structure in the 20th Century ° △ TB/1339
WALTER LAQUEUR & GEORGE L. MOSSE, Eds.: International Fascism, 1920-1945 ° △ TB/1276
WALTER LAQUEUR & GEORGE L. MOSSE, Eds.: The Left-Wing Intellectuals between the Wars, 1919-1939 ° △ TB/1286
WALTER LAQUEUR & GEORGE L. MOSSE, Eds.: Literature and Politics in the 20th Century ° △ TB/1328
WALTER LAQUEUR & GEORGE L. MOSSE, Eds.: The New History: Trends in Historical Research and Writing since World War II ° △ TB/1327
WALTER LAQUEUR & GEORGE L. MOSSE, Eds.: 1914: The Coming of the First World War ° △ TB/1306
FRANK E. MANUEL: The Prophets of Paris: Turgot, Condorcet, Saint-Simon, Fourier, and Comte TB/1218
KINGSLEY MARTIN: French Liberal Thought in the Eighteenth Century TB/1114
ROBERT K. MERTON: Science, Technology and Society in Seventeenth Century England ¶ TB/1324
L. B. NAMIER: Facing East: Essays on Germany, the Balkans, and Russia in the 20th Century △ TB/1280
L. B. NAMIER: Personalities and Powers △ TB/1186
NAPOLEON III: Napoleonic Ideas: Des Idées Napoléoniennes, par le Prince Napoléon-Louis Bonaparte TB/1336
FRANZ NEUMANN: Behemoth: The Structure and Practice of National Socialism 1933-1944 △ TB/1289
DAVID OGG: Europe of the Ancien Régime, 1715-1783 ** ° △ TB/1271
JOHN PLAMENATZ: German Marxism and Russian Communism. °△ New Preface by the Author TB/1189
PENFIELD ROBERTS: The Quest for Security, 1715-1740. * Illus. TB/3016
GEORGE RUDÉ: Revolutionary Europe, 1783-1815 ** ° △ TB/1272
LOUIS, DUC DE SAINT-SIMON: Versailles, The Court, and Louis XIV △ TB/1250
HUGH SETON-WATSON: Eastern Europe Between the Wars, 1918-1941 TB/1330
A. J. P. TAYLOR: From Napoleon to Lenin: Historical Essays ° △ TB/1268
A. J. P. TAYLOR: The Habsburg Monarchy, 1809-1918 ° △ TB/1187
G. M. TREVELYAN: British History in the Nineteenth Century and After: 1782-1919 △ TB/1251
H. R. TREVOR-ROPER: Historical Essays °△ TB/1269
ELIZABETH WISKEMANN: Europe of the Dictators, 1919-1945 ** ° △ TB/1273
JOHN B. WOLF: France: 1814-1919 TB/3019

Intellectual History & History of Ideas

HERSCHEL BAKER: The Image of Man TB/1047
R. R. BOLGAR: The Classical Heritage and Its Beneficiaries △ TB/1125
J. BRONOWSKI & BRUCE MAZLISH: The Western Intellectual Tradition: From Leonardo to Hegel TB/3001
NORMAN COHN: Pursuit of the Millennium △ TB/1037
C. C. GILLISPIE: Genesis and Geology: The Decades before Darwin § TB/51
FRANK E. MANUEL: The Prophets of Paris: Turgot, Condorcet, Saint-Simon, Fourier, and Comte TB/1218
BRUNO SNELL: The Discovery of the Mind: The Greek Origins of European Thought △ TB/1018

W. WARREN WAGAR, Ed.: European Intellectual History since Darwin and Marx TB/1297
PHILIP P. WIENER: Evolution and the Founders of Pragmatism. △ *Foreword by John Dewey* TB/1212

Literature, Poetry, The Novel & Criticism

JACQUES BARZUN: The House of Intellect △ TB/1051
JAMES BOSWELL: The Life of Dr. Johnson & The Journal of a Tour to the Hebrides with Samuel Johnson LL.D. ○ △ TB/1254
ERNST R. CURTIUS: European Literature and the Latin Middle Ages △ TB/2015
A. R. HUMPHREYS: The Augustan World: *Society in 18th Century England* ○△ TB/1105
RICHMOND LATTIMORE: The Poetry of Greek Tragedy △ TB/1257
J. B. LEISHMAN: The Monarch of Wit: *An Analytical and Comparative Study of the Poetry of John Donne* ○ △ TB/1258
J. B. LEISHMAN: Themes and Variations in Shakespeare's Sonnets ○△ TB/1259
SAMUEL PEPYS: The Diary of Samuel Pepys. ○ *Edited by O. F. Morshead. Illus. by Ernest Shepard* TB/1007
V. DE S. PINTO: Crisis in English Poetry, 1880-1940 ○△ TB/1260
ROBERT PREYER, Ed.: Victorian Literature TB/1302
C. K. STEAD: The New Poetic: *Yeats to Eliot* ○ △ TB/1263
PAGET TOYNBEE: Dante Alighieri: *His Life and Works*. Edited with Intro. by Charles S. Singleton TB/1206
DOROTHY VAN GHENT: The English Novel TB/1050
BASIL WILLEY: Nineteenth Century Studies: *Coleridge to Matthew Arnold* ○△ TB/1261
BASIL WILLEY: More Nineteenth Century Studies: *A Group of Honest Doubters* ○ △ TB/1262
RAYMOND WILLIAMS: Culture and Society, 1780-1950 ○ △ TB/1252
RAYMOND WILLIAMS: The Long Revolution ○△ TB/1253

Myth, Symbol & Folklore

MIRCEA ELIADE: Cosmos and History § △ TB/2050
MIRCEA ELIADE: Rites and Symbols of Initiation: *The Mysteries of Birth and Rebirth* § △ TB/1236
THEODOR H. GASTER: Thespis: *Ritual, Myth & Drama in the Ancient Near East* ○ △ TB/1281
DORA & ERWIN PANOFSKY: Pandora's Box △ TB/2021

Philosophy

G. E. M. ANSCOMBE: An Introduction to Wittgenstein's Tractatus. ○ △ *Second edition, Revised* TB/1210
HENRI BERGSON: Time and Free Will ○△ TB/1021
H. J. BLACKHAM: Six Existentialist Thinkers ○ △ TB/1002
CRANE BRINTON: Nietzsche TB/1197
ERNST CASSIRER: The Individual and the Cosmos in Renaissance Philosophy △ TB/1097
FREDERICK COPLESTON: Medieval Philosophy ○ △ TB/376
F. M. CORNFORD: Principium Sapientiae: *A Study of the Origins of Greek Philosophical Thought* TB/1213
F. M. CORNFORD: From Religion to Philosophy § TB/20
A. P. D'ENTRÈVES: Natural Law △ TB/1223
MARVIN FARBER: The Aims of Phenomenology TB/1291
PAUL FRIEDLÄNDER: Plato: *An Introduction* △ TB/2017
J. GLENN GRAY: The Warriors: *Reflections on Men in Battle. Intro. by Hannah Arendt* TB/1294
W. K. C. GUTHRIE: The Greek Philosophers: *From Thales to Aristotle* ○ △ TB/1008
G. W. F. HEGEL: The Phenomenology of Mind ○ △ TB/1303
F. H. HEINEMANN: Existentialism and the Modern Predicament △ TB/28
EDMUND HUSSERL: Phenomenology and the Crisis of Philosophy TB/1170
IMMANUEL KANT: The Doctrine of Virtue, *being Part II of the* Metaphysic of Morals TB/110
IMMANUEL KANT: Groundwork of the Metaphysic of Morals. *Trans. & analyzed by H. J. Paton* TB/1159
IMMANUEL KANT: Lectures on Ethics §△ TB/105

IMMANUEL KANT: Religion Within the Limits of Reason Alone. § *Intro. by T. M. Greene & J. Silber* TB/67
QUENTIN LAUER: Phenomenology TB/1169
MAURICE MANDELBAUM: The Problem of Historical Knowledge: *An Answer to Relativism* TB/1338
GABRIEL MARCEL: Being and Having △ TB/310
GEORGE A. MORGAN: What Nietzsche Means TB/1198
H. J. PATON: The Categorical Imperative: *A Study in Kant's Moral Philosophy* △ TB/1325
MICHAEL POLANYI: Personal Knowledge △ TB/1158
WILLARD VAN ORMAN QUINE: Elementary Logic. *Revised Edition* TB/577
WILLARD VAN ORMAN QUINE: from a Logical Point of View: *Logico-Philosophical Essays* TB/566
BERTRAND RUSSELL et al.: The Philosophy of Bertrand Russell Vol. I TB/1095; Vol. II TB/1096
L. S. STEBBING: A Modern Introduction to Logic △ TB/538
ALFRED NORTH WHITEHEAD: Process and Reality: *An Essay in Cosmology* △ TB/1033
PHILIP P. WIENER: Evolution and the Founders of Pragmatism. *Foreword by John Dewey* TB/1212
LUDWIG WITTGENSTEIN: The Blue and Brown Books ○ TB/1211

Political Science & Government

JEREMY BENTHAM: The Handbook of Political Fallacies. *Introduction by Crane Brinton* TB/1069
C. E. BLACK: The Dynamics of Modernization: *A Study in Comparative History* TB/1321
KENNETH E. BOULDING: Conflict and Defense TB/3024
CRANE BRINTON: English Political Thought in the Nineteenth Century TB/1071
ROBERT CONQUEST: Power and Policy in the USSR: *The Study of Soviet Dynastics* △ TB/1307
ROBERT DAHL & CHARLES E. LINDBLOM: Politics, Economics, and Welfare TB/3037
F. L. GANSHOF: Feudalism △ TB/1058
G. P. GOOCH: English Democratic Ideas in Seventeenth Century TB/1006
SIDNEY HOOK: Reason, Social Myths and Democracy △ TB/1237
DAN N. JACOBS, Ed.: The New Communist Manifesto & *Related Documents. Third edition, Revised* TB/1078
HANS KOHN: Political Ideologies of the 20th Century TB/1277
ROY C. MACRIDIS, Ed.: Political Parties: *Contemporary Trends and Ideas* TB/1322
KINGSLEY MARTIN: French Liberal Thought in the Eighteenth Century △ TB/1114
BARRINGTON MOORE, Jr.: Political Power and Social Theory: *Seven Studies* ¶ TB/1221
BARRINGTON MOORE, JR.: Soviet Politics—The Dilemma of Power ¶ TB/1222
JOHN B. MORRALL: Political Thought in Medieval Times △ TB/1076
KARL R. POPPER: The Open Society and Its Enemies △ Vol. I TB/1101; Vol. II TB/1102
JOHN P. ROCHE, Ed.: American Political Thought: *From Jefferson to Progressivism* TB/1332
CHARLES I. SCHOTTLAND, Ed.: The Welfare State △ TB/1323
BENJAMIN I. SCHWARTZ: Chinese Communism and the Rise of Mao TB/1308
PETER WOLL, Ed.: Public Administration and Policy TB/1284

Psychology

ALFRED ADLER: The Individual Psychology of Alfred Adler △ TB/1154
ARTHUR BURTON & ROBERT E. HARRIS, Editors: Clinical Studies of Personality Vol. I TB/3075; Vol. II TB/3076
HADLEY CANTRIL: The Invasion from Mars: *A Study in the Psychology of Panic* TB/1282
HERBERT FINGARETTE: The Self in Transformation ¶ TB/1177
SIGMUND FREUD: On Creativity and the Unconscious § △ TB/45

4

WILLIAM JAMES: Psychology: *Briefer Course* TB/1034
C. G. JUNG: Psychological Reflections △ TB/2001
KARL MENNINGER: Theory of Psychoanalytic Technique TB/1144
ERICH NEUMANN: Amor and Psyche △ TB/2012
MUZAFER SHERIF: The Psychology of Social Norms TB/3072

Sociology

JACQUES BARZUN: Race: *A Study in Superstition.* Revised Edition TB/1172
BERNARD BERELSON, Ed.: The Behavioral Sciences Today TB/1127
KENNETH B. CLARK: Dark Ghetto: *Dilemmas of Social Power.* Foreword by Gunnar Myrdal TB/1317
LEWIS A. COSER, Ed.: Political Sociology TB/1293
ALLISON DAVIS & JOHN DOLLARD: Children of Bondage ¶ TB/3049
ST. CLAIR DRAKE & HORACE R. CAYTON: Black Metropolis △ Vol. I TB/1086; Vol. II TB/1087
ALVIN W. GOULDNER: Wildcat Strike ¶ TB/1176
CÉSAR GRAÑA: Modernity and Its Discontents: *French Society and the French Man of Letters in the Nineteenth Century* ¶ TB/1318
R. M. MACIVER: Social Causation TB/1153
ROBERT K. MERTON, LEONARD BROOM, LEONARD S. COTTRELL, JR., Editors: Sociology Today: *Problems and Prospects* ¶ Vol. I TB/1173; Vol. II TB/1174
TALCOTT PARSONS & EDWARD A. SHILS, Editors: Toward a General Theory of Action TB/1083
ARNOLD ROSE: The Negro in America TB/3048
GEORGE ROSEN: Madness in Society: *Chapters in the Historical Sociology of Mental Illness* ¶ TB/1337
PHILIP SELZNICK: TVA and the Grass Roots TB/1230
HERBERT SIMON: The Shape of Automation △ TB/1245
PITIRIM A. SOROKIN: Contemporary Sociological Theories: *Through the first quarter of the 20th Century* ¶ TB/3046
WILLIAM I. THOMAS: The Unadjusted Girl: *With Cases and Standpoint for Behavior Analysis* ¶ TB/1319
EDWARD A. TIRYAKIAN, Ed.: Sociological Theory, Values and Sociocultural Change: *Essays in Honor of Pitirim A. Sorokin* ¶ o △ TB/1316
W. LLOYD WARNER & Associates: Democracy in Jonesville: *A Study in Quality and Inequality* TB/1129
W. LLOYD WARNER: Social Class in America TB/1013

RELIGION

Ancient & Classical

J. H. BREASTED: Development of Religion and Thought in Ancient Egypt TB/57
HENRI FRANKFORT: Ancient Egyptian Religion TB/77
G. RACHEL LEVY: Religious Conceptions of the Stone Age and their Influence on European Thought △ TB/106
MARTIN P. NILSSON: Greek Folk Religion △ TB/78
ERWIN ROHDE: Psyche △ § Vol. I TB/140; Vol. II TB/141
H. J. ROSE: Religion in Greece and Rome △ TB/55

Biblical Thought & Literature

W. F. ALBRIGHT: The Biblical Period from Abraham to Ezra TB/102
C. K. BARRETT, Ed.: The New Testament Background: *Selected Documents* △ TB/86
C. H. DODD: The Authority of the Bible △ TB/43
M. S. ENSLIN: Christian Beginnings △ TB/5
JOHN GRAY: Archaeology and the Old Testament World. △ Illus. TB/127
JAMES MUILENBURG: The Way of Israel △ TB/133
H. H. ROWLEY: Growth of the Old Testament △ TB/107
GEORGE ADAM SMITH: Historical Geography of Holy Land. o △ *Revised and reset* TB/138
WALTHER ZIMMERLI: The Law and the Prophets: *A Study of the Meaning of the Old Testament* △ TB/144

The Judaic Tradition

MARTIN BUBER: Eclipse of God △ TB/12
MARTIN BUBER: Hasidism and Modern Man. △ *Edited and Trans. by Maurice Friedman* TB/839
MARTIN BUBER: The Knowledge of Man △ TB/135
MARTIN BUBER: Moses △ TB/837
MARTIN BUBER: Pointing the Way △ TB/103
MARTIN BUBER: The Prophetic Faith TB/73
GENESIS: *The NJV. Translation* TB/836

Christianity: General

ROLAND H. BAINTON: Christendom: *A Short History of Christianity and its Impact on Western Civilization.* △ *Illus.* Vol. I TB/131; Vol. II TB/132

Christianity: Origins & Early Development

AUGUSTINE: An Augustine Synthesis. △ *Edited by Erich Przywara* TB/335
W. D. DAVIES: Paul and Rabbinic Judaism: *Some Rabbinic Elements in Pauline Theology* o △ TB/146
ADOLF DEISSMANN: Paul: *A Study in Social and Religious History* TB/15
EDWARD GIBBON: The Triumph of Christendom in the Roman Empire. § △ *Illus.* TB/46
EDGAR J. GOODSPEED: A Life of Jesus TB/1
ADOLF HARNACK: The Mission and Expansion of Christianity in the First Three Centuries TB/92
R. K. HARRISON: The Dead Sea Scrolls o △ TB/84
EDWIN HATCH: The Influence of Greek Ideas on Christianity § △ TB/18
GERHART B. LADNER: The Idea of Reform: *Its Impact on Christian Thought and Action in the Age of the Fathers* TB/149
ARTHUR DARBY NOCK: St. Paul o △ TB/104
ORIGEN: On First Principles △ TB/311
SULPICIUS SEVERUS et al.: The Western Fathers △ TB/309
JOHANNES WEISS: Earliest Christianity Vol. I TB/53; Vol. II TB/54

Christianity: The Middle Ages and The Reformation

ANSELM OF CANTERBURY: Truth, Freedom and Evil: *Three Philosophical Dialogues* TB/317
JOHN CALVIN & JACOPO SADOLETO: A Reformation Debate. *Edited by John C. Olin* TB/1239
G. CONSTANT: The Reformation in England △ TB/314
JOHANNES ECKHART: Meister Eckhart: *A Modern Translation by R. B. Blakney* TB/8
DESIDERIUS ERASMUS: Christian Humanism and the Reformation TB/1166

Christianity: The Protestant Tradition

KARL BARTH: Church Dogmatics: *A Selection* △ TB/95
KARL BARTH: Dogmatics in Outline △ TB/56
KARL BARTH: The Word of God and the Word of Man TB/13
RUDOLF BULTMANN et al.: Translating Theology into the Modern Age TB/252
NELS F. S. FERRÉ: Swedish Contributions to Modern Theology. *New chapter by William A. Johnson* TB/147
ERNST KÄSEMANN, et al.: Distinctive Protestant and Catholic Themes Reconsidered TB/253
SOREN KIERKEGAARD: On Authority and Revelation TB/139
SOREN KIERKEGAARD: Crisis in the Life of an Actress *and Other Essays on Drama* △ TB/145
SOREN KIERKEGAARD: Edifying Discourses △ TB/32
SOREN KIERKEGAARD: The Journals of Kierkegaard o △ TB/52
SOREN KIERKEGAARD: The Point of View for My Work as an Author § TB/88
SOREN KIERKEGAARD: The Present Age § △ TB/94

SOREN KIERKEGAARD: Purity of Heart △ TB/4
SOREN KIERKEGAARD: Repetition △ TB/117
SOREN KIERKEGAARD: Works of Love △ TB/122
WALTER LOWRIE: Kierkegaard Vol. I TB/89
Vol. II TB/90
JOHN MACQUARRIE: The Scope of Demythologizing: Bultmann and his Critics △ TB/134
WOLFHART PANNENBERG, et al.: History and Hermeneutic TB/254
JAMES M. ROBINSON et al.: The Bultmann School of Biblical Interpretation: New Directions? TB/251
F. SCHLEIERMACHER: The Christian Faith. △ Introduction by Richard R. Niebuhr Vol. I TB/108; Vol. II TB/109
PAUL TILLICH: Dynamics of Faith △ TB/42
EVELYN UNDERHILL: Worship △ TB/10

Christianity: The Roman and Eastern Traditions

DOM CUTHBERT BUTLER: Western Mysticism § o △ TB/312
A. ROBERT CAPONIGRI, Ed.: Modern Catholic Thinkers Vol. I TB/306; Vol. II TB/307
THOMAS CORBISHLEY, S. J.: Roman Catholicism TB/112
G. P. FEDOTOV: The Russian Religious Mind: Kievan Christianity, the 10th to the 13th Centuries TB/370
ÉTIENNE GILSON: The Spirit of Thomism TB/313
GABRIEL MARCEL: Being and Having TB/310
GABRIEL MARCEL: Homo Viator TB/397
FRANCIS DE SALES: Introduction to the Devout Life TB/316
GUSTAVE WEIGEL, S. J.: Catholic Theology in Dialogue TB/301

Oriental Religions: Far Eastern, Near Eastern

TOR ANDRAE: Mohammed § △ TB/62
EDWARD CONZE: Buddhism o △ TB/58
ANANDA COOMARASWAMY: Buddha and the Gospel of Buddhism. △ Illus. TB/119
H. G. CREEL: Confucius and the Chinese Way TB/63
FRANKLIN EDGERTON, Trans. & Ed.: The Bhagavad Gita TB/115
SWAMI NIKHILANANDA, Trans. & Ed.: The Upanishads: A One-Volume Abridgment △ TB/114

Philosophy of Religion

NICOLAS BERDYAEV: The Beginning and the End § △ TB/14
NICOLAS BERDYAEV: Christian Existentialism △ TB/130
NICOLAS BERDYAEV: The Destiny of Man △ TB/61
RUDOLF BULTMANN: History and Eschatology o TB/91
RUDOLF BULTMANN AND FIVE CRITICS: Kerygma and Myth: A Theological Debate △ TB/80
RUDOLF BULTMANN AND KARL KUNDSIN: Form Criticism: Two Essays on New Testament Research △ TB/96
MIRCEA ELIADE: Myths, Dreams, and Mysteries: The Encounter between Contemporary Faiths and Archaic Realities △ TB/1320
MIRCEA ELIADE: The Sacred and the Profane TB/81
LUDWIG FEUERBACH: The Essence of Christianity § TB/11
ÉTIENNE GILSON: The Spirit of Thomism TB/313
ADOLF HARNACK: What is Christianity? § △ TB/17
FRIDRICH HEGEL: On Christianity TB/79
KARL HEIM: Christian Faith and Natural Science △ TB/16
IMMANUEL KANT: Religion Within the Limits of Reason Alone. § Intro. by T. M. Greene & J. Silber TB/67
K. E. KIRK: The Vision of God △ TB/137
JOHN MACQUARRIE: An Existentialist Theology: A Comparison of Heidegger and Bultmann o △ TB/125
EUGEN ROSENSTOCK-HUESSY: The Christian Future or the Modern Mind Outrun. Intro. by Harold Stahmer TB/143
PIERRE TEILHARD DE CHARDIN: The Divine Milieu o △ TB/384
PIERRE TEILHARD DE CHARDIN: The Phenomenon of Man o △ TB/383
PAUL TILLICH: Morality and Beyond TB/142

Religion, Culture & Society

WILLIAM A. CLEBSCH & CHARLES R. JAEKLE: Pastoral Care in Historical Perspective: An Essay with Exhibits. New Preface by the Authors TB/148
C. C. GILLISPIE: Genesis and Geology: The Decades before Darwin § TB/51
KYLE HASELDEN: The Racial Problem in Christian Perspective TB/116
WALTER KAUFMANN, Ed.: Religion from Tolstoy to Camus TB/123
H. RICHARD NIEBUHR: Christ and Culture △ TB/3
H. RICHARD NIEBUHR: The Kingdom of God in America TB/49
TIMOTHY L. SMITH: Revivalism and Social Reform: American Protestantism on the Eve of the Civil War △ TB/1229

NATURAL SCIENCES AND MATHEMATICS

Biological Sciences

CHARLOTTE AUERBACH: The Science of Genetics Σ △ TB/568
W. E. LE GROS CLARK: The Antecedents of Man o △ TB/559
W. H. DOWDESWELL: Animal Ecology. △ Illus. TB/543
R. W. GERARD: Unresting Cells. Illus. TB/541
EDMUND W. SINNOTT: Cell and Psyche: The Biology of Purpose TB/546
C. H. WADDINGTON: The Nature of Life △ TB/580

History of Science

MARIE BOAS: The Scientific Renaissance, 1450-1630 o △ TB/583
W. DAMPIER, Ed.: Readings in the Literature of Science. Illus. TB/512
A. HUNTER DUPREE: Science in the Federal Government: A History of Policies and Activities to 1940 △ TB/573
ALEXANDRE KOYRÉ: From the Closed World to the Infinite Universe △ TB/31
A. G. VAN MELSEN: From Atomos to Atom: A History of the Concept Atom TB/517
STEPHEN TOULMIN & JUNE GOODFIELD: The Architecture of Matter o △ TB/584
STEPHEN TOULMIN & JUNE GOODFIELD: The Discovery of Time o △ TB/585

Mathematics

E. W. BETH: The Foundations of Mathematics △ TB/581
S. KÖRNER: The Philosophy of Mathematics △ TB/547
WILLARD VAN ORMAN QUINE: Mathematical Logic △ TB/558
FREDERICK WAISMANN: Introduction to Mathematical Thinking. Foreword by Karl Menger TB/511

Philosophy of Science

R. B. BRAITHWAITE: Scientific Explanation TB/515
J. BRONOWSKI: Science and Human Values △ TB/505
ALBERT EINSTEIN et al.: Albert Einstein: Philosopher-Scientist Vol. I TB/502; Vol. II TB/503
WERNER HEISENBERG: Physics and Philosophy △ TB/549
KARL R. POPPER: Logic of Scientific Discovery △ TB/576
STEPHEN TOULMIN: Foresight and Understanding △ TB/564
STEPHEN TOULMIN: The Philosophy of Science △ TB/513

Physics and Cosmology

JOHN E. ALLEN: Aerodynamics △ TB/582
P. W. BRIDGMAN: Nature of Thermodynamics TB/537
C. V. DURELL: Readable Relativity △ TB/530
ARTHUR EDDINGTON: Space, Time and Gravitation: An Outline of the General Relativity Theory △ TB/510
GEORGE GAMOW: Biography of Physics Σ △ TB/567
STEPHEN TOULMIN & JUNE GOODFIELD: The Fabric of the Heavens: The Development of Astronomy and Dynamics. △ Illus. TB/579